PRAISE FOR *REMOTE WORK*

'Insightful, informative and powerful. This book shares creative ideas and productivity tools that not only helped me optimize my output, but made my business more profitable and rewarding.'
Jamie Gwen, chef, author and television and radio host

'Chris Dyer and Kim Shepherd are culture building pioneers. *Remote Work* is timely and accessible and should be considered essential reading for people leaders charged with fostering culture virtually amid unprecedented life events.'
Michael Miller, Head of Talent Acquisition, Chipotle Mexican Grill

'Covid-19 has changed the way we work, whether we like it or not. To survive this new landscape, our companies must face the reality of our situation and innovate. Chris Dyer and Kim Shepherd's book will help you navigate the new world of remote working and remote leadership. Packed with examples, advice and stories from the field, this book will inform and entertain.'
Lisette Sutherland, Founder and Director, Collaboration Superpowers

'Think big and act – that's the charge of this new and exciting book. *Remote Work* could not have come at a more pressing time for the business world and will no doubt instil leaders with the wisdom needed to guide their teams to lasting success in an unpredictable future.'
Jennifer Brown, award-winning entrepreneur, diversity and inclusion consultant, speaker and author

'A book for our time! Chris Dyer and Kim Shepherd bring a stats-based approach peppered with their personal journeys as CEOs and C-suite advisers. *Remote Work* promises to be a must-read for businesses trying to adapt and cement workforce changes.'
Paul Gibbons FRSA, author and keynote speaker

'Chris Dyer and Kim Shepherd have poured their life's work into building and growing successful virtual-based businesses. Over the last ten plus years, they have worked tirelessly to cultivate a work from home (WFH) model that allows employees and customers to excel at what they do. Their experience in and passion for the WFH space is unparalleled.'
John Bernatovicz, President and Founder, Willory

'Full of research and rich case studies that cover any questions leaders may have about why and how transitioning to remote work will be successful for leaders, employees and the business. A must-read!'
Caryn Lee, Founder, Narrative and former Associate Partner, Accenture

'Thought leaders Chris Dyer and Kim Shepherd have cracked the code! In today's era of digital transformation and work-from-anywhere sensibility, this duo have architected a psychological, philosophical and physical WFH future-scape. *Remote Work* delivers brilliantly with practical, profitable and easy-to-adopt productivity tools for every business.'
Hope Frank, Global Chief Marketing and Innovation Officer, BlueTech Research

'The business world has changed for ever and this book could not be more timely. Every leader needs to read this book to revolutionize their organization.'
John R DiJulius III, bestselling author of *The Relationship Economy*

'Every leader needs to read this book. It is not only about leading in a remote work environment, it also has excellent advice on leading and building adaptive teams and cultures, as well as great stories and examples of leaders making a difference with these concepts.'
Annette White-Klososky, Forbes contributor, Partner at Future Point of View, Chair for Women on Boards and Women Presidents Organization

'Adapt and build a brighter future for yourself, your organization and your people by implementing the ideas captured here.'
Evans Kerrigan, CEO and Co-Founder, Integris Performance Advisors

'If you're a business or HR leader and unsure of how to unlock human potential and build culture, engagement and performance in a remote working world, this book is an absolute must-read.'
Deborah Hartung, leadership and culture changemaker

'*Remote Work* is a cookbook for leading organization structure into greater adaptability, productivity, employee engagement and profits. You'll read every word, take each of the many examples to heart and become smarter about how to move your people and your business forward successfully.'
China Gorman, Former CEO, Great Place to Work Institute

'Drawing on years of experience, the authors have codified their process of going remote to make it accessible for everyone!'
Mark McMillion, Principal, McMillion Leadership Associates

'If you're considering taking your workforce remote, or have already done so but still have questions, this book serves as a guide to doing remote work right!'
Annette Franz CCXP, Founder and CEO, CX Journey Inc

'With remote work becoming the "new black", Chris Dyer and Kim Shepherd provide a useful cheat sheet for employers to keep remote teams engaged while running their business more efficiently. Very insightful!'
LT Ladino Bryson, 'The Employment Therapist™', CEO and Founder, vCandidates.com

'Now more than ever, companies are looking for solutions to support a remote workplace while navigating its challenges and leveraging its unique opportunities. This book is your compass along that journey.'
Rob Catalano, Chief Engagement Officer, WorkTango

'*Remote Work* isn't a theoretical book. It comes from two people who have been very successful in establishing great organizational culture in the virtual workplace.'
David Harder, Founder and President, Inspired Work

'Your business bible for winning in this turbulent decade.'
Jill Ratliff, Senior Adviser, Beecher Reagan

'Chris Dyer and Kim Shepherd have come out with a fantastic book that is much needed in the current paradigm shift we are going through. Leaders will have to learn how to do great leadership remotely, and this book is a much-recommended read for that.'
Eduardo X Ibacache Rodriguez, author, writer, explorer and speaker of life, work and technology

Remote Work

*Redesign processes, practices and strategies
to engage a remote workforce*

Chris Dyer

Kim Shepherd

KoganPage

First published in Great Britain and the United States in 2021 by Kogan Page Limited

2nd Floor, 45 Gee Street
London
EC1V 3RS
United Kingdom
www.koganpage.com

122 W 27th St, 10th Floor
New York, NY 10001
USA

4737/23 Ansari Road
Daryaganj
New Delhi 110002
India

Kogan Page books are printed on paper from sustainable forests.

ISBNs

Hardback   978 1 39860 038 6
Paperback   978 1 39860 036 2
Ebook   978 1 39860 037 9

British Library Cataloguing-in-Publication Data

A CIP record for this book is available from the British Library.

Library of Congress Cataloging-in-Publication Data

Names: Dyer, Chris, author. | Shepherd, Kim, author.
Title: Remote work : Redesign processes, practices and strategies to engage a
  remote workforce / Chris Dyer, Kim Shepherd.
Description: 1 Edition. | New York : Kogan Page Inc, 2021. | Includes
  bibliographical references and index.
Identifiers: LCCN 2021008032 (print) | LCCN 2021008033 (ebook) | ISBN
  9781398600362 (paperback) | ISBN 9781398600386 (hardback) | ISBN
  9781398600379 (ebook)
Subjects: LCSH: Telecommuting. | Strategic planning. | Personnel
  management. | Organizational effectiveness.
Classification: LCC HD2336.3 .D94 2021 (print) | LCC HD2336.3 (ebook) |
  DDC 658.3/123–dc23
LC record available at https://lccn.loc.gov/2021008032
LC ebook record available at https://lccn.loc.gov/2021008033

Typeset by Integra Software Services, Pondicherry
Print production managed by Jellyfish
Printed and bound by CPI Group (UK) Ltd, Croydon CR0 4YY

This book is dedicated to a few special people
recently lost from our lives.

Chris would like to dedicate his portion to his dearly
departed mother-in-law Anita Caruso.

Kim would like to dedicate her portion to her departed brothers:
Jeff Timms and Scott Leggette.

CONTENTS

20 Paying it forward 253

LIST OF FIGURES

ABOUT THE AUTHORS

Chris Dyer

Chris Dyer is a recognized performance expert. Constantly intrigued by what makes some businesses and individuals more successful than others, Chris has dedicated years of research to uncovering what drives productivity and profits. He is the author of the bestselling and award-winning book *The Power of Company Culture*, published in 2018 by Kogan Page. He is also the Founder and CEO of PeopleG2, a background check company that has appeared on the *Inc.* 5000 list of the Fastest Growing Companies five times.

Chris was named the #1 Leadership Speaker by *Inc.* magazine in 2019 and has been a sought-after speaker and consultant for many years. As a consultant, Chris works with leading organizations to help them transform their cultures to boost performance and gain an even greater edge in the marketplace. He is also a recognized Remote Work Expert, helping startups to Fortune 500 companies with their remote work strategies and leadership. A certified Scrum Master, Chris is highly adept at helping teams work through obstacles and find solutions quickly and effectively. He leverages this experience in all aspects of his work, which has been shared by outlets including the BBC, *Forbes*, *Inc.*, *The Telegraph*, *Fast Company* and NBC.

A passionate talent management enthusiast, Chris is the host of *TalentTalk*, a popular weekly business podcast that features interviews with top executives about their strategies for hiring and promoting talent.

Kim Shepherd

A thought leader recognized by organizations nationwide, including the Human Capital Institute and the National Association of Women Business Owners, Kim is a regular speaker at national events on the topics of building virtual companies, the importance of cultural glue and attracting 'A' players.

As the CEO of Decision Toolbox, Kim took the company virtual in 2002 with more than 100 team members working across the United States and three other countries. This unique business model played a key role in the company being awarded the Alfred P. Sloan Award for Business Excellence in Workplace Flexibility three times. Decision Toolbox was also a three-time winner of *Inc.* 500/5000 Fastest Growing Private Companies, two-time winner of OCBJ Fastest Growing Private Companies and eight-time recipient of the HRO Baker's Dozen Award for Customer Satisfaction.

Kim was named the National Association of Women Business Owners 'Innovator of the Year' and was the recipient of the WomenSage Family Matters Award. She currently serves on the board of Habitat for Humanity – Orange County, and has served on the boards of Girls Inc. and Working Wardrobes.

Prior to beginning her career in business, Kim was a national television correspondent for 10 years with ESPN, NBC Sports and several syndication TV magazine productions.

FOREWORD

I have spent my life helping successful executives achieve positive, lasting change for themselves, their people and their teams. I am blessed to work with CEOs at Fortune 100 companies like Ford, Coca-Cola, Best Buy, Walgreens and GlaxoSmithKline. When I consult with senior executives, I am with them every step of the way, helping them stay on track.

No matter what level of management or leadership you're at in your profession, every leader needs help! That's why I am pleased to present this book, written for every leader. *Remote Work* focuses on resilience in a new business environment and gives you the tools you need to thrive through crisis and change. Leaders need this book and its powerful insights now more than ever.

Few events have challenged business leaders like the Covid-19 pandemic. Hopefully, when you're reading this, it is past us. The fact is, though, that the pandemic has made remote work a part of life. Kim and Chris both launched successful companies in times of crises. So whether you're still working to refine your remote organization or just starting out, you can probably benefit from their wisdom and experience. *Remote Work* delivers that insight in a practical, step-by-step approach. Keep the book handy, and Chris and Kim will be with *you* every step of the way.

Challenging times separate great leaders from good ones. I was with Alan Mulally, former CEO of Boeing Commercial Airplanes, as he joined Ford Motor Company which, at the time, was losing billions of dollars each year with a stock price that floated around $1. They were on the verge of collapse. When Alan left in 2014, the stock price was over $16 and the company had turned the corner, returning as a leading car manufacturer in the United States. Anyone can have passion and be an example when times are good. It's when times are hard that great leaders stand out.

Leading a remote company, or even a company that is partly remote, is different than leading a company with all the employees on site. To do it well, a lot of things will need to change – structure, culture, the way you run meetings and even your own leadership style. Kim and Chris have been through it. They took on the challenges, drove lasting change and created successful companies. *Remote Work* has inspiring stories, but most importantly, it is a meat-and-potatoes guide. I was so pleased to discover the go-to blueprint for leaders of any company, large or small. It can help you build a company that is better in just about every way: better leaders, better employees, better performance. And that gives you a competitive edge.

Here are some of the questions you may be looking to answer:

- How can I be sure that I'm making the best use of the talent?
- How do I know my employees are working if I can't see them?
- Will my current tools and technologies be effective when we go remote?
- Will my company culture survive when everyone is working from home?
- How can I help my employees succeed in their remote environment?

You can expect Kim and Chris to help you answer these questions and more, based on their years of personal experience.

In addition to drawing on their own experience, Chris and Kim interviewed a variety of proven leaders from diverse organizations, from global enterprises to non-profits. Those leaders provide insights, ideas and success stories from their own experiences making the remote transition.

Kim and Chris will also be there to guide you even after you've finished the book. They've created a platform where you can become part of the ongoing conversation. There you'll be able to share your own experiences and learn from others.

From my unique experience, I have learned that great leaders possess three important qualities: the courage to take a critical look in the mirror, the humility to admit that they can do better, and the discipline to do the hard work of getting better. *Remote Work* gives you the structure and tools, and provides inspiration and motivation. The rest is up to you.

Marshall Goldsmith
Thinkers 50 #1 Executive Coach and *New York Times* #1 bestselling author of *Triggers*, *Mojo* and *What Got You Here Won't Get You There*

ACKNOWLEDGEMENTS

So many incredible people came together to make this book possible. First and foremost, we have to thank Tom Brennan, Founder of Prowrite, for shaping our words and conveying our stories to make this journey sharable. Thank you to Kim's mother and sister, Bobbi and Kaleigh, for foregoing their morning phone calls while writing the book took precedence, and to Nita for her loving words of encouragement. Thank you to Chris's wife Jody and children Luba, Dmitri and Vladimir for accepting less time during this process and always providing loving support.

We thank the incredible business minds who shaped our growth: Dave Berkus, Adam Miller, Bob Kelley, Mimi Grant, Jay Barnett, Loren Miner, Nicole Cox, Jackson Lynch, Retired Major General Melvin Spiese, Courtney Seiter, Julie Fletcher, Sarah McVanel, Dr Aaron Lee, Jessica Hubbard, David Harder and a stable of brilliant authors who we reference throughout the book.

We also thank our team of proofreaders: Jody Dyer, Sharene Cleveland, Loren Miner, Kimberly Roush, Celine Williams, Lisa Perrine, Laura Neaubauer, Sarah Denton, Melissa Brunson, Sarah McVanel, Todd Milan, Nita Willis-Guell and Kristina Renee.

A special thanks to our Kogan Page team: Anne-Marie Heeney and Lucy Carter.

Introduction

2020: A study in chaos

When we wrote this book in 2020, it seemed the world had been turned upside down. The Covid-19 pandemic had taken many lives, precipitated a worldwide lockdown and sent many countries' economies into a tailspin.

On the West Coast of the United States, brush and forest fires destroyed more than 8 million acres in 12 states (Nijhuis, 2020). There were more tropical storms in the Atlantic than in any previous recorded year, with Hurricane Laura alone causing 77 deaths and $14.1 billion in damage (Aon, 2020). The monsoon season in Asia was one of the deadliest on record, with massive flooding killing thousands and displacing millions (Center for Disaster Philanthropy, 2020).

Some 33 armed conflicts raged around the world, with many of them ongoing for years (Comolli, 2020). There were humanitarian crises in Venezuela, Yemen and Rohingya, as well as on the southern border of the US. The year 2020 also saw an earthquake in Puerto Rico, wildfires in the Amazon basin, extensive bushfires across Australia, Cyclone Fani in India, Tropical Cyclone Idai in Southern Africa, famine in northeastern Africa and extensive civil unrest in the United States.

Often it felt like our world was a snow globe that someone kept shaking. But amid all these tragic disasters, there were some points of light. In a strange way, the Covid-19 pandemic brought people together, as we all were in the same mess. Anxiety went way up, but people were forced to slow down and focus on what matters: the ones we love.

Many businesses also proved to be a point of light. Unfortunately, some couldn't survive the shutdown. But others did, innovating new ways of interacting safely with customers. They proved their mettle, persisting and succeeding against the challenges.

No doubt you were impacted by Covid-19. You may recall when you first had to send people home to work, or were sent home yourself. For most, working from home was new, and it wasn't an option.

Sharing what we know

We had been toying with the idea of writing a book about taking a company remote, and 2020 brought new urgency to the project. Together we have 30 years of combined experience running remote companies, and we felt compelled to share what we have learned.

Crises are tipping points (we'll explore that more in the chapters that follow), and those who are bold and quick can seize the opportunities that lie behind the challenges. Speed is your friend when navigating obstacles, but it also increases risk. We hope our ideas will help you avoid some skinned knees.

We are sure that a lot of people have a lot of questions, so we're going to throw just about everything we know at you. The information is valuable whether your company is still working remotely, or considering a hybrid model combining office and home hours.

A little help from our friends

Some amazing people have shared some remarkable stories in the book, and we are deeply grateful. You'll hear from a human resources leader who helped staff up nurses in the heat of Covid-19. A CEO will talk about completing a merger involving thousands of employees while also setting everyone up for success at home. Another HR leader will share insights her global company has learned from being a remote organization for over 10 years. A Director of Programmes will tell how she led non-profit programmes from being completely in-person to being completely online. You'll hear from a Marine Corps general about the importance of training and culture in creating a culture like no other.

Pay it forward

We've known one another and have been swapping stories and ideas for over a decade. Even if your company has been remote for a while, we think there will be some new ideas. You'll definitely find some engaging stories, one-of-a-kind aphorisms and epigrams, and ideas ranging from common-sensical to crazy.

As you read the book, we encourage you to use sticky notes to mark the things that resonate for you and your company. Once you have finished reading, you can go back to your bookmarks and apply what you have learned. Of course, we fully expect you to take the ideas from the book and tailor them to your situation. You may even come up with some entirely new ideas.

Did you see the 2000 film, *Pay It Forward*? It's a feel-good story about a middle-schooler's effort to change the world by forming an ongoing chain made of acts of kindness. We love the idea, and because we have enjoyed success, this book gives us a chance to pay it forward. We're asking you, too, to pay it forward by sharing your ideas and responses in a community we've created on Slack: Remote Work Movement. Sign up at https://chrisdyer.com/remotework. Together we can maintain the momentum and continue to learn and share.

References

Aon (2020) Global Catastrophe Recap, September 2020, http://thoughtleadership.aonbenfield.com//Documents/20200810_analytics-if-september-global-recap.pdf (archived at https://perma.cc/MD7E-ZLN4)

Center for Disaster Philanthropy (2020) 2020 Monsoon Floods, *Disaster Philanthropy*, 17 December, https://disasterphilanthropy.org/disaster/2020-monsoon-floods (archived at https://perma.cc/D8GL-5GAN)

Comolli, V (2020) Armed Conflict Survey, Editor's Introduction, *IISS*, 27 May, www.iiss.org/blogs/analysis/2020/05/acs-2020-introduction (archived at https://perma.cc/7ZVX-L9MJ)

Nijhuis, M (2020) The West Coast wildfires are apocalypse, again, *New Yorker*, 20 October, www.newyorker.com/news/annals-of-a-warming-planet/the-west-coast-wildfires-are-apocalypse-again (archived at https://perma.cc/JK7A-AGWT)

01

Go home and work

Stay-at-home orders. Threats to public safety that were invisible but lurking. Daily reports on the number of people sick or dying. Injunctions to wear a mask if one must go out for essentials. Bare store shelves where basic necessities should be. Huge numbers unemployed. Businesses shuttered. Sounds like something out of a dystopian novel like George Orwell's *1984*. Unfortunately, it's not fiction, and we all lived through it.

IN THIS CHAPTER

We will cover:

- Crises drive innovation
- Cutting costs without cutting employees
- Creators, ideators and implementers
- Finding a vision in Swiss cheese

Looking for silver learnings

Few crises have had the worldwide impact on our personal lives and on business as the Covid-19 pandemic. The depth of the tragedy can't be overstated, particularly for those who lost loved ones to the disease. Many small businesses were unable to recover. Larger businesses lost significant revenue. Governments took their countries deeper into debt with large aid packages.

And yet, as humans we move forward, drawing on our resilience to recover and rebuild. We would like to take that one step further, and look for and learn from the silver linings. In fact, we believe that the massive shift to working from home (WFH) is a positive event and offers many 'silver learnings'. That's why we wrote this book.

The idea of working remotely is not new and wasn't spawned by the Covid-19 pandemic. We have both run remote companies for years. The idea has been met with strong resistance until the events of 2020 forced huge numbers of people to work from home. There is still resistance and, even more so, there is uncertainty. In general, people want certainty – from an early stage in prehistory, humans have held uncertainty as suspect, and for good reason. 'There might be a sabre-tooth cat in that cave,' was a good survival tactic. Several studies have confirmed this, such as that by University of Wisconsin psychology professors Grupe and Nitschke (2014). However, many very smart people have recognized the value in shaking things up and trying new things. Ralph Waldo Emerson wrote, 'People wish to be settled; only as far as they are unsettled is there any hope for them' (2000).

Crises drive innovation

Before Covid-19, people were uncertain about remote work, and few tried it. But desperate times came along and, facing those fears, millions of people went home, fired up the computer and made it work. The results surprised a LOT of people:

- people reported being more productive, and companies agreed;
- the old rhetoric against WFH collapsed in the face of lived experience;
- many people prefer it to going into the office.

We weren't surprised. Covid-19 is not the first crisis we've overcome, and it won't be the last. Kim took her company virtual in the wake of the 9/11 attacks, and Chris took his virtual following the 2009 mortgage recession. Those businesses thrive to this day, still virtual. Today neither of us would run a company any other way, or work any other way as individuals.

We believe that innovation flourishes in an unending circle made up of three roles: Creator, Ideator and Implementer. You might recognize those terms if you've read Tom Rath's 2007 book, *StrengthFinders 2.0*. You can think of Kim as the Creator, Chris as the Ideator and yourself as the Implementer – we'll explain this later in the introduction. However, the circle is constantly spinning, fuelled by the energy of innovation. Our hope is that, after implementing, you will create and ideate and implement some more. Just as important, we hope you will *share* your experiences with others. No need to recreate the wheel – we're already riding in it.

By the way, to avoid confusion, we're writing the book in a unified voice. 'We' and 'us' refers to both of us. When it's important to distinguish, we'll let you know if a story or idea comes from Chris or Kim.

When economic crises compel business leaders to cut costs, an obvious action is to make changes to staffing. However, as our experience shows, there are alternatives. When each of us took our companies virtual, a key goal was to save as many people – employees – as possible. Cutting costs was imperative, but cutting people was unthinkable. We both believe that people are the most important part of a successful company. A story from Kim's early years illustrates this.

MOM KNOWS BEST

'I learned a lot of business wisdom while working in the coffee shop run by my mom,' Kim tells us. 'She was a single mother raising four kids and running a successful business. The coffee shop was in Silicon Valley, although, at the time, the term 'Silicon Valley' wasn't yet widely used (Laws, 2015).

'Regular customers include Steve Jobs, Steve Wozniak, and the Divisional President of Lockheed Corporation. These executives had their favorite booths, and the kitchen started cooking their regular orders as soon as they pulled into the parking lot.

'One day, the Lockheed President walked up to the cash register with a sheepish look and told my mom that he had forgotten his wallet and couldn't pay for breakfast. He said he would go right home and get the money (we're talking about four or five dollars here).

'Mom said, 'Never mind, you'll be back tomorrow – just pay me then.' But as Locky headed for the door, Mom stopped him. 'The CEO of Lockheed can't go around all day without any cash.' She opened the register and handed him $100, which he repaid the next day... plus the cost of yesterday's breakfast.

'The lesson is that, while money and profits are important, people are even more important. Treating people right is an important part of any business plan, whether those people are customers or employees.'

Tough, awful choices

In 2001, Kim was CEO of recruiting firm Decision Toolbox (DT). After the al-Qaeda attacks, the firm's customers put a freeze on just about all hiring. With DT's survival at stake, Kim sat down with CFO Loren Miner and made a list of things they could do to cut costs. Kim will never forget that 'awful list' of tough choices. Kim asked herself, 'What would mom do? She would prioritize the people.' So that's what Kim did. With an eye to saving employees, they cut things like executive credit cards. Both Kim and her business partner, Jay Barnett, went without a salary. They owed the bank a bridge loan that they couldn't pay. When other creditors called to collect, they told them to get in line behind the bank.

One of the biggest steps was to move out of a beautiful showplace office. Not only did they move into a much more modest office, but they made the first step in going virtual. The office was too small for everybody, so instead of sitting on each other's laps, each person worked half the time at home. After about a year, everyone was WFH-ing full time, and they shifted to holding monthly in-person meetings. Pretty soon they let that small office go.

Decision paralysis

Chris's story is similar but also unique. As the CEO and founder of PeopleG2, a US company that provides employment screening and background checks to firms around the globe, decision making was embedded in his job description. But in 2009, as the economic recession truly materialized, Chris felt unable to figure out where to turn or what to do. The company was struggling with a major economic recession, better known in the United States as the 'heart attack of 2009'.

Mortgage lenders made up a large portion of PG2's clientele, and the recession was hurting clients in other industries as well. One client went, overnight, from hiring about 30 people a day to hiring none at all. After gruelling hours of reflection, he realized that this was a great opportunity to redesign the company. He also realized how little he knew about doing that.

In addition to doing a good deal of reading, he brought the problem to a CEO roundtable sponsored by the Adaptive Business Leaders (ABL), where he met Kim. She shared the story of taking DT virtual. With PeopleG2's office lease running out, Chris decided that was the way to go. He cut the phone lines, utilities, rent and more, and sent everyone home to work virtually. He was able to cut expenses by 38 per cent while eliminating 0 per cent of employees.

Not every employee stayed, but Chris didn't have to lay anyone off. In fact, the move to virtual revealed an issue that had remained hidden while the team worked in the office. There was one employee considered to be the best for high levels of productivity. Another employee had been under scrutiny because of low productivity. However, it turned out that the 'best' employee had been taking the easiest assignments out of the basket, leaving the hardest ones for their coworker. Once they went virtual, the tasks were assigned more systematically, and the scenario flipped: the 'best' employee's productivity plummeted while the 'worst' one's output skyrocketed.

These unexpected results prompted some serious reflection among leaders in the organization. Not only did they reconsider how they measured and evaluated employee performance, but they also had to hold some serious conversations with anyone underperforming. Most employees adjusted and made the transition, but the company did lose a few low performers early on.

Change or fail

Crises forced both of us to make changes or fail. There were no government bail-outs or economic stimulus programmes. We both had to look inward and reinvent our business models. Very few other companies were going remote, and there was no buzz around WFH the way there is today. In fact, we had to hide the fact we were remote in order to maintain credibility with clients. Imagine how desirable your company will be now that working remotely is a mainstream option.

For example, a common assumption is that virtual companies are essentially groups of slackers in pyjamas, but we saw improved culture, great productivity and increased profitability. That happened by design, however. Going virtual forced us both to become very sophisticated, particularly with culture and technology. We'll discuss both in more detail in upcoming chapters.

A lot of this creation and ideation was vetted at the ABL CEO roundtable. Not only did Kim and Chris meet there, but they shared ideas with the likes of Dave Berkus – 'super angel' investor and author of many books – and Adam Miller, Founder and CEO of Cornerstone OnDemand, which he grew from a one-person startup into an $850 million company, one of the largest cloud computing companies in the world (Condon, 2020).

Before landing at ABL, both of us had tried other CEO groups. Chris found that there was a lack of diversity in the groups, which meant a lack of diversity in thinking. Kim tried several groups, but none challenged her. At ABL they found diverse ideas and sharp people who motivated them to work harder and become better. As Kim says, 'At ABL, I often felt I was just barely clinging to the caboose, flapping in the wind. That group motivated me to pull myself into the train and push on until I reached the locomotive.'

Since this is a how-to book, here's our first recommended action step: spend time around people who are sharp and will challenge you. Hire smart people and join groups that force you out of your comfort zone.

Creators, ideators, implementers

These stories put a little more context around our assertion that Kim is a Creator and Chris an Ideator. At a time when there were no other models available to her, Kim had to create a virtual model for her company. Chris looked at a large number of different ideas; though many might find that overwhelming, Chris has a knack for quickly homing in on the right one. Moving forward in the book, we will explore a number of ideas and share many stories. We encourage you, Dear Reader, to do some creating and ideating on your own, and implement the ideas in ways that will work for your organization.

We'll close out this chapter with a story about Swiss cheese – you know, the cheese with holes in it. We use it as a metaphor for a great approach to identifying opportunities. Most leaders focus on the cheese – the aspects of the business that are visible and present. However, many opportunities exist in the holes – things that you don't see right away. You have to look hard at the holes, and the following story is a great example.

THE GENERAL AND THE CHEESE

Several years ago, Major General Melvin Spiese, while serving at Camp Pendleton, asked Kim to give a motivational speech. Kim recalls: 'The audience was officers who would soon be transitioning out of the military and into the private sector. He had heard me speak before and thought my message would resonate with his officers. I was thrilled, recognizing what an honour it was even to be invited to speak at the officers' club at a major military base.

'I reached out to the general, asking what he would like me to address with the group, and how long he would like me to speak. The general replied, "120 minutes. We know there's something we don't know, but we don't know what it is."' Kim assumed that there was something lost in translation, so she asked him to repeat it. His response: 'We know there's something we don't know, but we don't know what it is.'

'I was taken aback. It wasn't the first time I would be flying by the seat of my pants, but this was a tall order. The general was asking me to motivate a roomful of men (yes, they were all men that night) who had spent most of their adult lives leading, disciplining and motivating others. How would I even begin to address whatever it was that they "don't know"?

'I spent hours going through my bag of tricks for anything that could give me at least an outline of something to say. With absolutely no success, I decided to walk into the room unequipped, hoping that divine inspiration would guide me for two hours.'

Reading the room

'To most civilians, Camp Pendleton's officers' club is majestic and overwhelming. When I arrived, I felt I was walking on hallowed ground. Standing alone onstage for what seemed like an eternity, I took in the emotion of the room. There was a mood of fear and trepidation. Seizing on what I thought was an opportunity, I emphatically told the officers that they were all about to make the biggest mistake of their lives: "Feeling insecure about a transition to the private sector, you are going to step down into smaller roles than you currently occupy." With invisible encouragement from the group, I sensed that I was onto something.

'I warned that most of them would accept managerial roles within an organization, leaving their roles as leaders behind. I explained that managers "do" and leaders "think". Managers take marching orders while leaders give them. I asked, "When was the last time you had to take orders from somebody else?" In silent unison, they prompted me to keep going.

'The business world is fraught with astonishingly poor leadership. I told them one bad apple at the top creates sour fruit throughout the entire company. That, in turn, creates a culture that includes a bad work ethic, lack of discipline, political correctness, disloyalty... the list goes on. Taking a job as a manager under a boss whose character is less than yours will erode your strengths and keep you in a constant state of frustration.

'I insisted, almost demanded, that they NOT make this horrible mistake. Citing my 20 years of experience working with CEOs from around the country, I told them that their talents were a commodity that is in great demand. Stopping once again to gauge the mood of the room, I noticed that everyone's posture was a little more erect. The sense of despair that had filled the air just 15 minutes earlier was beginning to leave.'

A whole lot of hole

'It was then that I asked everyone to stand up, take the white napkin on their laps and hold it in front of them like a flag. "Pretend that you're holding a giant piece of Swiss cheese," I instructed. After a bit of rustling and confusion, I asked them to imagine there were large holes in that piece of cheese. Focus on the holes, not the cheese, I said. In business, opportunities arise in the holes. The job of a leader is to identify what's missing and determine how to fill it. Many businesses have failed by merely trying to create more cheese.'

Often we are so focused on what is present and visible – the cheese – that we forget to look at what is NOT visible – the holes. Kim created this concept in 1988 in the most unusual of situations and locations. She was the Director of Entertainment for Club Med, a French-based resort corporation with over 100 all-inclusive properties around the world. She led a team of choreographers, set decorators, costumers and sound and lighting directors, but her talents were not needed with them. Their skills in those areas far surpassed hers.

Where she was needed, however, was in filling holes to make the guests less restless and every resort had myriad holes. On the island of St Lucia, for example, most guests were scuba divers who left early each morning, before breakfast, for a dive. They returned an hour before lunch was offered, and they were hungry and irritable. What was missing – the hole – was a diversion. Kim invented a character named Claire, who would schlep a bucket and mop to the pool shortly after the divers' arrival.

She would lazily dredge her mop into the pool, whipping it out and over her shoulder, knocking over four or five lounge chairs in the process. All eyes were now on Claire, who repeated this action several times, much to the delight of the onlookers. Before they knew it, lunch was served. During her two years with Club Med, Kim probably created 20 or 30 diversions around the world. She was just filling holes.

FIRST-NAME BASIS

'With the officers of Camp Pendleton now fully engaged with their napkins of Swiss cheese, I decided to take things a step further. I asked how many people had entrepreneurial aspirations to start their own companies. About a third of the room held up their hands. Staying with the "hole" concept, I encouraged them to look towards current events to help identify gaps around the world. Brazenly, I offered to try to create an imaginary company in real time and asked for a volunteer.

'The most decorated officer in the room, a two-star general, raised his hand. I asked the general his first name. "Thaddeus," he replied – Thad. "Thad," I asked, "What do you want to be when you grow up?" It was as if all the oxygen had been sucked out of the room.

'But after a moment of reflection, he admitted that he had absolutely no idea. I offered that when we come to a place in our lives where we don't know what we want to do, it's best to then ask ourselves what we *don't* want. The general had a ready answer for this: "I don't want a boss, a cubicle, military work, poverty, or geographical isolation." Those answers gave me something to work with.

A vision emerges

'Collaborating in front of the other officers, the general and I started to create a vision. The general wanted to start his own business involving global travel, to lead a team of people and earn a decent salary. I told him to hold up his napkin once again, and asked him to look for the current event holes in his now "global" piece of cheese.

'After a pause, I shared that at that very moment there was a cruise ship called the *Concordia* sitting atop a rock off the coast of Italy. There were air marshals patrolling the skies, but there were no cruise marshals patrolling the seas. That was a major hole in need of filling. I suggested that he take a handful of his fellow officers and create a cruise marshal training curriculum. He could then present the concept to four cruise lines with the caveat that the first to accept his proposal would be the first one to offer the world the safety of security on the seas. The last I heard, the former general was doing just that.'

We'll be exploring how to use the Swiss cheese exercise in remote work. For example, you can look at what's missing from your staff, finances, operations, projections, culture and just about any other part of your company – and then figure out how to fill the gaps.

Leave a trail – and share it

As you read this book, you may still be in the midst of the Covid-19 pandemic, or maybe it is just a deeply imprinted memory. We hope you have a good idea of what we mean when we talk about working remotely – just about everyone had to do it when Covid-19 hit. We plan to share our experiences and insights around just about all aspects of going remote, from who should and shouldn't do it to the importance of a strong culture. We'll explain why we think remote is best for leaders, companies and employees.

We don't see this book as the final word, or even a crystalized theory, but rather as a process, and the beginning of an ongoing conversation with many creators, ideators and implementers contributing. If you are going to go remote, or put more intentionality around a team that is already remote, share your experience with us. As Emerson said, 'Do not go where the path may lead. Go instead where there is no path and leave a trail.'

References

Condon, S (2020) Cornerstone OnDemand taps former Saba chief Phil Saunders to serve as new CEO, *ZDNet.com*, 11 May, www.zdnet.com/article/cornerstone-ondemand-taps-former-saba-chief-phil-saunders-to-serve-as-new-ceo (archived at https://perma.cc/N6WQ-2FB5)

Emerson, R W (2000) *The Essential Writings of Ralph Waldo Emerson*, Random House, New York

Grupe, D W, and Nitschke, J B (2014) Uncertainty and anticipation in anxiety:

An integrated neurobiological and psychological perspective, *HSS Public Access*, 24 December, www.ncbi.nlm.nih.gov/pmc/articles/PMC4276319 (archived at https://perma.cc/YMA2-CUEU)

Laws, D (2015) Who named Silicon Valley? *Computer History Museum*, 7 January, https://computerhistory.org/blog/who-named-silicon-valley (archived at https://perma.cc/W3ZY-QYW3)

Orwell, G (1961; originally 1949) *1984*, Signet Classic, New York

Rath, T (2007) *StrengthFinders 2.0*, Gallup Press, New York

02

Coming to terms

Some people use the terms 'remote', 'virtual' and 'work from home' interchangeably, while others have their own definitions of each. For our purposes here, we're going to use the term 'remote' and define it as:

A situation in which someone works independently and, on a regular basis, in an environment where there are no coworkers. This includes working from home, executive offices, coffee shops, etc. The person is part of the company and collaborates with their team, but not in an office on a regular basis.

IN THIS CHAPTER

We will cover:

- What remote is *not*
- Old-school resistance
- Deliberate design
- New ways of thinking
- Step by step
- New ways of seeing
- Culture: the key to performance
- Follow the leader

What remote is *not*

There aren't quite 31 flavours of remote/virtual/WFH, but there are quite a few. To help ensure that we're all on the same page, let's get out some tiny spoons and taste a few. First are some flavours that involve remote work, but aren't the focus of this book. People in these models can, and we hope they do, take advantage of insights here, but our message will be much clearer with a defined focus. Spoons ready?

The **digital nomad** is that glamorous person using their laptop in a beach chair in Fiji between the ocean swell and the coconut palms. This is the freelancer, the one-person show, and this is what we consider 'virtual'. In fact, some digital nomad roles have been with us so long that most of us don't realize they are remote workers; independent plumbers or electricians, journalists, consultants, writers/editors, translators, designers and others can be digital nomads. However, our focus is on companies with multiple employees working in a consistent or regular manner.

Part-time or **gig work** is a growing sector in the economy and many gig workers ply their trade in the field, such as Uber or GrubHub drivers or InstaCart shoppers. Gig workers often can choose to take an assignment or not. While gig workers typically use a shared infrastructure, our attention will be on companies whose success depends on teamwork and collaboration among remote employees.

Field workers include salespeople and employees who travel to different locations to do their job, like field service technicians or cleaning services. This is a hybrid model in which most (usually) employees are on site and a smaller percentage on the road. While this model is not our main focus, it does highlight a challenge: how do you ensure that off-site employees are just as engaged as those on-site?

The **remote CEO** is more common than you might think, and both Chris and Kim have run across this scenario: the CEO claims the company is remote, but all the employees work on-site – it's only the CEO who is remote. The CEO may face some of the remote challenges we'll explore later, such as isolation or poor communication. Just the same, our mission in this book is to share insights about remote culture and infrastructure, and those don't apply unless the majority of the company is working from home.

What we're talking about is a company in which the majority of employees work successfully at home, sharing an infrastructure and culture. Success requires the same level of teamwork, communication and knowledge sharing that's needed in a sticks-and-bricks model – in fact, it requires more of those things.

Old-school resistance

Before Covid-19, a lot of people were adamant that working from home was not viable. They claimed that remote models would undermine discipline, productivity, creativity and communication.

A famous example of efforts to suppress remote work occurred when Marissa Mayer, then President and CEO of Yahoo!, eliminated remote work as an option in 2013. This policy reversal drove good talent away (many into the arms of welcoming competitors) and couldn't have been good for morale (Silverman, 2013).

If your company builds jet aircraft, you need to have a lot of people in the hangars getting their hands dirty. But Yahoo! builds internet services. All that their employees need is a laptop and a broadband connection. Unfortunately, a lot of other CEOs told themselves, 'If Yahoo! can't do it, we can't do it.' Best Buy, for example, cancelled their work-from-home option shortly after Mayer's announcement (Pepitone, 2013).

Mayer's stated reason was pretty standard old-school anti-remote rhetoric: people can't collaborate unless they are face to face. But think about it. In 2013 (and still today), in brick-and-mortar buildings around the world, CEOs were brainstorming with other executives via instant message, email and phone – even when the other execs were in the office just across the hall.

Today, however, forced by Covid-19 to go remote, executives have realized that collaboration is possible. In fact, overall company performance can improve.

Deliberate design

Another thing many people learned from the Covid-19 pandemic is that it's one thing to send everyone home to work, and quite another to *do it well*. Everyone was scrambling to adjust processes and, to their credit, most people and companies kept it together and got things done.

Now, however, you have a chance to put some thought into it. An effective remote model should be a combination of philosophy, tools and talent leveraged in a deliberate way to achieve optimal outcomes. The key word in that definition may be 'deliberate'. Shortly after the 9/11 attacks, Kim and her business partner, Jay Barnett, were brainstorming about how to keep

FIGURE 2.1 Design what you want, or deal with what you get

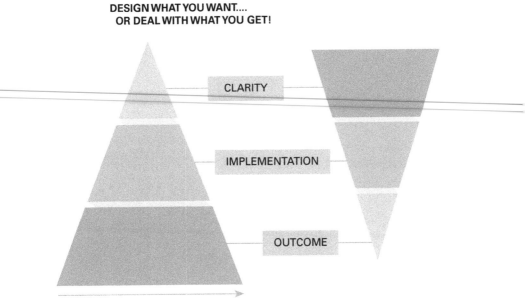

their recruiting firm, Decision Toolbox, afloat. It was at that time that they came up with the maxim: *design what you want, or deal with what you get.*

During that same brainstorming session, Kim and Jay applied the approach to create a unique business development strategy. In general, hiring had slowed significantly, but they knew that some companies were, in fact, hiring. What they wanted was knowledge about who these companies were. What they designed was this: they first identified 100 prospective client companies that they considered in their 'sweet spot'. Then Jay used his technical savvy to create a 'spider' that would crawl the web, constantly looking for increases in job postings.

When the spider reported that one of the 100 companies had posted a few new jobs, Kim and Jay got on the phone and offered their assistance. These targeted cold-calls helped them increase revenue by $2 million. 'Design what you want or deal with what you get' became a core business practice for them.

Chris arrived at a similar epiphany in 2009 as he struggled to steer his firm, PeopleG2, through the treacherous waters of the subprime mortgage crisis. He had started a remote model and it quickly became apparent that there was a major bottleneck: him. Employees were bringing just about every decision to him. It hadn't been as noticeable in the sticks-and-bricks office, but once these requests started piling up in his email inbox, the bottleneck was clear.

Designing the new process involved delegating responsibilities and clarifying which decisions needed approval and which could be made by an employee. The biggest change, however, was a cultural one that involved empowering employees. This was more than just new processes.

New ways of thinking

It also involved new responsibilities and new ways of thinking. Chris had to do a good deal of coaching, and he heard 'But that's the way we've always done it' a lot. Still, before too long, the inadvertent bottleneck gave way to designed efficiency – and a less cluttered inbox.

In another example, Chris wanted to grow sales by expanding his client base. The mortgage industry had been early adopters of employment background checks, but in 2001, few other industries used this service. Using newspapers and other sources, he found the fax numbers for several targeted prospects. The message he sent was more educational than sales-oriented. It basically said, 'Here's why you NEED to do background checks' rather than pitching his company.

Chris got two kinds of responses. In a lot of cases, people just told him not to do it again. However, a fair number of people said they didn't really appreciate the fax, but they were interested in knowing more. The strategy helped Chris increase revenue by $1 million. By the way, things have changed since then, and you don't want to send unsolicited faxes, texts or any other communication unless the recipient has opted in. But the point of these examples is that creative thinking and some calculated bold risks can help you achieve your goals.

Step by step

Taking your company remote should be a deliberate, curated process. There are steps to follow when designing what you want in your remote model. A lot of people think the first step is setting up the technology, but we disagree. The best sequence to follow is **people, process, tools and technology**. Bring in technology last. If, for example, you have bad processes, technology will only make those bad processes faster.

Instead, start by considering your people. Who are they? What can they do? What can't they do? What do they need to succeed? That leads to processes, which should leverage your people's talents. Rather than being a burdensome checklist, processes should be a smooth flow that makes sense. It frees your people from having to wonder what happens next so that, instead, they focus on being good at what they do.

Next up come the tools that people need in order to keep the process flowing. Tools can be many things, like a laptop or access to industry databases. With people, process and tools in place, you can lock it all down with the technology.

Another good practice in going remote is to bring the strengths you had in your sticks-and-bricks model. Identify what was effective when everyone came into the office, and make sure it translates to the remote model. This includes culture. You'll find that culture is a recurring theme throughout the book. We believe that it is just as important as budgeting and sales and operations. Most likely, even a strong in-office culture will need to evolve to be effective in a remote model. At this point, however, we want to urge you to be just as deliberate about culture as you are about other aspects of your business.

New ways of seeing

We also encourage you to take a fresh look at your company every quarter. Look at everything you have in place, and then shake it up. Scramble the puzzle pieces. Don't assume anything is right. What was right three months ago may not be right today. Another analogy here is to take your cabin apart piece by piece, and then reassemble it. Whichever analogy you use, the process can help you identify duplication of effort, bottlenecks or other inefficiencies. It can also prompt insights into things that are missing or lead to some great new ideas. The remote model is much more malleable and agile than most brick-and-mortar models, allowing for constant revision.

You can think of designing your remote model as a process of visualizing your optimal organization and then painting it on a virtual canvas. Of course, as artful as your business may be, it is more than a painting. It is dynamic and needs oversight every day. For example, how will you know your employees are working? In the office you could survey the cubicles and see everyone hard at work. But was that really effective? Lots of people are good at looking busy, when they're really browsing Amazon.

In a brick-and-mortar model, the emphasis is on input, on workers putting numbers in the database, putting orders in the system, putting reports in the boss's inbox. The remote model puts the emphasis on *output*.

You don't see how your employees work, but as long as the organization is achieving goals, you don't need to see.

When Kim's company went virtual in the early 2000s, the leadership team suddenly had blinders on. They couldn't see how people were spending their time. Yet it turned out to be one of the best things that happened to the company. They realized that they had to come up with new ways of monitoring performance. As a matter of fact, you need to monitor performance even more closely in a remote model.

Even if your company has solid performance metrics in place, try putting on blinders for a day. It will help you find out what you don't know. For example, you may have a best-in-class financial dashboard, but it still doesn't show you what's going on in operations, or what business development is up to today.

While you're focusing on metrics, make sure what you're measuring is valuable. If a metric doesn't add value, don't waste time and money monitoring it. For instance, the time clock mentality doesn't really apply in a virtual model. True, employees have to be available to customers and vendors, but some people may do their best work during off hours. If those people are delivering at a high level, do you really need to know what time they punched in and out? Many companies have found that employees invest *more* time in work when they work at home.

Culture: the key to performance

Your metrics should track progress to defined goals and this brings us back to culture. A robust virtual culture creates team spirit not by the quantity of hours people spend together, but by the quality of the shared mission. If you hire passionate people and they are driven by your mission, they will perform without much micromanagement.

For example, in a remote model you want teamwork, but it's just as important, if not more so, to promote and reward individual growth and excellence. Remote work is similar to on-site work, but it's also different, in the same way that water polo is similar to but different from competitive swimming. While he was in college, Chris coached water polo and swimming at the high school where he had earned the MVP title for water polo. He realized that the difference may be subtle, but it's important.

In water polo, teamwork is essential. Players need to know the team strategies and their responsibilities within the strategies. They need to know where their teammates are at all times, and understand what any teammate is likely to do next. They need to be of one mind.

In contrast, competitive swimming is a more individualized sport. The swim team practises together, helping and encouraging one another, but when the 50-metre freestyle race starts, it all comes down to individual performance.

Your remote team should become like competitive swimmers. There should be collaboration, but an effective remote team depends on solid individual performance. In fact, it's likely that this scenario will reveal those who thrive and those who struggle to work remotely. You may have to coach and encourage those strugglers to adapt, but overall your remote culture should promote pride in individual performance, and allow those performers to stand out.

Kim claims that those who do well in a remote model have a 'Me, Inc.' mentality. They approach their career as if it were a company and they were the CEO. They are motivated not only to excel, but also to develop their skills on an ongoing basis. The virtual model is the ideal place for Me, Inc. thinkers, as their personal talent and tenacity will be revealed and rewarded.

Like everything else, you need to design what you want in culture. Many people hear the word and think, 'warm and fuzzy'. Not necessarily. For example, Steve Jobs created the culture at Apple to be highly demanding. In essence, he told people that they would work like dogs, but they would be part of something unique and amazing.

It's important in a remote model that you have a culture that is clearly defined. It has to be good, if not great, and you have to be proactive about promoting, cultivating and keeping it robust. It will require a shift in thinking on your part and on the part of every employee – that's what we'll explore in Chapter 3.

References

Pepitone, J (2013) Best Buy ends work-from-home program, *CNN*, 5 March, https://money.cnn.com/2013/03/05/technology/best-buy-work-from-home (archived at https://perma.cc/DJN8-5986)

Silverman, E S (2013) At Yahoo, working from home doesn't work, *Wall Street Journal*, 25 February, www.wsj.com/articles/BL-ATWORKB-750 (archived at https://perma.cc/EQR4-K8QE)

03

Spoiler alert – CEOs beware

Remote work is much more than just a change in venue. Everyone in your organization will need to change the way they think. It will be challenging for all, but if you're the CEO, you need to gather your courage, emotional strength and tenacity. Take your company remote, by all means, but don't enter this endeavour lightly.

IN THIS CHAPTER

We will cover:

- It starts at the top
- Global team building
- Challenge your brain
- Output vs input
- Measuring the intangible
- Embrace your inner dragon slayer
- Servant leadership or visionary leader?
- Work *on*, not *in*, your business
- Focus on what is important
- Strengths and compassion

It starts at the top

As a CEO, you already know that it can be lonely at the top. It's similar to being the conductor of an orchestra. You're leading a group of individuals who are experts at their particular instrument. They rehearse in order to be on the same page, but ultimately each performer plays their specific part on their specific instrument. Your job is to hear the entire combined output, the symphony as a whole. If the violins are too fast, you bring them into line. If the percussion is too heavy, you tell them to lighten up. Even in the middle of a concert, the conductor has to be a beat or two *ahead* of the orchestra (Roberts 2017).

Ultimately, the conductor is responsible for selecting the music and defining the interpretation. If the critics pan the performance, the blame falls on the conductor. Like the conductor, the CEO has to see the big picture, set the strategy and guide the organization forward.

Obviously this is a top-down view of things. We're taking this view not to advocate rigid hierarchies, but to help CEOs prepare for the isolation they are bound to experience. A CEO can experience loneliness at the top in a brick-and-mortar model. However, in addition to talking about running a business, we're throwing in leading a major shift in thinking as well as the literal isolation of working from home.

Returning to the analogy, there is some hope for relief from the isolation and loneliness. The orchestra conductor isn't an absolute dictator. Each member of the orchestra is an accomplished professional, and collaboration is valuable. If a trumpet player approaches the conductor with some insight or ideas, the conductor would be foolish to ignore it. Your team should be made up of strong talent, so you can take the same approach. In fact, team building and collaboration will be essential.

With a team of virtuosos who enjoy making beautiful music together, you can get rid of any notion of 'Do this because I say so'. That would be easy. Guiding a team via motivation is much more difficult, even if team members are highly self-motivated. Sometimes it will feel like herding cats – very talented cats, but not always easy to herd.

Global team building

In the remote model you aren't restricted to local talent. The best oboist in the world may be in Poland, and now you can add her to your team. Kim had a VP of Creative Services at one point who came to her almost in tears. The VP and her husband had decided to move to New Zealand to be near his family, and she was devastated about having to quit her job at Decision Toolbox.

'Why would you quit?' Kim asked. 'It's a remote model.' After a few days to move and get settled, the VP opened DT's brand-new Auckland office... in the VP's home.

Challenge your brain

To do this well, you have to be always on, always working to keep the culture fresh and sticky – that is, keep it so interesting and engaging that no one will want to leave. We don't want to discourage you (after all, we're presenting a whole book about how to go remote), but frankly, we both found that being the CEO of a remote company is exhausting. It's lonely. In Kim's words, 'It hurts your brain'.

You can have an advisory group, or tiger's den, as Chris calls it, and that's a great idea. But the responsibility for the decisions still falls on you. You can delegate, and you should. But even though your leadership team then delegates to others, the delegation chain leads back and ultimately ends with you.

It's pretty rare that a team member comes to you and asks, 'How are you doing?' Yet whenever you hear discord or stress in the ranks, you are the first to dive in and sort things out. These things are true in the stick-and-bricks model, but they are even more important in the remote model.

Before taking his company remote, Chris focused his attention on products, customers and sales. In the process of going remote, he realized that his focus had to be on people. Your employees will take care of the products and everything else, so your job is to support them. You need to be able to spot trouble. Kim calls this 'sixth sense moments', when you can see dead people. Well, not really dead, but stuck, frustrated or floundering.

Output vs input

That's when you, the CEO, provide the input needed to get the right output from employees. Kim developed a great way to formalize and apply this idea in the days after 9/11, calling it the Performance Driven Workforce. In PDW, the emphasis is on output rather than input, and employees are rewarded for performance.

For example, her company made it so that a meaningful portion of the team's compensation was based on performance metrics. Those metrics created an index score, and they assigned projects based on those scores.

There were three positive results. First, the frontline people were motivated to perform at a high level, so they could get more work – and, as they were paid by the project, more income. Second, any of them with consistently low scores found the going rough, so they moved on. Third, but not least, high-performing frontline customer-facing people meant highly satisfied clients and repeat business.

In a virtual model you need people who are independent and self-motivated, and the PDW encourages that. If you want to implement PDW, you have to define and communicate the performance metrics clearly to your team. Everyone, team members and leadership alike, has to understand the system, the things you measure, the rewards and the consequences. It's true that collecting all that data requires micromanaging, but your people should use those numbers to micromanage *themselves*. That way you can micro-train but macro-manage.

Another tool to help you and your employees change to a focus on output is Results Over Observed Time, or ROOT. CEOs in brick-and-mortar models tend to look at day-to-day metrics: did the inside sales group make X number of calls, did operations meet today's productivity goals, etc. Kim developed ROOT to get out of that day-to-day micromanagement. By monitoring output, ROOT puts your focus on *what* your company is putting out instead of focusing on *how* you're putting it out.

If you've got a nagging thought trying to surface in your mind, it may be this: we're talking about measuring some very fuzzy things, like teamwork, motivation and culture. A lot of people don't think you can measure those things, and that's the reason a lot of business leaders ignore them. Not only do we disagree, but we believe that, in a remote model, you have to measure many things, including the intangibles.

Measuring the intangible

Chris believes so strongly in measuring that he made it one of the seven pillars of culture success in his book, *The Power of Company Culture*. Measurement counterbalances our human inclination to make sense of things we don't understand. Given a set of facts, we try to make sense of them by applying our experiences and what we have learned in order to fill in the gaps. Sometimes we are right, but very often we are wrong. Consider the halo effect.

If you have a salesperson who brings in a big, new account, does that prove they are a top performer? You might think so – right now they seem to be wearing a halo. However, if you look over relevant spreadsheets, you might conclude that this salesperson missed their goals, failed to reach quota for the year, and consistently underperformed. The numbers tell you to overlook the timely account win and make a better decision about that salesperson.

Similarly, if someone is very good at one thing, it doesn't automatically mean they'll be good at anything you might delegate to them. Someone might be a whizz at managing projects, but they may fall flat when trying to handle sales. As CEO, you need to minimize your bias and see past your assumptions, and measuring helps you do this.

To apply measurement to less tangible things like culture, consider an exercise Google carried out. They used deep data analysis to find out why some teams were highly effective and others were less so. According to Julia Rozovsky (2017), manager of People Analytics at Google, they studied about 180 teams, conducting 200 interviews and looking at 250 personality traits.

They found that team effectiveness had nothing to do with some magic combination of extroverts and introverts, or management with technical expertise. Instead, it hinged on a team's ability to interact effectively. In turn, effective interaction depended on some very fuzzy concepts, such as team members being comfortable taking risks, the personal importance of the work to each member, and the belief that the work will make an impact.

In their book *Work Together Anywhere*, Sutherland and Janene-Nelson (2018) agree with these ideas. For them, remote-only work requires strong collaboration and teamwork so that employees maintain a sense of belonging to and making an impact on the organization. They also agree that the remote model 'focuses on output instead of input'.

Step back to assess

Coaching people on sales technique or teaching them a new accounting system is relatively easy, compared to creating and tending culture. As CEO, you need every advantage, and remote gives you a big one: the ability to step back, see what is working well, where the problems are, and what might be missing (Swiss cheese, remember?).

The remote model gives you time to think. In the sticks-and-bricks model, there is a constant flow of people coming to you for input and advice. Once you go remote, you may still have people reaching out to you, but you can better manage how and when you respond. And you'll rarely be put on the spot.

Embrace your inner dragon slayer

Chris admits that he used to get irritated when people brought him the big issues. But once his company had gone remote, he realized that the big issues are his job. People should be able to solve the smaller issues on their own – the trolls, the big bad wolf. But the dragons? The CEO has to be the dragon slayer. Now Chris enjoys taking on the big issues, in part because he doesn't also have to deal with the smaller ones.

Besides, if you get exasperated every time someone brings you a big issue, they'll avoid it. Thank them. Welcome it. Bask in the glory of your shining armour. At least until you remember that it's a two-edged sword: there can be only one dragon slayer, increasing your CEO isolation.

Servant leadership or visionary leader?

Well-known angel investor and business guru Dave Berkus (Berkus and Shepherd, 2015) adds yet another burden to this grim vision of the lonely CEO: that of being a servant leader. Servant leadership is an approach in which leaders view themselves as the servant of those they lead. They share their power, put the needs of their employees before their own, and help people develop the skills they need to thrive.

To follow the philosophy, you need to empower your people and engage them in decision making. However, Berkus feels that servant leadership is only one of several leadership styles in a CEO's toolbox, and the CEO should use different approaches for different situations.

Writing that there is 'a very thin line between abdication of responsibility and participative leadership', he cites Steve Jobs and Elon Musk as examples of bold leaders. Both had visions with which others disagreed. However, they ignored those people – even members of their senior leadership teams. By following their own vision, even when contrary to employee input, they changed the world.

Ultimately, Berkus believes that a leader can employ servant leadership effectively, but not as a primary leadership style. Otherwise the leader risks being perceived as soft and indecisive.

Work *on*, not *in*, your business

The remote model compels you to work ON your company instead of IN it. For example, once Decision Toolbox (DT) had grown back to the $2 million mark, Kim felt she should bring on a number two to share the growing responsibilities. She got pushback on that idea from her ABL colleagues – conventional wisdom says to hire a number two leader at $4 million. However, Kim trusted her own vision and hired Nicole Cox to lead the growing team of recruiters.

During the interview, Kim glossed over Nicole's strong recruiting experience and instead asked about her parenting skills. The result: Nicole leveraged her 'tough love' mothering approach to build an amazing recruiting team, and Kim was free to stay two beats ahead of the orchestra. In a remote model, employees need both direction and support. Nicole established performance standards and held people accountable, while at the same time promoting a culture that rewarded accomplishments.

Focus on what is important

Along similar lines, Chris came up with the concept of Teams–Relationships–Speed (TRS) to help the business thrive in his new remote model. This contrasts with People–Proximity–Bureaucracy, which is the default emphasis in sticks-and-bricks. Instead of eavesdropping on the conversation in the next cubicle, or worrying who is jockeying for promotion, TRS helps employees focus on what is important.

As Google discovered, what is important is in the relationships, such as team members being comfortable taking risks and believing in the impact of their work. Perhaps just as important in TRS is the speed factor. Chris's efforts in encouraging his team to keep their eye on the prize helped PeopleG2 become a better company *faster*.

At DT, Kim formed several small 'pods' of employees, to promote TRS as well as collaboration and the important feeling of being part of something. A pod consisted of two to four people who met (via conference call) weekly for about an hour to help one another with challenges and share success stories. There might be a little kvetching and personal sharing, too, and all of that builds the relationships and promotes the cultural glue you need to keep the team tight.

Strength and compassion

Both the remote model and TRS need a strong focus on strengths. One of the great lessons from Tom Rath's *StrengthsFinders* book is to stop focusing on the weaknesses and failings you need to remedy, and focus instead on your strengths. You'll need to get a good picture of both individual and team strengths.

Part of that process is a shift in thinking about each employee's goals and, maybe even more importantly, their overall life situation. We often assume that everyone is interested in climbing the corporate ladder and taking on new responsibilities. That isn't always the case. You may already have employees who are very happy doing their current job today, and will be happy in it for years to come. Assuming they are good at it, these people lend stability to your organization.

At the same time, some of your people may be working through life situations like starting a family, getting divorced or caring for ageing parents. In the future they may be interested in taking on new challenges and opportunities, but for right now a status-quo job is just what they need.

Making assumptions about what employees want can cause you to misunderstand their strengths and develop inaccurate expectations. On the positive side, if you become the kind of CEO who supports people in both their professional *and* personal growth, it can become a competitive advantage. You don't have to become a counsellor, but you should be empathetic and willing to give people the space they need. The compassion you show today should motivate the employee to maintain strong performance. It also will engender loyalty and, a year from now, you might have an employee who is driven to take on new responsibilities. We will take a deeper dive into these ideas later in the book.

Hopefully we haven't terrified anyone out of taking their company remote. We both believe thoroughly in the benefits, and neither of us has any regrets. And, in today's landscape, there may not be a lot of choice. Assuming you're still with us, let's move on to Chapter 4 and look at what remote is, and what it isn't.

References

Berkus, D and Shepherd, K (2015) *Get Scrappy: Business insights to make your company more agile*, Berkus Press, Los Angeles

Dyer, C (2018) *The Power of Company Culture: How any business can build a culture that improves productivity, performance and profits*, Kogan Page, London

Rath, T (2007) *StrengthsFinder 2.0*, Gallup Press, Washington DC

Roberts, M S (2017) Why do conductors always conduct ahead of the beat? *Classic FM*, www.classicfm.com/discover-music/why-conductors-beat-ahead (archived at https://perma.cc/RUP7-G8XN)

Rozovsky, J (2017) The five keys to a successful Google team, *re:Work*, https://
    rework.withgoogle.com/blog/five-keys-to-a-successful-google-team (archived at
    https://perma.cc/V3MC-9FQK)
Sutherland, L and Janene-Nelson, K (2018) *Work Together Anywhere: A handbook
    on working remotely–successfully–for individuals, teams, and managers,*
    Collaboration Superpowers, The Hague

04

Scrumming Swiss cheese

Sound delicious? By the end of the chapter it should. We're going to share some practical and structured ways you can focus on the holes in the cheese, design what you want and make it happen. In addition to drawing on our own experience, we'll also share insights from people we respect.

IN THIS CHAPTER

We will cover:

- Scrumming against Covid-19
- Numbers tell the truth
- Deliberate structure
- The Scrum Master
- It's okay to fail
- Blue sky or shippable product
- Finite and infinite
- Welcome to the 'why not?' world

Before going on, think of a couple of problems you face in your organization. Hold those in mind as you read. We're going to introduce a great method for attacking and solving problems (bonus: it has other applications, too). As you read through, your real-life problems should create a strong context for understanding the method. More importantly, once you're done with the chapter, we encourage you to try it on one of those problems. We're confident you'll find it effective.

We believe a remote model is ideally suited to take advantage of all the best tools, leadership models and opportunities for innovation that are available and emerging today. It can flex and change quickly and easily, without the burden of geography, infrastructure, and top-heavy command and control.

Covid-19 actually helps underscore our belief that working remotely helps clear away the clutter. Kim heard Sarah McVanel, an expert on employee recognition, present on the positive relationship between recognition, engagement and bottom-line results. McVanel made the comment that 'Covid-19 has lowered the water line and allowed us to see cracks'.

When companies rushed to send everyone home in response to the pandemic, the sudden change revealed weak spots. It's a blessing in disguise: Covid-19 has made it easier for us to look past the cheese and focus on the holes.

One of the tools that lends itself well to remote work is Scrum, a very effective method that teams can use to define objectives, chunk up the work and get it done quickly. It isn't about the cheese – that is, your day-to-day business, such as background checks or recruiting. It's about focusing on what is NOT there right now, whether it is a gap to fill, a problem to solve, a product to develop or upgrade, or a better way of doing things.

Chris is a Certified Scrum Master, so we'll focus on that approach, but you can use other methodologies or approaches, such as Six Sigma, Lean or Kanban. The important thing is to use a structured approach to the process, from initiating ideas to implementing actions. By 'structure' we don't mean an obsessive/compulsive approach, but you do want a framework that helps the team maintain focus and also promotes a positive, productive team dynamic.

SCRUMMING AGAINST COVID-19

A great example of the power of Scrum comes from mortgage lender Quicken Loans and contact centre innovator Rock Connections (Juan, 2020). They partnered with the City of Detroit to create an efficient process for managing drive-through Covid-19 testing – and they did it fast.

According to David Juan, Director of Engineering at Quicken, some of the challenges included getting the word out, identifying locations, scheduling appointments, keeping people safe during appointments, sharing patient information among multiple stakeholders, and more. They pulled together a team from Quicken and Rock, as well as community stakeholders.

Initially the team planned to accomplish this large feat in 10 days, but it became clear that the need was even more urgent. Through a lot of dedicated hard work, they delivered the system in *five* days. They attribute this to Scrum methodology. There was an almost overwhelming number of issues to be worked out, from making the service public to integrating health records to automating the process of making appointments. Juan writes: 'Using the Scrum methodology, we broke the development down into one-day sprints and committed to delivering working software within each sprint. We had working software by the end of the first day, and every day after that we continued to iterate.'

Their solution allows for efficient and safe mass testing, without patients having to wait in long lines. On the first day the city was able to conduct 200 tests. By constantly learning and adjusting, they soon were at 400 a day and currently handle about 1,000 tests a day.

Numbers tell the truth

The first step, even before you start using the Scrum method, is to identify potential issues. Your experience and intuition can be very useful, but as we said in the previous chapter, measurement is essential. For one thing, it serves as a reality check for your intuition, helping you see past any biases.

Chris put it very well in his book, *The Power of Company Culture*: 'When it comes to business performance, the numbers tell the truth, and valuing this combination – numbers and truth – is a hallmark of great company culture.' For much more detail about measuring, have a look at that book. Meanwhile, here's a quick summary:

- Measuring key performance indicators (KPIs) is highly valuable as an objective way to collect and analyse data, and implement solutions. KPIs are metrics to monitor the most important areas of performance. They can be quantitative, such as a percentage of defects in manufactured parts, or qualitative, such as scores on customer satisfaction surveys. They lend objectivity that brings teams together, rather than dividing them by casting blame. Sharing results encourages individuals to account for their own progress while recognizing that of others.

- Focus on KPIs known to affect the success or failure of your business. Assessments can record performance after the fact, as with customer satisfaction surveys, or they can track in-progress activities such as website analytics. Frequent, periodic evaluation affords comparative and ongoing insights.
- Make sure data collection and analysis are an integral part of your operational framework by using short weekly surveys or a project management system such as Scrum.

Deliberate structure

If you've never heard of Scrum, it was created as a software development methodology, but has proven useful in managing all kinds of projects. It brings teams together to concentrate on a specific topic. In fact, the term originated in rugby to describe a face-to-face physical struggle in which one team tries to advance the ball while the other tries to prevent it. The analogy emphasizes the need for teamwork.

Typically the process starts with an individual who has an idea. It may be about a new product, a problem to be solved, a capital purchase to be made or a variety of other ideas. This individual, known in the Scrum approach as the product owner, reaches out to others to be part of the team.

Right off the bat there is a built-in reality check regarding the new idea. Participation in a Scrum team is voluntary. If the idea is not able to get even a small group excited about and committed to the idea, it may not be worth pursuing.

Let's assume that it is, however. If the topic touches all areas of the company, the team should have cross-functional representation, and each Scrum team should include a different mix of employees, and even partners, vendors and customers. This offers several advantages:

- it strengthens your culture by enabling people to work together in a positive way (more on that in a moment), and brings together people from different departments who otherwise might not interact;
- it ensures a richer mix of ideas;
- it helps ensure broad support across departments;
- it encourages transparency, which can help less assertive employees be more forthright;

- it can provide team members with professional development opportunities;
- it promotes engagement by allowing people to step out of their daily routine, do something a little different, and see the impact of their contribution;
- it can help you achieve inclusion and diversity goals.

The Scrum Master

Once the team is formed, they need to select a Scrum Master. While some companies have certified Scrum Masters on staff, anyone can do the job. The Scrum Master (SM) needs to be objective, so the team often adds a person. If one of the original team members has strong opinions about the topic, that person probably should wait and play the Master role on another Scrum. It definitely should *not* be the product owner. The SM will keep the group on task, assign responsibilities, ensure tasks are completed and help remove obstacles.

The product owner (PO) now provides the team with a list of requirements and tasks, often presented as a story. For example, let's say the PO's idea is to purchase a new customer relationship management (CRM) tool. The PO has some clear ideas about the features that will make their job easier. After massaging, the initial story may be, 'Let's manage client relationships more efficiently. Let's ensure we are capturing the information we need.' It's very common for requirements and stories to evolve during the Scrum. For example, in this case the team probably would decide that more input from the user community is needed.

The Scrum Master (SM) leads the team, at the beginning, in refining the requirements/stories, including defining what success would look like, what failure would look like, and potential options. From there, the SM facilitates the process of breaking down the work into segments known as sprints. The SM assigns tasks at the beginning of each sprint. The length of the sprint can vary (one week is common), but the idea is that, during the sprint, team members work hard and fast – sprint – to accomplish the sprint goal in a timely manner.

Scrum teams should gather daily for a stand-up meeting. It also can be called a daily Scrum. The meeting should be no more than 15 minutes and it's up to the SM to keep everyone focused. Each team member should answer three basic questions:

- What did you accomplish yesterday?
- What are you working on today?
- What is keeping you from accomplishing tasks?

It's okay to fail

One of the things we like best about Scrum is that the focus is on achieving goals, and not on blame or shame. The SM is responsible for ensuring the team dynamic makes each person feel safe to share any information, good or bad. Recall the Google study we discussed in Chapter 3. One of the characteristics of their most effective teams was that everyone felt comfortable sharing. If a team member shares that they were unable to accomplish yesterday's task, the SM takes point on identifying and removing the roadblock, with the help of the team.

In 2017, IBM started transitioning to Agile. You might hear 'Scrum' used interchangeably with 'Agile', and that's somewhat accurate, although there are differences. However, among the things they have in common is a belief in embracing mistakes as learning opportunities. IBM's transition is about much more than software development. They believe Agile has applications across businesses, and see it as a way to transform their culture. In a YouTube video produced by the Scrum Alliance (2017), Marcel Greutmann says that a key goal was 'reinventing IBM'.

Greutmann is General Manager and Global Leader, Agile Professional Services, and explains that Agile 'assumes failure by design. Learn from it, change, and then move forward' (Scrum Alliance, 2017). His group is one of many in IBM that help clients with Agile transformation.

A lot of employees are reluctant to bring bad news to anyone, particularly a boss. At one point, Chris found it helpful to have employees practise giving him bad news. Even when the problem was fictitious, some people struggled. However, by demonstrating a constructive approach during the role play, Chris was able to teach them that the emphasis always would be on creating solutions, not on pointing fingers.

The Scrum method also allows the SM to rein people in as necessary, ensuring that everyone has a chance to speak, and that the conversation doesn't get derailed. That means the SM has to be assertive and diplomatic, and willing to say things like, 'Let's park that design idea for now, since this 15 minutes is focused on the budget'. On the other side of the coin, the SM should be able to get more reluctant team members to open up.

At the end of each sprint, there should be a similar meeting that may last a little longer. The team discusses how things went, what they might need to do differently and lessons learned. Again, the SM's job is to keep the meeting on track and promote a comfortable, transparent dynamic. You need to learn from things that did *not* go well, but also take time to celebrate the successes. Chris's employees report that it feels awesome when they get to share what went well. Then you start on the next sprint.

Blue sky or shippable product

You can use Scrum to achieve a tangible result, like a software product, or to encourage brainstorming. Kim put a fun but also fruitful twist on Scrum at quarterly in-person all-staff meetings. She had everyone break into groups deliberately organized so each team had two members from the same department. Then she asked each group to imagine that they had a million dollars to spend on making the company better.

Kim calls exercises like these 'tsunami planning' rather than Scrums, but the similarities are the essence of our message. For example, a million dollars is a lot of blue sky, so it helped people feel free to throw anything onto the table. It also helped people gain insight into how other departments work, and strengthened people's sense of belonging to a team.

The result was a LOT of great ideas, and about 80 per cent of them didn't cost a penny to implement. However, it took the tsunami planning exercise to draw the ideas out. Participants discovered that others were thinking about the same things. They also discovered differences, by design, in a space that was safe.

Chris also put his own spin on the idea by combining Scrum with tsunami planning. He poses topics that involve big, hypothetical events, such as 'How will we respond if a competitor takes away 30 per cent of our market share?' The events don't have to be negative. What if revenues suddenly jumped by 40 per cent? If your response to that is 'Dream on, buddy', that's exactly the idea. Whether you are Scrumming or tsunami planning, you have to provide a box so big that your people have to really stretch to think outside it.

The tsunami planning sessions also resulted in great ideas, and Chris kept (and continues to keep) records for future reference. If something happens, he can skip the panic step and go right to solving it. Chris still does this monthly, and not only do his people look forward to the sessions, but they also get better at it each time.

Scrum levels the hierarchy, at least within a Scrum team. That means no one is exempt from being the subject of a solution. For example, Kim's leadership team seemed to be getting tangled in their own underwear, creating a bottleneck that impacted the rest of Decision Toolbox. To figure out what was going on, Kim created a Scrum team to go out and get input from across the organization. The commission determined that certain leaders were causing major bottlenecks. Kim's leadership team made changes based on this input. Sometimes you need to let employees 'boss around' executives – even the CEO.

Finite and Infinite

It's important to distinguish Scrum teams, which are finite, from infinite teams, like Sales, Customer Service, Marketing, Finance, etc. Infinite teams may change, but they are a consistent part of your company. Typically they are established by the CEO or other executives and managed by a single leader. They include team members that are specialists in the specific area, and team member responsibilities remain the same over time.

In contrast, once the goal is achieved, a Scrum team dissolves. The teams are self-forming, and people join because they care about the topic. They are facilitated by a Scrum Master, but should operate with a good deal of independence from leadership. Teams have cross-functional membership, team members' tasks can change from week to week, and tasks aren't necessarily assigned according to a team member's area of specialization.

The finite nature of Scrum teams helps ensure that nobody, including the CEO, always dips into the same pool of A players, which could limit opinions, ideas and outcomes. Participation is optional, which ensures that people are motivated. Scrum levels the field, making team members equal in rights and responsibilities to encourage transparency. For example, in a standup meeting, any team member can call what Lisette Sutherland terms ELMO: 'Enough – let's move on'. In the rules of Scrum, everyone has to respect that request.

Scrum teams enable you to promote Swiss cheese thinking at all levels. Infinite teams focus on the cheese, but Scrum teams allow employees to step away from the daily cheese and get creative in the holes. The hierarchical design of most infinite teams can discourage open employee feedback, but Scrum creates a safe place for exactly that. IBM's Greutmann puts it this way: 'We welcome employee pushback. We want ideas coursing their way up.'

Welcome to the 'why not?' world

When you implement intentional and structured processes like Scrum, you empower your people to deal with problems and drive positive change. The remote model is the ideal platform for this. Away from the office, there is less noise and fewer politics. It makes it easier for people to think, 'Sure, why not?'

Without those distractions, people can – and do – focus more on core work.

The makers of RescueTime, a productivity/time tracking tool, searched their data to confirm this. According to Jory MacKay (2020), their data comes from millions of users. They found that knowledge workers are more productive when working at home than in the office. 'More productive' is defined as focusing on the key responsibilities in one's job description.

They also measured how much time remote and in-office employees spend in communication, which includes meetings, email and chat. They found that remote workers spend 4 per cent more time on core work and 18 per cent less time on communication than office workers. When you look at that over the course of the average 261 working days in a year, it translates to 58 more hours (1.4 weeks) on core work and 256 fewer hours (6.4 weeks) on communication.

Does this mean we're advocating the elimination of communication? Of course not. But it turns out that Zoom-type meetings tend to be more efficient than in-person ones. More people show up on time, there are fewer distractions, and meeting leaders seem to be more committed to staying on point. Perhaps even more importantly, the RescueTime data shows that 'People who work from home report finishing more daily tasks and feeling better about their accomplishments'. Greater productivity, happier employees, no commute – it's hard to argue with that.

While we're at it, why not join the Remote Work Movement community on Slack? We're making sure the community is a safe space for exploring the holes in the Swiss cheese – sharing ideas and solutions about better ways of leading and working in a remote model. Sign up at https://chrisdyer.com/remotework.

In Chapter 5, we'll help you answer the question, 'Who's in your orchestra pit?'

References

Juan, D (2020) Rocket Mortgage Technology team creates open-source COVID-19 mass testing platform [blog] *Rocket Mortgage Technology Blog*, 11 May, https://medium.com/rocket-mortgage-technology-blog/announcing-mass-testing-platform-an-open-source-covid-19-drive-through-testing-platform-and-593d49a318 (archived at https://perma.cc/Q4SB-YQB6)

MacKay, J (2020) Work from home productivity data: Why you (and your manager) shouldn't be afraid of remote work, *RescueTime Blog*, 1 April, https://blog.rescuetime.com/work-from-home-productivity-data/ (archived at https://perma.cc/XQ3L-STHL)

Scrum Alliance (2017) IBM's agile transformation (online video) www.youtube.com/watch?v=Xu0nxyebc6g (archived at https://perma.cc/M2YG-HWRV)

05

Who is in your orchestra pit?

If you've been waiting for some action steps, here they come. Hopefully you tried a practice Scrum, as we suggested in Chapter 4, but now we're moving away from practice. It's game time. We're going to share two exercises that will help you understand the talents and strengths of the players in your orchestra. Remember we said, 'You should be working ON your business, and not IN it'? Well, get suited up.

IN THIS CHAPTER

We will cover:

- SWOT: entering the matrix
- DiSC: by the Spear of Athena!
- StrengthsFinder 2.0: accentuating the positive
- Staying fluid
- Pulling it all together
- Remote makes it easier

It's important to know your talent, particularly in a remote model. You want each person to invest their time in what they do best and what they love doing. Everyone has tasks they're not crazy about, even CEOs. But we're not talking about the administrative things everyone has to do, like documenting a call in the CRM system. We're talking about each person's main focus, whether it is closing deals or closing the books.

When employees use their strengths and enjoy doing so, they will be energized and engaged. However, if someone does a great job on one task, it's easy to think they will want responsibility for more projects, even those that are completely different. One example might be, 'Maria did a great job on updating the employee handbook. I'll ask her to lead the employee events committee.' You just assumed Maria is good at just about anything, right?

Not necessarily. Take a moment to imagine you are Maria, and you are really uncomfortable when people come to you for direction. Now you're saddled with a project that fills you with dread. Now imagine you are sitting all alone in your home office, with no idea where to start. Can you feel your motivation starting to fizzle? On the other hand, give Maria another manual to update, and she'll go above and beyond, putting in extra time and effort because she enjoys it.

That's why it's important to know each employee's strengths. Then you can say, 'Marcus is great at building relationships and collaborating. He would be perfect to lead the events committee.' And chances are good that Marcus will jump on the task with enthusiasm.

This level of insight is true CEO enlightenment. However, there are several steps you'll need to take to get to that level, in this order: SWOT 1, StrengthsFinder, DiSC and SWOT 2. You may or may not be familiar with these tools and methods. You may have used them. Either way, we're about to describe each of them. We're suggesting you apply them to your entire organization, or at least to a group within the organization, such as your leadership team.

Here's the really fun part: each exercise provides you with insights, and each exercise is a great team builder and motivator. You can spread the exercises over a month of Friday afternoons, getting together via videoconference. While we are advocates of remote models, we recognize the value in getting the team face to face periodically. These exercises would be great for a two-day retreat – it might be a lot for one day. Our recommendations assume that your team is gathered in one location, as some parts help you visualize your company in different ways. We also recommend you have participants complete the DiSC and StrengthsFinder assessments online prior to the gathering.

The journey of a thousand miles starts with a SWOT assessment of your company. The StrengthsFinder and DiSC tools are for individuals, but SWOT is for your company. It can be used by departments, such as IT, or at the outset of a new initiative, such as a marketing campaign. However, in this exercise, you want an overall view of your workplace.

SWOT stands for strengths, weaknesses, opportunities and threats. MindTools.com (nd) suggests that you 'use SWOT analysis to assess your organization's current position before you decide on any new strategy'. As the acronym suggests, it helps you make the most of your strengths, address weaknesses, capitalize on opportunities and manage threats.

It's free and relatively easy, and we recommend bearing in mind a couple of things when you work on it. First, this is NOT something to do on your own. There is a degree of subjectivity inherent in the assessment, so you want to minimize the subjectivity by involving people from different areas and levels within your organization (Grant, 2020). Make sure your SWOT team is diverse so you get input from people with different backgrounds and world views.

Second, this is not something the CEO can delegate. It is essential that leadership is represented on the team, if only to ensure the CEO hears the different input. However, you may want someone other than the CEO to lead the process to help promote an open forum.

SWOT: entering the matrix

Start your SWOT process by drawing a four-square matrix, one for each of the elements: Strengths, Weaknesses, Opportunities and Threats. Engage your team in brainstorming about where your company stands, right now, with regard to each element. List the input and ideas in the appropriate square. It may help to point out that strengths and weaknesses are internal, while opportunities and threats are usually external.

To get the brainstorm started, you should ask some of the following questions. Participants can think about the questions in terms of themselves as an individual, their department or team, and/or the company overall. At this stage, there are no wrong answers. Later you'll be able to prioritize the most crucial ones.

Strengths

- What do we do very well?
- What do customers or partners see as our strengths?
- What is our unique value proposition or competitive advantage?
- What are our chief assets and resources?

Weaknesses

- What could we do better?
- What expertise do we lack?
- What are our most common customer complaints?
- In what ways is our financial picture weak?

Opportunities

- Is there an emerging trend (technology, consumer preferences, etc) we can take advantage of?
- Are there features and/or benefits of our products or services that we might consider changing or adding?
- Is there a niche market we're overlooking?
- Are we hearing requests from customers that suggest new products or services?

Threats

- Are there emerging trends that might threaten our market position?
- Are employees happy and loyal, or are we at risk of losing them to competitors?
- Can we anticipate things our competitors might do differently?
- What factors might interrupt our supply chain?

But wait, there's more…

Ideally, at the end of the brainstorm, you'll have plenty of ideas/issues in each quadrant. Save the detailed list, but for right now spend time narrowing each quadrant down to the top two or three most important items. Normally, this is the point where you should start developing a strategy to respond to the items, although we'll ask you to hold on for now. You can cross-reference the items, such as looking at how to leverage a strength to mitigate a threat. For example, if one of your threats is a new, up-and-coming competitor, and one of your strengths is an exceptional reputation over 25 years, you might want to develop a marketing strategy that emphasizes 'the brand you've trusted for 25 years'.

However, in this exercise, we want you to hold onto that analysis just a little longer. In general, input used for a SWOT analysis is subject to change, so you should update it on a regular basis. In fact, we suggest you re-do the analysis (SWOT 2 in our sequence) after you've used the StrengthsFinder and DiSC tools. With deeper insight into strengths and weaknesses, we're 99 per cent sure you'll get a different SWOT picture. It will prove interesting, and it might very well prompt you to rethink your strategy.

DiSC: by the Spear of Athena!

Now that you have an overall assessment of your company, you need to get a good understanding of your individual employees. We recommend you do the DiSC assessment next. It gives an individual assessment that is also based on the environment – on each person within a professional context.

This stems from the theories of William Moulton Marston (1928), presented in his book *Emotions of Normal People*. Marston's research led him to develop DiSC so that it assesses a person's behaviour in relation to their environment (Gupton, 2013).

An interesting aside: Marston was also involved in the development of the lie detector and the DC Comics character Wonder Woman. 'By the Spear of Athena' is one of her catchphrases. According to Angela Robinson (2017), who wrote and directed the film *Professor Marston and the Wonder Women*, Marston incorporated DiSC concepts into the character and the early comic books. A word of warning: the film, rated R, is *not* intended for young fans of Wonder Woman.

So grab your Lasso of Truth (available anywhere they sell Wonder Woman paraphernalia) and let's dive into DiSC, which stands for dominance, influence, steadiness and conscientiousness. A lot of websites claim it is useful for identifying leadership styles, and it is, but it is broader than that. We're using it to help you and your employees discover individual working styles.

It also can help you improve team performance and is well suited for working remotely. As early as 2006, Janet Duck, Director, Excellence in Teaching & Learning at Pennsylvania State University, described how it can help virtual teams be more effective in academic settings: 'The assessment information can be translated into behavioural cues to be used by team members in virtual teams.'

The DiSC assessment uses a 'forced choice' format and consists of a series of statement groups, each including four statements. For example, one set may be:

- People look up to me.
- I tend to be a kind person.

- I accept life as it comes along.
- People say I have a strong personality.

You review each set of four statements and then select the one that you feel applies *most* accurately to you. Then you select the one that *least* applies. In some sets you may find it hard to choose – none may apply, or several may apply equally in your mind. Nonetheless, you are instructed to do the best you can – that's why it's called a forced answer test. Also keep in mind that there are no right or wrong answers. The only way to fail a DiSC case is to be untruthful in responding.

There are different versions and the number of statement groups can vary. Some can be done in 15 minutes, but it shouldn't take more than an hour. We suspect that the shorter ones may not provide the depth and accuracy of longer ones, but we'll leave it to you to decide which version is best.

Assessment results will indicate how each person 'scored' in each of the four areas, or personality types. 'Score' may not be the best term because we tend to associate it with winning and losing, or better and worse. People don't fall into one type or another. Rather, they will have a mix of all four types, with an emphasis on one or two. With DiSC, you're getting a profile. It doesn't tell you who your best employees are; it helps you understand what each employee may be best at doing, and suggests the best way to communicate with each one.

Type profiles

There are traits associated with each of the four personality types. These traits suggest the kinds of tasks or assignments that may be easier or harder for each person. We'll get to that in just a bit, but first let's understand the four types with the following summaries that are based on Fallon (2015) and Rohm (2013).

Dominance

- People who score high in this type tend to be highly motivated and competitive. They enjoy challenges and adding accomplishments to their résumé. They are adept at commanding groups and audiences, and value action, competency and concrete results.
- D-types will have to work a little harder when faced with tasks that require patience and attention to detail. Others may consider them direct, demanding and maybe even insensitive.

- To communicate successfully with a D person, get directly to the bottom line and avoid generalizations, and focus on solutions rather than problems.

Influence

- I-types display enthusiasm, optimism, collaboration and warmth. They appreciate approval and bring energy, affirmation and an action orientation. Often they are good at coaching and counselling.
- People in this type can fear disapproval and become frustrated when they are unable to influence others. They may be challenged to follow through completely and speak candidly.
- For communication success, make a connection by sharing your own experiences with them and allowing them time to ask questions and share their thoughts. Stay positive, minimize details and don't interrupt them.

Steadiness

- People in the S group enjoy cooperating with others on defined tasks, helping and being appreciated for it. They typically are calm, deliberate and predictable, and they value loyalty, security and group acceptance.
- They may be uncomfortable with change, unclear expectations, multitasking or confrontation, and are more inclined to humility at the cost of self-promotion.
- Communication success: be amiable and show your interest in them as people. Ensure your messages and expectations are clear, be polite and avoid being confrontational.

Conscientiousness

- Those with high C scores value accuracy, quality and details, and prefer to work independently and systematically. They enjoy knowledge gain and personal growth, and they respect diplomacy.
- They can, however, overanalyse situations and themselves, slowing the decision-making process. They may have a hard time delegating, fear being wrong, and are not entirely comfortable in group social events. People may consider them standoffish and they can become isolated.
- When communicating with your C people, emphasize facts and details and avoid emotional or pep-talk language. Be patient and persistent.

Put a finer point on it

Some people will have scores so high in one area that their personality type falls squarely into one of the four above. However, most people will have higher scores in two areas. We can get an even more accurate summary of each person's score by using 12 personality subtypes.

For example, a person whose strongest score is in influence and second-strongest score is in steadiness is said to be an IS. However, those with very strong scores in a single area and very weak scores in the other three can be assigned a single letter.

Each type also has a name that helps summarize the type. According to LinkedIn (2019), they are:

- DC: The Challenger
- D: The Winner
- DI: The Seeker
- ID: The Risk Taker
- I: The Enthusiast
- IS: The Buddy
- SI: The Collaborator
- S: The Peacekeeper
- SC: The Technician
- CS: The Bedrock
- C: The Analyst
- CD: The Perfectionist

Line 'em up

Once everyone has completed their assessment and has a DiSC profile, it's helpful for you to visualize the array of types in your organization. The next step is to arrange the team according to their personality types. DiSC assessments often are summarized graphically in a circle divided into four quadrants. If you are doing this exercise in person, such as at an all-staff meeting, you might draw a circle on the floor.

If your team is bigger, you can have all the Ds stand together, all the Is stand together, etc. In addition, have them line up according to sub-type. In the D category, for example, you would have the DCs on one side, the Ds in the middle, and the DIs on the other side. Next would come the IDs, Is, ISs and so on.

In a remote group, you can use the illustration features available in many video conference platforms. After the meeting, you might have someone refine them so that you can distribute them among your team. Either in person or on a chart, the visualization should provide you with some insights.

Most of your executives will be high on dominance and influence. The challengers, winners, seekers, risk takers, enthusiasts and even buddies are results oriented, driven, commanding and enthusiastic. They see the bigger picture, but they also see what isn't there (to refer back to our analogy, they spend a lot of time working in the holes of the Swiss cheese). Conversely, those in the steadiness and conscientious categories are the ones who get things done, handling the details, working dependably and systematically. These team members work in the cheese. You also may find that people in the same categories tend to be friends, even if they are in different departments.

This exercise helps you see who is in your orchestra pit, but it also can help you spot potential ways to improve team and individual performance. For example, are the right personality types in the right roles? It's an extreme example, but if your head of sales is not a D or I, there may be something wrong. You also can assess balance in your organization and departments. If you're heavy in one type, you can focus recruiting efforts on bringing in more of the types in which the company is light.

A key message in this chapter is to ensure your people are doing what they love. You may see from completing this exercise with your team that there are people who might be happier and more fulfilled in a different position. Even a couple of minor adjustments can make an individual, team or department more effective. The insight provided by this and the other tools (below) is especially valuable in a remote model, since communication and interpersonal dynamics are different than they are in an office.

StrengthsFinder: accentuate the positive

Next up is StrengthsFinder, now rebranded as CliftonStrengths to honour Don Clifton, who developed the concept while CEO of Gallup, Inc. Tom Rath, Clifton's grandson (Publishers Weekly, nd), updated the work and it was published in 2007 as *StrengthsFinder 2.0*. According to Dan Kopf (2016), it is the only book to appear on Amazon's list of top 10 bestsellers for 10 years running, from 2007 to 2016. In this regard, it outperformed books in immensely popular series like *A Song of Ice and Fire* (aka 'Game of Thrones'), *Harry Potter*, *Diary of a Wimpy Kid* and *The Hunger Games*.

One reason for its popularity is the fact that it doesn't tell you what's wrong with you. Instead, it helps you understand what your key strengths are, so you can use them to excel. It helps you know what's awesome about you. In fact, the American Psychological Association honoured Clifton with a Presidential Commendation, calling him 'the father of strengths-based psychology and the grandfather of positive psychology' (University of Nebraska – Lincoln, 2018).

The actual StrengthsFinder assessment takes 30 to 45 minutes, and is completed online. It is made up of 177 questions covering 34 strength themes divided into four domains: Strategic Thinking, Relationship Building, Influencing and Executing. Like DiSC, it is a forced response format, presenting pairs of phrases that may describe you. Some pairs are straightforward, such as 'I am a sensitive person' and 'I am a logical person'. Others require a bit more thought, like 'I dream about the future' and 'People are my greatest ally'. Still, you make your best choice and indicate the extent to which that choice describes you.

Once you've completed all the questions, you'll receive a report indicating your five top strengths along with information about your particular strength mix. In fact, the report reveals how all 34 themes are combined in your unique profile. However, for our purposes, we'll focus on an individual's top five. It is those, we believe, that really reveal a person's work style and preferences, what energizes them and how they connect with others.

To give you some examples, here are some of the 34 strength themes, divided into the four larger domains (Gallup, nd):

Strategic thinking

- Analytical
- Context
- Ideation

Relationship building

- Positivity
- Relator
- Individualization

Influencing

- Command
- Maximizer
- Communication

Executing

- Achiever
- Belief
- Responsibility

Real stories from real people

To put all this StrengthsFinder information in context, we'll share our own strengths.

Kim's strengths:

- Ideation: A fascination for ideas and the ability to find connections between things most consider unrelated.
- Belief: Having certain unchanging core values that provide a purpose in life.
- Communication: A knack for putting thoughts into words. People with this strength are good presenters and conversationalists.
- Positivity: Contagious enthusiasm that motivates and engages others.
- Achiever: Stamina, a strong work ethic – achievers love to be productive.

Chris's strengths:

- Ideation: A fascination for ideas and the ability to find connections between things most consider unrelated.
- Command: Strong presence and the ability to take control and make decisions.
- Individualization: Strong interest in what makes each person unique, and an ability to determine how diverse people can work well together.
- Responsibility: Psychological commitment to doing what they say and a commitment to values such as honesty and loyalty.
- Relator: Appreciation for close relationships and satisfaction in working with friends to reach a goal.

Seize the whiteboard

We'll get to the group exercise shortly, but this story shows the strengths at work. Chris and Kim were both supporters of Working Wardrobes, a non-profit based in Irvine, California that helps people overcome difficult challenges so they can achieve the dignity of work and the 'Power of a Paycheck'. As members of the board of directors, they were in a meeting to find ways to raise funds.

In fact, Kim was leading the brainstorm. The room had board members, volunteers, employees and others, and there were many good ideas. However, the group was getting bogged down and they weren't moving forward. Kim was thinking, 'We're all rowing, but don't know where we're going.'

Chris was thinking something different: 'We're just *talking* about rowing – no one is doing it.' He asked, 'Kim, can I take over the process?' She gladly agreed.

Kim and Chris are both ideators, so getting the flow of ideas going wasn't a challenge. But Chris's second strength is command. He stepped up to the whiteboard and, within a few minutes, led the group to map out some tangible goals and actions. Chris wasn't bossy or aggressive, he just leveraged his command presence to get things done. According to Kim, the transformation in the meeting was as smooth as silk.

Make your mark

At your StrengthsFinder meeting, put up a banner that has all 34 strengths listed across the top. Give everyone two sticky dots and ask them to put their name on both. Now ask them to go up to the banner and put their dots under their number one and two strengths.

You now have another visual tool for understanding your company as a whole. Is there a balance of strengths, or do three or four personality types make up the majority of your staff? Are there important strengths missing? The results can be insightful.

For example, when Kim did this exercise at a Decision Toolbox all-staff meeting, not one single dot out of about 200 was under competition. As the group talked about the lack of competitiveness, they realized most people competed with themselves, wanting to be better tomorrow than they were today. Like members of the violin section in the orchestra, they didn't compete with other violins, or with the woodwinds or brass. Even the strong sales team was more focused on sharing a good solution than on beating the other guy.

Chris discovered that StrengthsFinder helped him achieve a diversity of goals. He, too, did the banner exercise and recognized that PeopleG2 was short on some important strengths. He decided, moving forward, that he would only hire people if they had at least one of the strengths the company needed. He wanted people who thought differently in order to mix things up. Within a relatively short time, his team included a broader mix of strengths. The team also had much more diversity in ethnicity, gender, orientation and other areas. The remote model makes it easier to accomplish this, simply by making the whole world your talent pool.

When your orchestra is well balanced, it is a special thing. Not only is the music much more vibrant and impactful, but the players are much more enthusiastic. A virtuoso clarinettist knows the piece and music theory, and could probably do an adequate job if asked to play the timpani. But there is a reason the clarinettist became a virtuoso: the instrument is the right fit for their personality type. It gives them satisfaction and fulfilment to play it, and play it very well.

When your team works remotely, it is essential to understand personality types. For example, Kim's personality type means she loves to present. Give her a microphone, sit back and enjoy the show. But she doesn't enjoy creating the presentations and slides. Decision Toolbox's revenue depended on Kim's speaking engagements, so she found Sharene Cleveland, a professional with a passion for organizing strong growth for both of them.

Leverage individual strengths

Remember Maria and Marcus? Maria has the strength input, according to StrengthsFinder. Input is a drive to collect and organize information. Her DiSC assessment places her in the conscientiousness quadrant, suggesting she appreciates accuracy and therefore has a strong detail orientation. No wonder she did a great job on the manual.

But C people also can have a hard time with delegation and social events. Asking her to lead the events committee is likely to lead to poor results. Worse, it's almost torture for Maria. Like all your employees, Maria deserves to do the kind of work she loves.

On the other hand, Marcus's DiSC assessment puts him in the influence quadrant, meaning he's big on collaboration, good at influencing others, and generally optimistic. His top strengths may include arranger or connectedness. We don't even have to define those – you know he would be ideal for the events committee. Is he the best choice for creating a manual? Probably not.

Stay fluid

Both DiSC and StrengthsFinder are fluid. Recall that DiSC assesses an individual's behaviour within an environmental context. If you complete one DiSC in the context of your company and one in the context of a non-profit you support or your church, you may get different results. It's also possible to use the results to fine-tune your personality.

Chris worked for his uncle when he was 16 and his uncle asked him to do the DiSC assessment. He has always scored highest in dominance, but at age 16 he also scored high in steadiness. That didn't sit well with Chris, as it suggested a low level of comfort with change and a reluctance to try new things. Spurred by a kind of cognitive dissonance with those results, Chris deliberately began being more adventurous. Over the next few years he went to new places, met new people and ordered food he'd never tried before. In college he took the assessment again and his steadiness score was much lower.

Pulling it all together

These are big exercises, but worth doing periodically to ensure the entire organization is aligned with strategy and to keep the orchestra well tuned. SWOT assessments can be useful in starting a new project or initiative. All the assessments are valuable for both finite and infinite teams.

Here, pull together the insights you have from the exercises and use these suggestions for putting them to work in the context of your overall company. Many of these apply to projects and Scrum events as well:

- Ensure the right people are in the right roles, the roles that will keep them engaged and enthusiastic. Solutions may involve changing jobs completely, but you also can consider divvying up the responsibilities differently.

- Ensure you and your leaders and managers adjust their communication strategies to each individual employee's personality type. Not necessarily a simple task but one that pays big dividends.

- Ensure you and your team know what success looks like to avoid rowing without knowing where you're going.

- Ensure you and your team know what failure looks like, so you can predict what might go wrong or identify changes needed regarding your team, processes, marketing dynamics, competitors, etc.

- Ensure everyone knows how the group has agreed to deal with conflict. You can use any strategy, but everyone needs to know what it is. This will promote the open, safe atmosphere you want, and help you row when the waters get choppy.

Remote makes it easier

These tools are important in your remote model, and we believe they work even better in a remote environment than they do in sticks-and-bricks companies. For the CEO and other leaders, working remotely requires you to be able to step out of the rat race and think big picture. It requires that you focus on purpose, coaching and performance in different ways, rather than on 'office politics'.

Remote work compels you to focus on human nature, as well as group and individual strengths. Remote situations need trust, clear processes, strong communication, discipline and proactive leadership. It's harder when you're starting out and you have to do it right because your company won't survive in a bad culture.

You shouldn't go into a remote model lightly; in the next chapter we'll help you find out if you have what it takes.

References

Duck, J (2006) Making the connection: Improving virtual team performance through behavioral assessment profiling and behavioral cues, *Developments in Business Simulation and Experiential Learning*, **33**, pp 358–59, https://absel-ojs-ttu.tdl.org/absel/index.php/absel/article/view/544 (archived at https://perma.cc/LUN9-S9CL)

Fallon, N (2015) DiSC assessment: What kind of leader are you? *Business News Daily*, 30 December, www.businessnewsdaily.com/8692-disc-assessment.html#:~:text=overview%20of%20each.-,Dominance,focuses%20on%20the%20bottom%20line.&text=Learn%20more%20about%20the%20Dominance%20style (archived at https://perma.cc/R2Y7-G6PH)

Gallup (nd) The 34 CliftonStrengths themes explain your talent DNA, *Gallup*, www.gallup.com/cliftonstrengths/en/253715/34-cliftonstrengths-themes.aspx (archived at https://perma.cc/TDJ3-R9MK)

Grant, M (2020) Strength, weakness, opportunity, and threat (SWOT) analysis, *Investopedia*, 24 February, www.investopedia.com/terms/s/swot.asp (archived at https://perma.cc/YND2-CCEN)

Gupton, C (2013) Understanding DISC personality test, part 1 – DISC profile model of behavior, *DiSCPersonalitySource.com*, 11 December, www.discpersonalitysource.com/understanding-disc-profile/tag/disc-assessment (archived at https://perma.cc/RVD9-L2PR)

Kopf, D (2016) Only one book has made the Amazon Top 10 every year for the past decade, *Quartz*, 21 December, https://qz.com/868736/strengthfinder-2-0-is-the-only-book-that-has-made-the-amazon-top-ten-every-year-for-the-last-decade (archived at https://perma.cc/P5C9-6M57)

LinkedIn (2019) All about the 12 DISC personality types, *LinkedIn*, 12 December, www.indeed.com/career-advice/career-development/disc-personality-types (archived at https://perma.cc/U2VU-BZ74)

Marston, W M (1928) *Emotions of Normal People* (2012 reprint), Target Training International, Ltd, Scottsdale, Arizona.

Mind Tools (nd) SWOT analysis: How to develop a strategy for success, www.mindtools.com/pages/article/newTMC_05.htm (archived at https://perma.cc/MK68-VSMH)

Publishers Weekly (nd) How full is your bucket? Positive strategies for work and life, *Publishers Weekly*, www.publishersweekly.com/9781595620033 (archived at https://perma.cc/B4EA-YAEU)

Robinson, A (2017) *Professor Marston and the Wonder Women*, Annapurna Pictures, Los Angeles

Rohm, R A (2013) What is DISC? It is a powerful way to understand people and their personality types! *Discovery Report*, www.discoveryreport.com/introduction-to-disc-personality-types.html (archived at https://perma.cc/UUX5-5765)

University of Nebraska – Lincoln (2018) Don Clifton Legacy, UNL College of Business, 29 April, https://business.unl.edu/news/don-clifton-legacy/?contentGroup=clifton_strengths_institute (archived at https://perma.cc/5JZF-Z859)

06

Why not remote?

Between us we have more than 25 years of experience leading successful virtual companies, with all our employees working remotely. We also have 25+ years of hearing people tell us why their company *can't* go remote. And you know what? Some of them may be right.

IN THIS CHAPTER

We will cover:

- Structural obstacles
- Cultural obstacles

Even now, when remote appears to be the new fad and everybody seems to be doing it, some resist. Ninety per cent of this book is about why you should and how you can. Here's the 10 per cent about why you may not be able to.

We believe that the obstacles to going remote fall into two categories: structural and cultural. As we describe first the structural and then the cultural obstacles, evaluate your company and your own mindset. Even if you already have decided to go remote, you'll get some insights into challenges you'll face. We only ask that you keep an open mind and be honest with yourself. At the end of the chapter, if you're convinced you can't go remote, feel free to stop reading. If you're still with us, much of what follows in the next chapters will be how to overcome these barriers.

Structural obstacles

Structural obstacles generally involve tangibles such as location or tools. Although it may not be easy, you can overcome most obstacles in both categories. However, some structural obstacles are absolute, and change simply isn't possible.

'The work has to be done at a specific location.' If you want to make wine, someone has to be in the vineyard. If you want to make aeroplanes, someone has to be in the hangar. Keep in mind that many employees in such organizations may be able to work remotely, such as accountants, marketers and IT professionals.

'The work has to be done with team members in the same room.' This was one of the reasons cited by Yahoo! when they changed their work-from-home policy: 'We need to be one Yahoo!, and that starts with physically being together' (Newport, 2020). We don't find this to be a very compelling objection. Many companies have teams that are dispersed in multiple cities – not 'in the same room' – and the work gets done. However, some specific situations require that people be together. For example, some software developers do dual coding, working next to one another with shared screens.

'Direct command and control is required.' This is not just about bosses needing to feel in control – that's a cultural obstacle. Instead, think about the person operating and supervising a flight simulator for trainees.

'The right tools don't exist or are not affordable.' If your job requires you to use Google for internet research, you can't do that remotely in China. That's an extreme example, but there may be locations where there is no infrastructure available. Your company may not be able to afford to set everyone up with the equipment to work from home. For example, the State of California requires employers to reimburse workers for all 'necessary' and 'reasonable' expenses, including the costs of working from home (National Law Review, 2020).

'There are legal, compliance or geopolitical complications.' The ideal programmer for a unique coding language may be in Iran – but there are sanctions against doing business there. If you have remote employees in multiple locations, you may need a business licence for each state. A highly talented project manager may live in New York, but your human resources team may not have the bandwidth to learn the complex employment laws there.

'Working across multiple time zones is impractical.' Chris, who is on the West Coast, has one employee on the East Coast who works from 6 am to

9 am. He has arranged to touch base with her periodically at a time that works for both. Kim, working from California, had an employee in New Zealand. That employee was one day ahead but several hours earlier in the day. Not only could this cause issues with arranging client conversations, but it could also impact on your own schedule. If you can't make this work, you probably don't want to go remote.

'We don't have the resources or bandwidth to do the restructuring' required for remote success. Creating remote teams requires that you create new processes and structures. Routines will need to be built, refined and rebuilt. Expectations need to be updated and communicated. It takes much more than installing Zoom. Think back to Chapter 4 on Scrum: you need to be very clear about goals and expectations up front, and carve out time to evaluate processes periodically. Take meetings for example. You'll need to determine how meetings will work, and ensure everyone is up to speed on whatever technology you're using. In addition, you'll need to be very, very organized, with a clear agenda. A loosey-goosey approach to leading a meeting won't work. We think it's worth the investment to drive increased output and efficiency. But if you don't have time to do it, you're probably better off not doing it.

'Mixed or hybrid models bring unique challenges.' As we write this, the Covid-19 pandemic is still with us, and there is uncertainty about when it will be safe for large numbers of people to work together on-site. Some companies, like software giant Slack, will offer the choice of on-site or remote indefinitely. Facebook and Twitter have made similar announcements (Manfredi, 2020). At Nanjing University, administrative staff are working rotation schedules to have some time in the office and some at home, which makes social distancing easier (Newport, 2020). However, some companies may adopt this or similar approaches even after Covid-19 is behind us. In our minds, a CEO has to give the hybrid approach serious thought. In essence, you'll need two or even three times the infrastructure to enable on-site work, remote work, and processes to ensure strong interaction between the two.

'We need a physical space for the sake of clients, investors or potential employees.' Maybe your success depends on having a showroom or demonstration space – you feel you could do it online, but clients won't buy in. Investors are often wary of things they can't touch or feel. You may find that prospective talent doesn't care for remote work. Maybe they aren't tech savvy enough, or they just don't like it. In another example, a law practice may think it is essential to meet face to face with clients.

'I don't have my own on-point home office.' One of Ernest Hemingway's (1933) characters put a high value on 'a clean, well-lighted place', but that's just the beginning for a remote office. You need the infrastructure, such as a broadband connection, but you also need a haven from distractions. Clockify, makers of time-tracking software, asked users about their biggest challenges in working remotely, and distraction was a big one (Kojic, 2020). These include family members, pets and chores. Everyone needs a place they can go to work and think, and it is especially true for CEOs. If you can't create this space at home, you will suffer and struggle.

'We don't have the digital security to protect your internet connection.' David Grober (2020), writing on ZDNet, reported that the use of remote access technologies (like virtual private networks, or VPNs) increased by at least 33 per cent in the four months following the outbreak of the Covid-19 pandemic. But hackers are smart, and they know that the 'newly remote' are vulnerable. Even if you use a personal computer, cybercriminals can use stolen information to get at your own resources and those of your company. Hackers, phishers and bears – oh, my! If you aren't able to ensure a secure connection from home, stay in the office.

'Remote is *more* stressful for workers, not less.' One of the big selling points of remote is that it is less stressful – no commutes, crowded cubicles or micromanagement. However, according to Eric Rosenbaum (2020), the *transition* from office to remote can be very stressful. He reports that Arianna Huffington's company, Thrive Global, is partnering with Qualtrics to track the experience of employees of more than 7,600 companies. As of April 2020, the study has demonstrated that the transition stress is significant. And, of course, stress impacts productivity and creativity. Huffington claims that the solution has to come from company leadership. We're getting into the grey area between 'structural' and 'cultural' obstacles here, and we'll address the cultural aspect shortly. The structural point is that, if you are not in a position to dedicate time and energy to minimizing the stresses of remote for employees, it's probably not the right time to go remote.

'Remote doesn't provide the traditional in-office social interaction your employees need.' It's possible to create virtual water coolers, but you need to set expectations that the company may not be the source of friendships and social interaction that employees want. We will provide ideas for promoting teamwork – in fact, it is essential – but 'teammate' and 'friend' are not the same thing. If you are unable to set this expectation, or your employees are totally reliant on the workplace for friendship, you'll want to keep the sticks-and-bricks model.

Cultural obstacles

Depending on the situation, cultural obstacles may be harder to overcome than structural ones. Going remote requires a change in thinking, and not everyone is prepared to make that change. Adapting can be overwhelming for both leaders and employees. When Kim first took Decision Toolbox remote, there were a handful of employees who just couldn't make the transition, and chose to leave. Here are the cultural obstacles we run across most often.

'I can't manage what I can't see.' This idea is given weight by the phrase 'If you can't measure it, you can't improve it.' According to Don Peppers (2018), some attribute the phrase to Total Quality Management (TQM) guru W. Edwards Deming, and others to management guru Peter Drucker. It has achieved the status of maxim. In our approach to remote, managing people and leveraging metrics and measurement are essential. But if that belief is not negotiable for you, we'll agree to disagree – don't go remote.

'Business as usual is working fine.' This may be a great reason not to change anything, although agility is important. Most likely you had to make some changes in response to the Covid-19 pandemic, but going remote as a model is a major change. If your satisfaction and engagement results are through the roof, you may not want to rock the boat.

'The magic only happens when we are all in one room.' In the next chapter we'll share a story about making magic happen remotely. We believe that there are collaboration tools and processes (like Scrum, for example) that help teams be highly effective. On the other hand, if you and your team truly need and want face-to-face interaction, keep your office.

'I can't even imagine what it would look like.' We think this stems from an overall fear of the unknown, and call it 'virtualophobia'. After this chapter, we're going to help you imagine it and make it happen – that is, if you are open-minded and willing to venture into new territory.

'My team is not independent enough – the team lacks the right talent.' This may be a lack of trust, and our remote model incorporates KPIs to overcome that. We believe that, if you set expectations and hold people accountable, most people can do it. But if you are being honest with yourself, and you are convinced that the team is not capable of handling the change, remote is probably not for you.

'We'll all be too lonely and isolated.' This is another obstacle we'll help you overcome and the solutions can be fun, too. In our minds, it falls to the leader to create the culture that prevents this – to be the light in the dark place. It's not a small commitment. If you're not interested in that role, or if you just crave the face-to-face (or socially distanced) interaction, leave things as they are.

'We don't have enough structure.' It may seem like this one would belong in the structural obstacles list above, but sometimes people have a hard time separating structure and culture. And there is a space where culture and structure morph into one another, fuzzing the line. Either way, this book is about creating both, and in ways that complement one another.

'There isn't enough leadership in our org chart.' What if we can show you how to create a structure that makes it easier to manage people and operations, and a performance-driven culture that rewards self-sufficiency in employees? That might even increase the bandwidth of your existing leadership team. However, if your leadership team is truly too small, then you probably want to maintain the status quo.

'We just want to get our work done.' Hard to argue with that. But since you're reading this, you must have some interest in going remote. If you want a better way to get work done, stick with us.

'Employees will have work guilt.' That is, they'll log onto your system so it looks like they're working, and then they'll go run errands or watch TV. Interestingly, Yahoo! found the opposite was true (Newport, 2020). Reportedly, Melissa Mayer's no-remote decision was driven in part by a review of their network logs – remote employees were logged off for long periods. In both cases, however, we feel that leadership is measuring the wrong thing. Our model focuses on accomplishing goals, not logging hours. And it frees you, the CEO, to have much more flexibility in your days. Intrigued? We hope so.

'We'll address it in the future.' We can identify with having so much to do that it's hard to think of anything else. And as we mentioned previously, the transition requires time and effort. But once implemented, your company will be incredibly agile. Still, if right now isn't the right time, or agility isn't an essential ingredient in your industry, come back when you're ready. We'll be here.

'Employees won't be able to separate work life from home life.' This is definitely a valid point. For example, Chris had an account manager whose numbers suddenly dropped. Let's call him Nick. It turned out that Nick's wife would hand over responsibility for their child to him every afternoon. Nick didn't even realize what the problem was. Don't get us wrong: fathers have just as much responsibility for childcare as mothers do but it's important to recognize that you can't work and provide various forms of care at the same time. The point is that employees of all genders need to balance work and life responsibilities, and it falls to leadership to facilitate that. We'll show you how to set expectations and help your people find balance. We're not expecting you to become a life coach for each person, but if you're not prepared to invest some time and effort in this area, remote may not be for you.

Ready for a renaissance?

You probably have noticed that the distinction between structural and cultural is not always absolute. However, we have reached something of a crossroads. Here, defining categories is less important than your reaching a clear and honest assessment of your ability and willingness to take your company remote. If the obstacles are too great, then we don't judge if you choose the different path. However, if you're still on the fence, the rest of the book may help you decide.

Still with us? Great. Now we'll shift gears and share why we believe you *should* go remote. After all, technology has given us the means to launch a renaissance in how we work…

References

Grober, D (2020) Roundup: Covid-19 pandemic delivers extraordinary array of cybersecurity challenges, ZDNet, 24 June, www.zdnet.com/article/roundup-the-coronavirus-pandemic-delivers-an-array-of-cyber-security-challenges (archived at https://perma.cc/3RK2-FFRZ)

Hemingway, E (1933) *Winner Take Nothing*, Charles Scribner's Sons, New York

Kojic, M (2020) Remote workers share their biggest challenges (Blog) *Clockify*, 26 March, https://clockify.me/blog/remote-work/challenges-remote-work (archived at https://perma.cc/GKD8-RHAT)

Manfredi, L (2020) Slack to offer permanent work from home to most employees, *Fox Business*, 14 June, www.foxbusiness.com/technology/slack-permanent-work-from-home-most-employees?utm_medium=remote-how.com&utm_source=remote-how.com&utm_campaign=remote-how.com (archived at https://perma.cc/378N-RC24)

National Law Review (2020) California employers' duties to reimburse employees working from home during the Covid-19 pandemic, *National Law Review*, 19 April, www.natlawreview.com/article/california-employers-duties-to-reimburse-employees-working-home-during-covid-19 (archived at https://perma.cc/9Z4L-M3TE)

Newport, C (2020) Why remote work is so hard – and how it can be fixed, *The New Yorker*, 26 May, www.newyorker.com/culture/annals-of-inquiry/can-remote-work-be-fixed (archived at https://perma.cc/SBN2-4752)

Peppers, D (2018) Why 'You can't manage what you can't measure' is bad advice, *LinkedIn*, 31 August, www.linkedin.com/pulse/why-you-cant-manage-what-measure-bad-advice-don-peppers (archived at https://perma.cc/Q6Y6-M2UN)

Rosenbaum, E (2020) What we've learned about how remote work is changing us, *CNBC*, 15 April, www.cnbc.com/2020/04/09/heres-what-we-know-about-how-remote-work-changes-us.html (archived at https://perma.cc/MDG9-4Y5R)

07

A collision of intelligence
and creativity

A few years ago, Chris and his wife Jody toured Florence and its art museums, including the Uffizi Gallery and Palazzo Pitti. One of the wealthiest and most influential cities of the middle ages, Florence emerged in the late 14th century as the birthplace of the Renaissance. The influence of that heady period was present in so much of what the Dyers saw that Chris asked one of the guides, 'Why did the Renaissance happen? Why here?'

IN THIS CHAPTER

We will cover:

- Utopia is possible...

- Yes we can

- Agility and technology

- Rapid ramping

The full answer to that might fill an entire book, but the guide said that one of the most important reasons is that there were many smart, creative and talented people there at the same time. They shared their own ideas and built on the ideas of others. In the earliest days, the likes of Dante, Petrarch and Boccaccio rubbed elbows. Later, the city was home to da Vinci, Machiavelli, Michelangelo and Guicciardini – imagine the café where those minds chatted over macchiatos, reshaping the Western world.

It was then that Chris had an inspiration of his own: today, great minds can 'rub elbows' using technology – even if they are on the other side of the world. Today we have the technology to create our own Renaissance, to reshape our companies and our work life.

Utopia is possible …

… But only in a remote model. Not only can you bring great ideas together across distances, but you also can simplify your life and clear your mind of daily minutiae. Michelangelo and da Vinci had wealthy patrons, freeing them from worry about Florentine rent and groceries. They were able to withdraw from the hustle and bustle, into studios and workshops. There was only so much gas in their tanks for brilliant ideas, and they didn't waste it on micro-decisions.

There are more contemporary examples of remarkable people minimizing micro-decisions to save gas for the macro ones. In his book *Daily Rituals: How artists work*, Mason Currey (2013) says that Albert Einstein followed a regular daily routine during his years as a Princeton professor, from 1933 to 1945. It included breakfast and catching up with the newspapers, a few hours of work in his office, lunch, a nap (yes, a nap – every day), tea, visitors and correspondence, supper and more work. His long hair minimized visits to the barber, and he never wore suspenders or socks, considering them unnecessary.

According to Vincent Carlos (2019), Steve Jobs' turtleneck, jeans and sneakers were more than a brand image: 'Steve also understood that he had a finite capacity of brainpower to make well thought out decisions.' By wearing the same thing day in and day out, he could eliminate a set of daily decisions. Jobs was a regular in the coffee shop owned by Kim's mom, and she still remembers that he (and other rising Silicon Valley innovators) would order the same breakfast every day.

Successful people tend to have ways of avoiding decision fatigue, the process that weakens your decision-making power with each decision. John Tierney (2011) explains the reality of decision fatigue: 'No matter how rational and high-minded you try to be, you can't make decision after decision without paying a biological price.' Humans have only so much brain power for making decisions in a day. The more decisions one makes, the more likely it is that decision quality will diminish. Decision fatigue is associated with poor decisions, impulse buying and decision avoidance.

When you go remote, however, you create an oasis that minimizes the kind of micro-decisions required to go into an office every day. Not only decisions about what to wear, but also things like:

- Do I need to shave/put on mascara today?
- Do I need to stop and get gas, or can I make it one more day?
- Should I take the freeway or stick to the surface streets?
- Is Bob bringing the doughnuts, or should I pick them up?
- Should I stop by Kerry's desk this morning, or later this afternoon?

In your home office, you can go on autopilot, diminish decision fatigue, and save the gas for big decisions, like 'If we make Mona Lisa's smile a little bigger, will we sell more?'

If all this talk of renaissances and utopias sounds too good to be true, let us share the story of a project Kim's company took on. The story exemplifies how the structural and cultural aspects of a well-designed remote model come together to create real-life business success. It will also add context for the next three chapters, which explain why a remote model is best for leaders, for the company and for employees.

Yes, we can

In 2015, Northrop Grumman came to Kim with a very tall order. They needed to hire 1,000 aerospace engineers quickly, and they needed a partner to augment their internal team's efforts. Was Decision Toolbox up for the challenge of filling a portion of that number? Before responding, Kim's first step was to take the question to the team. Decision Toolbox had just landed another large engagement to hire 300 store associates to accommodate a major expansion by 99 Cents Only Stores. The Northrop engagement would stretch every individual in the organization.

She not only asked leaders and managers, but also recruiters, sourcers, media specialists, marketing writers, accountants – everyone in the company. Kim was concerned that there would be pushback. There wasn't. NO ONE said no to the project. By inverting the decision-making pyramid, Kim shared the Swiss cheese, asking everyone to focus on the holes: given that there is nothing there now, can you all envision what might be possible?

Design what you want...

With all hands on deck, Kim turned to Nicole Cox, Chief Recruitment Officer (CRO), and Loren Miner, Chief Operations Officer (COO). Keeping in mind DT's philosophy – design what you want or deal with what you get – this team plotted out a strategy. The first step was to build a team of 10 aerospace recruiters at supersonic speed. The request from Northrop came in on Thursday. On Friday morning Nicole assembled her managers to talk through the details. Then she reviewed the team's StrengthsFinder profiles to identify the right people for the various tasks. By 2 pm Friday, the project was launched.

Kim made sure everyone knew that they would have to share in the hard work, but that they would also share in the rewards the company would reap. She aligned those rewards to performance, such as the accomplishment of specific goals. That helped motivate people to work over the first weekend and beyond. That first weekend, the team accomplished some key tasks:

FIGURE 7.1   Design what you want, or deal with what you get

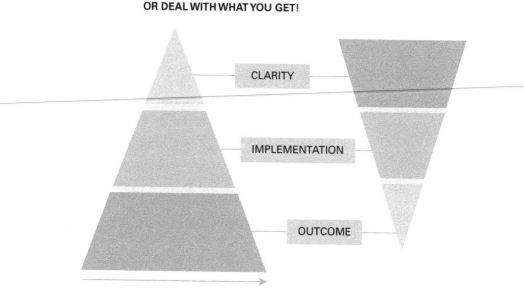

DESIGN WHAT YOU WANT....
OR DEAL WITH WHAT YOU GET!

CLARITY

IMPLEMENTATION

OUTCOME

TIME

- opened a requisition and created marketing materials to attract talented aerospace recruiters;
- started sourcing and reaching out to candidates in DT's existing database and on job boards like LinkedIn and Indeed;
- researched the best job boards and the top cities for aerospace and defence recruiters (as a virtual company, DT had a nationwide pool to draw from);
- started screening applicants.

Rapid ramping

In retrospect, Nicole says, 'We truly created a process from scratch that we had never thought of before.' In order to implement, refine and ensure the success of the new process, Nicole flattened the hierarchy. She got into the trenches alongside her team and 'poured waffle batter' into the nooks and crannies to hold it all together. As she helped the team navigate obstacles, she kept pace with her CRO duties by 'managing up' to COO Loren, who covered them.

Early the following week a core group of new aerospace recruiters started. Over the next three weeks, that team sourced and screened 216 candidates for 29 different positions across a variety of competencies. In the course of the project the client asked DT to take on 225 per cent more jobs than originally expected. 'We earned 100 per cent on the client satisfaction survey, achieved a 48 per cent profit margin, and all members of the team made good money.'

COO Loren summarized the project very well, writing, 'This is what differentiates DT. No one can ramp up to serve a client as quickly and seamlessly as we can!' The virtual model allowed DT to procure the necessary resources quickly, without having to worry about office space, desks, computers, etc. Loren also wrote, 'The whole "design what you want" philosophy behind DT allowed me to tell the client that we could start working for them the moment they gave us the green light. Instantaneous turnaround with little implementation. Our competitors' implementation takes weeks and weeks.'

Agility and technology

The virtual model makes your company agile and able to land new business quickly, because you don't have to worry about procuring additional office space, desks, computers, etc. You also need a culture that promotes the kind of all-hands spirit we saw in the example. Culture is a big part of our remote model, and we'll share more insights on the topic later.

The technology that makes this renaissance possible, of course, is the internet. We'll spend more time on these tools in future chapters, but the internet is behind video conferencing, document sharing, collaboration tools and more. It also makes it possible for your team members to log onto your key systems, such as enterprise resource planning (ERP), customer relationship management (CRM), accounting software, business intelligence tools and more.

The remote model enables you to focus on people, processes and technology in order to make the magic happen and create your renaissance. It gives you a competitive advantage, promotes loyalty among your employees and might just establish you as an industry trend-setter.

References

Carlos, V (2019) Why so many successful people wear the same outfit every day: There's a smart strategy behind it, *Thrive Global*, 30 May, https://thriveglobal.com/stories/why-successful-people-often-wear-the-same-outfit-every-day (archived at https://perma.cc/PZ2E-SHKR)

Currey, M (2013) *Daily Rituals: How artists work*, Knopf, New York

Tierney, J (2011) Do you suffer from decision fatigue? *New York Times Magazine*, 21 August, www.nytimes.com/2011/08/21/magazine/do-you-suffer-from-decision-fatigue.html (archived at https://perma.cc/Y4JP-WJVA)

08

Top-down leadership: why remote is best for leaders

Flipping conventional thinking

In 2017, Chris was approached by Dr Aaron Lee, then a graduate student, who was studying the relationship between employee engagement and remote work (Lee, 2018). He wanted to survey and talk with employees of different remote companies, including PeopleG2. Dr Lee's hypothesis was that working remotely will undermine employee engagement. Going into the study, Dr Lee posited that, in general, people ranked higher-order engagement needs as is shown in Figure 8.1.

The most important needs were assumed to be personal connection and personal satisfaction, while work–life balance comes in at number six.

IN THIS CHAPTER

We will cover:

- Time: My gift to me
- Time: My gift to my team
- Goals vs busywork
- Having your team's back
- Voted off the island
- Autonomy, mastery and purpose
- Competitive advantage
- Case study: AMN rides the Covid-19 coaster

FIGURE 8.1 Traditional work

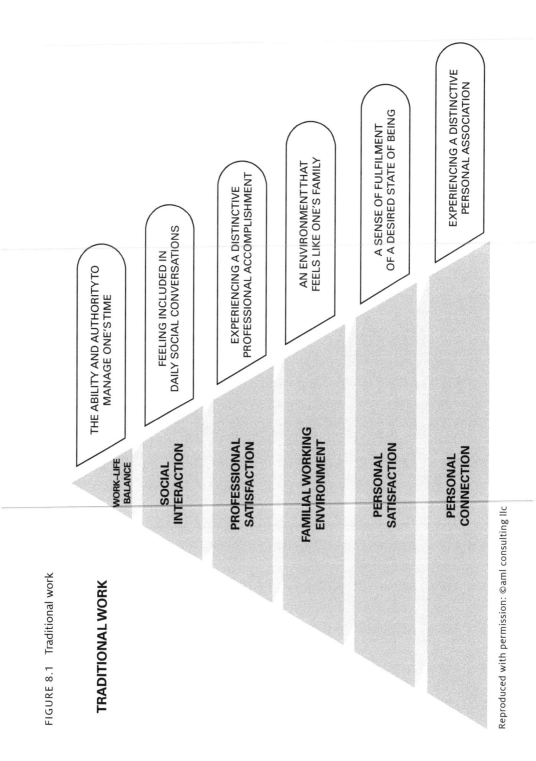

TRADITIONAL WORK

WORK-LIFE BALANCE — THE ABILITY AND AUTHORITY TO MANAGE ONE'S TIME

SOCIAL INTERACTION — FEELING INCLUDED IN DAILY SOCIAL CONVERSATIONS

PROFESSIONAL SATISFACTION — EXPERIENCING A DISTINCTIVE PROFESSIONAL ACCOMPLISHMENT

FAMILIAL WORKING ENVIRONMENT — AN ENVIRONMENT THAT FEELS LIKE ONE'S FAMILY

PERSONAL SATISFACTION — A SENSE OF FULFILMENT OF A DESIRED STATE OF BEING

PERSONAL CONNECTION — EXPERIENCING A DISTINCTIVE PERSONAL ASSOCIATION

FIGURE 8.2 Remote work

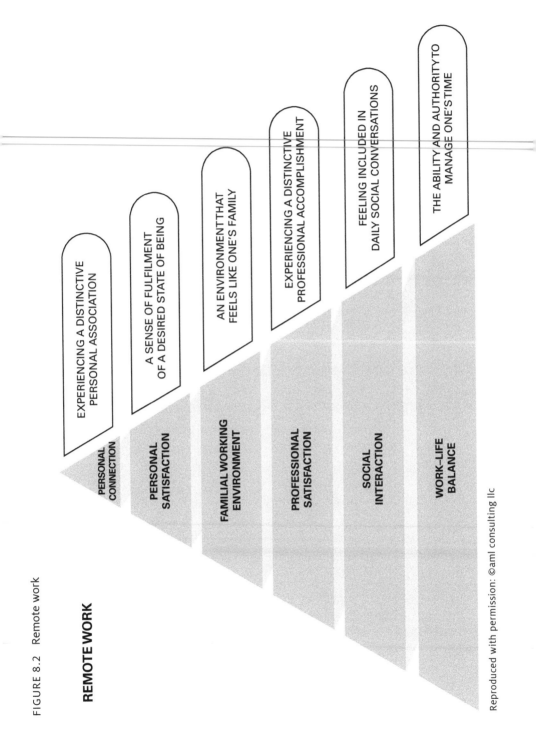

REMOTE WORK

EXPERIENCING A DISTINCTIVE
PERSONAL ASSOCIATION

PERSONAL
CONNECTION

A SENSE OF FULFILMENT
OF A DESIRED STATE OF BEING

PERSONAL
SATISFACTION

AN ENVIRONMENT THAT
FEELS LIKE ONE'S FAMILY

FAMILIAL WORKING
ENVIRONMENT

EXPERIENCING A DISTINCTIVE
PROFESSIONAL ACCOMPLISHMENT

PROFESSIONAL
SATISFACTION

FEELING INCLUDED IN
DAILY SOCIAL CONVERSATIONS

SOCIAL
INTERACTION

THE ABILITY AND AUTHORITY TO
MANAGE ONE'S TIME

WORK-LIFE
BALANCE

We'll explore Dr Lee's study results further in future chapters, but he found that engagement is actually higher in remote models. We feel that the most important finding was that the pyramid was, in fact, flipped. The most important factor in high employee engagement is work–life balance: the ability and authority to manage one's time.

If you are like we were, pre-remote, that phrase sounds like the fabled city of El Dorado. We want desperately to believe in it, but our experience tells us it's a pipe dream. Then, forced to go remote (like many today), we stumbled upon a treasure that would make a golden city look like a run-down trailer park.

Working remotely hands you control of your time. In fact, it demands that you manage it well. Before we go into that, however, try this thought experiment. Imagine that your company would magically go remote tomorrow. Looking at today, what are the time-consuming activities that would go away in that transition? First to mind for many is commute time, but there are others, like shaving and putting on makeup, deciding what to wear, stopping for a bagel, going out to lunch, and others. Add up the hours you would save. Is it in the region of two hours a day?

Time: my gift to me

Now take half of that time, say five hours a week, and give it back to yourself. An hour a day just for you – definitely one step closer to the utopia we claimed in the previous chapter. You can go to the gym, take a nap, catch up on a television show or meet one of your da Vinci-like friends for a macchiato. Be sure to take it for yourself; like taking a personal day, it's a personal hour. You need it to relax, recharge and renew.

Once you go remote and 'take back the time', you need to defend it. We believe the best way to do that is through discipline. Think of your time as Lego® bricks, and fit the half-hours and hours together in a structure that works for you. Put a brick in for mascara if you have a video meeting. Add another brick for the Scrum stand-up. Include personal bricks – dinner with friends, meditation, dog walking – so that you have a clear structure every day. If you like, you can use the red bricks for the high-priority items. Don't glue it, of course, as you may need to shift things around. The key thing is that YOU do the shifting.

Now put the wall up where everyone can see it. You probably already use a shared calendar and perhaps your email signature provides a link so people can book an appointment with you. With this metaphorical wall, you're not blocking people out, you're just owning and managing your time. You don't have to put 'walk the dog' if you think it might give the wrong impression. Just put 'personal'.

Back to the other five hours you liberated by stepping out of the rat race. This is time you can work on (not in) your business. Imagine an uninterrupted hour of strategic thinking. As CEO, that's really your job, right? Put in a brick for professional development (or perhaps finally read Stephen Covey's *The 7 Habits of Highly Effective People* (2013)). You also could practise the habits, like 'sharpening the saw'– what Dr Covey calls 'principles of balance self-renewal'. Hone your leadership skills. Work on personal excellence.

Time: my gift to my team

Share this exercise and the insights with your leadership team. Not only will it help them perform better, but it will also help ensure that you all are working in the same direction. In essence, you are eliminating the worst parts of work – what better way to promote engagement and loyalty?

It may not be enough to tell your team to practise good time management habits – you may need to teach them. Here's a time management tool for yourself and your team. Get an egg timer and set it for 45 minutes. During that time, work hard on your project or task. When it rings, set it again for 15 minutes and use that time to step away from the work and recharge. It might be part of the hours you reclaimed in the exercise above. Make a sandwich. Put clothes in the washer. The point is to take a break and reset your mind.

Another point for you, and for your team, is that working remotely will push you to leave observational management behind, in favour of performance-based management (PBM). We'll get into the details of PBM in later chapters, but the point is to establish outcome-based metrics for all employees. Then, rather than monitoring attendance in an office, you monitor whether or not employees meet their metrics.

Goals vs busywork

Gazing out across the sea of cubicles is no way to manage performance. People can look very busy, whether they are achieving goals, posting to Snapchat, or floundering in confusion. In order to flip the engagement pyramid, you need to (1) let go, (2) trust your people, and (3) empower them to do their best work. You can do this in a bricks-and-mortar model, but you *must* do it in a remote one.

We're not alone in this belief. Siemens AG, one of the world's largest companies, recently announced that, moving forward, they would allow employees around the world to work remotely two to three days a week (Bariso, 2020). Looking beyond the Covid-19 pandemic, CEO Roland Busch attributed the decision to a desire to enhance company culture and his memo echoes our beliefs exactly: 'These changes will also be associated with a different leadership style, one that focuses on outcomes rather than on time spent at the office. We trust our employees and empower them to shape their work themselves so that they can achieve the best possible results' (Bariso, 2020).

Justin Bariso, who wrote the Inc.com article above, is a consultant, speaker and author of the book, *EQ Applied: The real-world guide to emotional intelligence* (2018). Bariso called the Siemens move 'a master class in emotional intelligence'.

Another advantage for you is that, when an employee asks for help, they don't pop their head into your office and interrupt you. We're not saying that helping employees is not important but it's equally necessary to establish a structured process for this. Even with something as simple as sending you an email, employees should have a look at the bricks in your schedule wall to see when they might expect a response. You can then manage your schedule to give that employee the help they need.

A remote model requires a level of discipline that is almost military. Discipline can help you eliminate:

- your bad habits;
- getting caught up in personalities;
- being sidetracked by impromptu meetings;
- wasting time in two-hour lunches;
- informal and unofficial hierarchies and teacher's pets.

Having your team's back

Before anyone gets the wrong idea, you still need to be present as a leader, even if you are not visible and a remote model requires that you reimagine your leadership style. In part, you need to be a coach and facilitator rather than a micromanager. Instead of 'counting beans' and monitoring minutes, you should help your employees create an environment that is as pure as possible to help them work effectively. This includes not only providing resources and removing obstacles, but also helping your team feel safe and protected.

One of Kim's most important moments at Decision Toolbox occurred as she arrived at a quarterly face-to-face all-staff meeting. Pausing just outside the door, she listened to the conversations going on inside. The staff members were not office buddies – they rarely interacted in person. Some were meeting one another for the first time. But the conversations were all centred on compliments for one another. 'Great job landing that client!' 'What a clever way to attract candidates.' People weren't talking about themselves or worrying about impressing anyone. They felt safe, they trusted their leadership team, and their leaders trusted them.

Chris recalls a scenario at PeopleG2, when he discovered that everyone in a particular department referred to their supervisor as 'Dear Leader'. Knowing that this was also a nickname associated with Kim Jong-il, the late dictator of North Korea, he started looking into it. As it turns out, the moniker was based in true affection and respect. The team knew the supervisor had their backs and they didn't have to worry about psychological safety. The supervisor had purposely created this sense of safety for the remote environment.

VOTED OFF THE ISLAND

For a while after going remote, Kim was the sole business development resource at DT. She picked up a new client, the CEO of a swimwear producer. Not long into the new engagement, one of Kim's employees asked to be taken off the account. 'The CEO is mean,' the employee explained. Kim asked around and, sure enough, this new client had quickly developed a reputation for disrespect and putting people down. Kim quickly scheduled a meeting with the CEO.

'Do you ever watch the TV show *Survivor*?' Kim asked. Yes, why do you ask? 'Because we held an immunity challenge, and you've been voted off our island. No one beats up my people. You're fired as a client.'

The CEO retorted, 'I still owe you $35,000.' Kim quickly responded, 'That may be, but come Monday morning, you'll still be seriously short-staffed.' The CEO paid the money, DT delivered the candidates they had sourced to that point, and the two organizations parted ways.

Autonomy, mastery and purpose

Once you have provided for the psychological safety of your employees, you can focus on higher levels of leadership. In *The Power of Company Culture*, Chris cites some powerful advice from Daniel H Pink, speaker and author of several books on various work-related topics. In 2019, Pink was named the sixth most influential management thinker in the world by Thinkers50 (2019).

Pink's work resonated with Chris because he reveals that a commonly accepted motivator – the carrot and the stick, or the theory that punishment and reward compel better performance – is more false than true (2010). It turns out that encouraging individual satisfaction is actually the better motivator – and Pink cites respected scientific studies to prove it. Pink suggests that, instead of a bonus and penalty system, employers enact policies that allow staff three proven motivators: autonomy, mastery and purpose. Pink notes that their motivational force comes from the fact that they are each something that human beings naturally want and actively seek in life.

'Autonomy' doesn't mean doing whatever you want. it means the licence to work autonomously, in your own way, or to make certain decisions for yourselves. This often results in greater innovation, as employees feel free to offer insights that may not occur to policymakers. Autonomy works when we clearly lay the boundaries for a position and allow freedom within those parameters. For employees, those boundaries provide clarity on what to do, and on what defines success, but being trusted to work in ways that most suit them within those boundaries provides motivation.

An appreciation of autonomy has been around for millennia. Taoist sage Lao Tzu, who lived sometime between the fourth and sixth centuries AD, had this to say: 'The wicked leader is he who the people despise. The good leader is he who the people revere. The great leader is he who the people say, "We did it ourselves"'(2007).

Giving your people the chance to specialize and master certain skills, rather than working assembly-line style or performing only part of a task, keeps them continually seeking improvement. Everyone has something at which they want to get better. Whether it's in the context of work or not, overcoming obstacles and gaining mastery is a rewarding and fulfilling part of being human. In fact, we believe upward mobility should apply across all aspects of an individual's life. Chris, for example, plays guitar and writes songs. Kim rides with cross-country cycling clubs. Being unable to move forward in the skills or activities we are learning can be demotivating and unpleasant. As a leader, you should provide people with opportunities to master new work-related skills.

Defining an overarching purpose for what a company or staff member does is a key driver of self-motivation. In his book, *Start With Why* (2011), Simon Sinek argues that money should never be the sole driver behind achieving work objectives. It is actually a less powerful motivator than that amorphous sense of fulfilment we all yearn for. Sinek uses 'why' the same way we're using 'purpose'. Your company's mission statement should have some trickle-down effect to every member of the enterprise. If an employee can't recite or express his or her purpose in the context of the company mission, they will never be a great employee.

The whole point of giving your people autonomy, mastery and purpose is to help them become better employees. That means that, at some point, they may outgrow their role or even your company. If you can provide them with a new opportunity within your organization, great. If not, as you write them a letter of recommendation, take pride and satisfaction in knowing you helped them grow. We have both found that our approach creates strong loyalty. In more than one case a good employee left in pursuit of new opportunities but then found their way back – the grass wasn't greener.

Competitive advantage

Another benefit that remote offers leaders is related to employee loyalty. Good employees are always vulnerable to being poached. Our remote model helps you protect your assets by giving employees what few others are offering. Working at home is the ultimate in convenience, but when you add in a culture that promotes autonomy, mastery and purpose, you have a powerful employment value proposition. It helps you both retain the people you have and attract top talent for new positions.

Going remote also puts you in the vanguard of the evolution of the workforce. It provides you and everyone on your team a chance to grow and develop, and to achieve new levels of personal excellence. You and your team will develop unique skills that will help your company be more competitive. That means you will be able to take your vision of your company to a new level. The entire team can also add valuable experiences to their résumés.

Chris found that going remote helped him become better in some areas where he was weak. For example, remoteness requires savvy use of technology.

Before going remote Chris had a hard time remembering birthdays and anniversaries. Now he uses an app that helps everyone be aware of these important events, and provides ways to send a card. It also reminds Chris to set up a celebration in the virtual breakroom.

The following case study offers several examples of how a strong leadership team stepped up, taking a large company remote while also answering the clarion call for nurses at the outbreak of the Covid-19 pandemic.

CASE STUDY
AMN Healthcare: riding the Covid-19 coaster

Crises separate the great companies – and leaders – from the merely good ones. But what happens when you throw an already very good company into the eye of the storm? If that company is AMN Healthcare, what happens is pretty remarkable.

We talked with Julie Fletcher, Chief Talent Officer at AMN, the US's largest healthcare staffing company and providers of healthcare total talent solutions (NYSE: AMN). Staffing makes up a major part of the business, with an emphasis on nurses but also into the physician and allied healthcare professional space. When the Covid-19 pandemic hit, they were faced with two major challenges at the same time:

- Responding to desperate demands for nurses, particularly in emergency departments, ICUs, telemetry and related areas. In just a few short months, AMN sent over 10,000 nurses to support hospitals and healthcare facilities across the country. They received requests for thousands of nurses for New York alone, which was then the epicentre of the pandemic.

- Sending some 3,000 team members home to work, setting them up for success in a whole new environment in a very short timeframe.

Even before Covid-19, AMN had proved itself to be a great company, as evidenced by appearing on the Fortune 1000 list for several years and winning an array of awards for most admired, best place to work, best and brightest in the nation, and others. They are also recognized for corporate responsibility in multiple areas, including LGBTQ+ and gender equity, diversity, equality and inclusion (DE&I), sustainability, and community engagement. In addition, they are one of a handful of healthcare staffing firms to be accredited by the Joint Commission for consistently meeting national standards of excellence.

Engaging nurses

However, Covid-19 created an opportunity for AMN leadership to shine even more brightly. As Julie put it, 'never waste a good crisis'. We'll go into detail about AMN's deliberate and proactive approach to going remote, but their proactive efforts to find nurses for clients deserve some attention as well.

Recruiting and engaging nurses always has been a challenge, with demand far outstripping supply. Among other heightened outreach efforts, AMN CEO Susan Salka was invited to appear on two television broadcasts to talk about the urgency. Fortunately, most consider the profession a calling, and it was gratifying for Julie to see how many nurses stepped up. AMN had a massive response from nurses and healthcare professionals who expressed interest in possibly responding to positions to support Covid-19. Some came out of semi-retirement or other careers to help out, and Julie heard one story of a nurse who lived on a farm who bought supplies, made a number of homemade face shields, hitched up her trailer and drove to New York because 'it was where she needed to be'.

Going remote

Prior to the Covid-19 pandemic, remote was the exception for corporate employees. AMN was beginning to develop leaders to be more effective at telecommuting and leading remote teams, but was still in the infancy stages. Slightly less than 20 per cent of their full-time team members were working remotely. However, sending ALL 3,000 team members home within two weeks created a whole new set of challenges, and an unprecedented level of urgency.

The two key focuses relating to team members revolved around personal/ professional engagement and productivity. AMN already had an approach by which most team members could embrace telecommuting (ad hoc work from home 1–2 days/week) if they were meeting or exceeding productivity goals. The executive team found that, for the most part, people truly stepped up as they went remote full-time for Covid-19, and productivity stayed solid or improved in some areas.

While acknowledging the hard work and dedication of AMN team members, Julie also attributes the consistent productivity to AMN's culture and high employee engagement. In her mind, productivity and culture are two sides of the same coin: the deliverables are important, but equally important is how you go about delivering. Results and values-based behaviours weigh equally in the balance.

A company's culture attracts people who share the same cultural values. AMN fully embraces the social and political environment, in contrast to some leaders in other companies, who are sometimes afraid to take a stand. For example, while many companies track gender data to support DE&I efforts (and that's good), AMN is among the first tracking LGBTQ+ data – and they are confident that employees trust them enough to voluntarily share the information yet keep it confidential.

On the whole, AMN employees feel strongly about social responsibility – it's part of what drew them to AMN. Julie believes that a large number of AMN employees believe in doing the right thing, and this helped them step up to the challenges of

Covid-19. In addition, seeing leadership do the right thing and being transparent was further motivation. The teams truly rallied around the AMN mission of supporting patient care in a time of crisis, and Susan often reminded the organization, 'This challenge is what we have been training for our whole careers'.

Translating a great culture to remote

More challenging was transitioning the strong, high-touch culture at AMN from in-person to fully remote. To paint the picture, Julie described the third, fourth and fifth floors of their San Diego office, where team members handled recruiting, credentialling and all back-office functions as high-passion, high-energy functional teams. When leaders walked the floor, energy levels were high and everyone was busy. It's demanding work, and supervisors provide as much attention and care as they can with a balance on values and productivity.

After Covid-19, the location changed, but the demanding nature of the work remained the same or became more intense to match the intense demand of their clients. Not only did they have to find nurses, but they had to confirm the nurses were properly credentialled to fill the roles and serve patients.

To take the high-touch culture online, they realized that it was better to over-communicate than leave people feeling disconnected. They encouraged managers and supervisors to stay committed to communication, to ramp up where needed and to check in with individuals even MORE frequently. How were they doing with their work, home, family balance? How could AMN support them with more equipment if needed? What else could they do to help them? Susan, Julie and the rest of the executive team held Senior Leadership Forums more frequently (monthly went to every three weeks), and AMN Live meetings (any question, any topic and proactive messaging cascaded) went from monthly to every three weeks or ad hoc if needed on a special announcement. These meetings were not only to convey information but also to share uplifting messages and promote engagement.

In addition, their employee support groups developed and shared information and resources specific to making the transition, covering mental health, supporting work–life balance, child and family care and more. Julie believes that, while there were logistical issues like equipment and connectivity, most challenges were personal. For example, supervisors had to understand that parents of school-age children were trying to balance work with homeschool responsibilities. Leaders had to be flexible with meetings if an employee had to step away briefly and help their school-age child jump onto a Zoom class session.

Communication had to be two-way, and they made a point of listening carefully to team members. In addition to the one-on-one check-ins by managers mentioned above, they sent a lessons learned survey out, asking how the company did on transitioning to work from home. They asked how the company did on supporting them with communications, facilities, IT & HR support, and also asked, 'What can we do better to support you as you work from home?' After analysing the responses, they summarized and sent the five most frequent responses by area to each leader.

Transparency also took on greater importance in the remote model, and Julie said they used the Senior Leadership Forums and AMN Live sessions to promote it. In addition, leadership teams had to develop a clearer focus on priorities and share that information with the organization. An upside of the pandemic was that it forced departments to break down barriers and collaborate more. Overall, the company moved faster and with greater purpose.

As of this writing, AMN has settled into remote work, and employee surveys indicate that 95 per cent are doing well. Leadership is still evaluating when they will come back or how long they will stay remote. Things seem to happen in waves with Covid-19 – AMN calls it the 'Covid-19 coaster'. While they are taking things one day at a time, they are not waiting to take action. Proactive efforts to optimize remote work will continue.

Leadership in the (remote) crucible

Julie found that shifting to remote created an interesting dynamic among leaders as well as employees. When everything is running smoothly, leadership is relatively easy, but in crises leaders truly earn their stripes. AMN has a strong culture and has always set the bar high for leaders, and that helped. In addition, the experience of dealing with Covid-19 and going remote made most of their leaders better. It also shone a light on some other opportunities for leadership training.

Supporting leaders

To help leaders during both the remote transition and spike in demand, AMN mobilized quickly. They established a 'command centre' with multiple swim lanes that were focused on clients, healthcare professionals and employees. They put tools in the hands of leaders to help them promote engagement and productivity, including tools and training for online meetings, tips for staying engaged, and 'Daily Dose of Leadership' emails from the senior executives to keep leaders motivated, inspired and engaged through the crisis.

They also moved resources around, including putting about 250 existing employees into new roles and bringing on about 150 temporary hires. That meant lots of virtual training, and fast, so they put resources in place to support leaders in training others.

They digitized the training programmes for many temporarily redeployed so they could move faster. Some more traditional leaders needed support with remote leadership, and weekly articles, videos and interviews highlighting best practices were quickly created, and a lot of emphasis placed on optimizing leading remotely. It took a little extra effort to help everyone realize the way of work–life integration was becoming the new normal. As long as leaders stayed focused on engagement and productivity, we knew the organization would get through this.

AMN also focused on team member wellness – providing guidance and resources to help team members stay physically, emotionally and mentally healthy via webinars, free access to online exercise and meditation programmes, daily Zen@AMN meditation sessions, and activities like step challenges and walk at lunch days. They also made sure team members had access to on-demand crisis counsellors through EAP.

New ways of thinking

The reality is that AMN is a different company now. The executive team are listening to their teams daily as they always have and planning for returning to on-site work at some point when the time is right. There will likely be a combination of hybrid workers coming and going from AMN offices if they live in an area where that makes sense. Likely some roles and individuals may work from home longer-term and some with individual unique home situations may also need special accommodation. At this point, the future may be uncertain, but it is highly unlikely that things will ever go back to the way they once were.

Julie feels that everyone – at AMN and anywhere else – has to move from a mindset of 'temporary' to one of 'for the time being'. That means moving from the kitchen table to a more formalized workspace, creating structure for the children's days, and more.

Supporting productivity and engagement

That also means leaders need to accept even greater responsibility for engagement and productivity as the situation evolves. Whether people continue at home or work in the office, these changes can be unsettling. Team and individual engagement is the number one most important thing leaders should focus on. Leaders have to check in regularly and, when necessary, help people if they are having a rough, emotional day. Productivity is tied directly to engagement. Leaders know their most engaged team members are typically their most productive as well. Adaptability and flexibility are always characteristics of great employees, and now that they are even more important, leaders need to help their people develop those traits. Julie believes that leaders who win the hearts and minds of their teams will find the team gives 110 per cent.

For Julie, going remote has other upsides. She believes that it will support diversity and inclusion efforts, which are front and centre at AMN, since companies will be able to draw from a larger geographical pool.

At AMN, the C-suite has developed habits and skills that enable them to make higher-quality decisions at a faster pace than before. For example, they changed their meeting routine and now hold shorter but more frequent meetings. They also had to understand one another's worlds a little better. Not only did they have to break down work silos, but they also had to get to know each other's families and personal lives a little better... now that the work world is physically embedded in the personal world.

One of the highlights of this case study is the remarkable performance of AMN in recruiting and hiring nurses for the clients in the face of dire need. They also created strong success in moving to a fully remote model. A couple of things stand out to us as being particularly relevant here. First, Julie credits a strong culture and high employee engagement as key factors in that success. We'll go into more detail about culture in Chapter 13, but there is no question in our minds that the right culture is essential for any company to thrive, and culture is even more important in a remote model.

Second, their approach was deliberate. We've already used that term and we'll continue to do so throughout this book because it is an important difference between strong and weak leadership. It's one thing to send everyone home to work, but something very different to take the time to set up a robust remote model. Throughout this book, but particularly starting in Chapter 14, we'll give you ideas and suggestions for designing what you want, so you aren't stuck dealing with what you get.

A third point that stands out is the fact that AMN leadership recognized that they needed new ways of thinking as they went remote. Not only did they define new ways of thinking, but they also supported leaders in adopting those ways. That enabled the leaders to help their own teams think in new ways. Also important to note is that they adopted new ways without abandoning or eliminating their core values.

In the next chapter we'll explore why remote is the best model for your company. Interested in lowering costs? Stick around.

References

Bariso, J (2018) *EQ Applied: The real-world guide to emotional intelligence*, Borough Hall, New York

Bariso, J (2020) This company's new 2-sentence remote work policy is the best I've ever heard, *Inc.com*, 27 July, www.inc.com/justin-bariso/this-companys-new-2-sentence-remote-work-policy-is-best-ive-ever-heard.html (archived at https://perma.cc/N6TP-96AH)

Covey, S R (2013) *The 7 Habits of Highly Effective People: Powerful lessons in personal change*, Simon & Schuster, New York

Dyer, C (2018) *The Power of Company Culture: How any business can build a culture that improves productivity, performance and profits*, Kogan Page, London

Lao Tzu; Sam Hamill (translation) (2007) *Tao Te Ching*, Shambhala, Berkeley CA

Lee, A (2018) *An Exploratory Case Study of How Remote Employees Experience Workplace Engagement*, The George Washington University, 2004 BA, The University of Virginia, 2000 Dissertation Submitted in Partial Fulfillment of the Requirements for the Degree of Doctor of Philosophy Management Walden University August 2018

Pink, D H (2010) RSA ANIMATE: Drive: The surprising truth about what motivates us, *YouTube*, www.youtube.com/watch?v=u6XAPnuFjJc (archived at https://perma.cc/SY8B-QNNW)

Sinek, S (2011) *Start With Why: How great leaders inspire everyone to take action*, Portfolio, New York

Thinkers50 (2019) Award winners of 2019, *Thinkers50.com*, https://thinkers50.com/awards/awards-2019 (archived at https://perma.cc/7AQ6-JQ9Y)

09

Company health: why remote
is best for the company

Studies demonstrating the benefits that companies gain from going remote have been around for years. But a new flurry of studies has arrived since the Covid-19 pandemic. There are also studies that argue that going remote is a guaranteed disaster. It all depends on which models and cases you look at. It's one thing to send people home to work, but it's something quite different to design what you want, such as a successful remote model. We suspect that the disasters occurred when leaders didn't realize that they had to be very deliberate about it.

IN THIS CHAPTER

We will cover:

- Top and bottom line
- Enhanced operational strength
- Unpoachable staff
- Growing painlessly
- Plug-and-play flexibility
- Increased productivity

As we work through this chapter, we'll look at both the old and the new. However, it seems that, whether remote is an independent choice or born of necessity, it can make a big difference to your company's performance in many ways.

Top *and* bottom line

One thing you want to be deliberate about is your competitive strategy. According to Umar Farooq (2018), writing on MarketingTutor.net, there are four approaches you might take:

A **cost leadership strategy** involves underpricing the competition to drive volume. Farooq suggests that this strategy is better suited to larger organizations that can take advantage of economies of scale, citing Walmart as an example. However, Kim used this strategy to good effect at Decision Toolbox – when everyone else was raising prices, DT dropped theirs.

Differentiation leadership strategy is useful when you have powerful differentiators to distinguish your products or services from those of your competitors. Superior quality or value-added features cost you more, but you should be able to charge premium prices that cover the costs. An example here is Apple.

Cost focus strategy is similar to cost leadership, but it involves targeting a specific segment of your industry. You offer that segment the lowest price. Farooq's example suggests that a producer of bottled water might target markets where people *must* buy bottled water, like Dubai.

Differentiation focus strategy is similar to cost focus in that you target a specific market segment, but instead of offering the lowest price, you differentiate your company from your competitors to attract customers. Farooq's example is Breezes Resorts, whose 'no children' policy appeals to couples.

Whichever strategy you choose, you need to control the dynamic between the top and bottom lines. That's where a remote model shines. Your infrastructure costs go down significantly when you go remote. No more office lease payments, no more furniture outlays, no more utilities. Meanwhile, you are more agile, and therefore it's easier to land new business, as we saw in Kim's experience with Northrop Grumman.

You can hire better talent for less by targeting markets where the cost of living is lower. We both started in Southern California, where the cost of just about everything is high. When you go remote, however, not only can you draw from a larger talent pool, but you can often get more for your money.

One survey (McQuaid, 2020) found that almost a third of employees in the United Kingdom would take a pay cut in order to work remotely. A similar study, sponsored by Platform.sh, a DevOps automation platform, got an even higher figure in the United States: 47 per cent (Silver, 2020). While the UK survey took place after Covid-19 had hit, and the US one before, both articles claim that a key reason for this willingness is the fact that employees save money when they work remotely, such as by not commuting, buying a lot of work clothes or paying for childcare. Your company saves money, your current people save money, and future candidates may see your remote model as a significant attraction when applying for a role... sounds like a win-win to us.

The flexibility of remote also makes it easier to outsource functions. Chris made a significant investment in recruiting for marketing talent. What he found, however, was that anyone who had the expertise he wanted was very expensive. Instead, he engaged a marketing firm and has been very happy with the results. An outsourced model resembles a remote one in many ways, making it an easy fit.

Enhanced operational strength

When you go remote, your company may quickly resemble a sasquatch, with a very big footprint. It may be that the majority of your employees are still in one local area, but over time you can expand to have employees in every time zone you do business in. You can go global if it makes sense, and ensure that the sun never sets on your empire.

There are several advantages, such as being able to offer expanded time coverage to customers. Some global IT firms have development teams around the world, enabling them to work 24/7 on projects. Code sets are passed from team to team. In addition, with a little forethought, you can have managers in each time zone, expanding the hours during which your company can solve problems and make decisions.

We mentioned scalability and adaptability above, referring back to the Northrop Grumman example from Chapter 7. Flexibility may be one of the most important characteristics of business success today. Writing about small business, Angela Stringfellow, Chief Ideation Officer of CODA Concepts, says, 'The importance of flexibility in business simply can't be overstated. Whether that means changing your business model, lowering prices, outsourcing or leveraging innovative, value-added pricing strategies, today's small businesses may want to consider embracing corporate flexibility to survive' (Stringfellow, 2017). The remote model has exceptional flexibility because it is free from the burden of traditional office infrastructure, such as leased space, furniture, etc. Taking your company remote makes it highly scalable and adaptable.

Remote also makes your business more resilient to natural disasters and, as was demonstrated clearly in 2020, global pandemics. In their book *Remote: Office not required*, Fried and Hansson (2013) describe the concept of a single point of failure (SPoF) in systems theory. Since everything breaks eventually, engineers and others concerned with high reliability invest a good deal of time in eliminating SPoFs. 'Forcing everyone into the office every day is an organizational SPoF,' they argue. If the power or internet go down, no one in the office is able to get anything done. You may have back-up computer servers or other redundant systems, but no one can afford a back-up office. If your offices are in areas prone to severe weather or natural disasters – hurricanes, floods, earthquakes, etc – the risk is even higher.

The SPoF argument extends beyond major disasters. Personal issues crop up more frequently, and they can create a conflict for employees who are required to go into the office. These include catching a cold, having a sick child home from school, or a plumbing emergency. In the words of Fried and Hansson, 'Whatever the world throws at it, be it a blizzard or the requirement to be home for the exterminator, a distributed workforce is one that can keep working regardless.'

Unpoachable staff

When a good employee leaves, they can leave you bleeding in multiple ways. Search Solution Group, a recruiting firm, states that vacancies can have a cultural effect, causing apathy, disengagement, overwork, stress and lowered productivity. Externally, a vacancy can cause partners and customers to lose confidence in your business.

The direct costs can be significant, and this is clear using even the most basic of cost of vacancy calculations. Dr John Sullivan, writing on ERE.net (2005), says you can start by calculating your company's revenue per employee (your total revenue divided by the number of employees) and then dividing that by 220, the typical number of working days in a year. That gives you the average daily revenue produced by an employee. Let's say your company's revenue is $10 million and you have 50 employees. That means your average annual revenue per person is $200,000. Now divide that by 220, and your average daily revenue is $909. That means a position left vacant for 28 days costs your company $25,452.

Add to that the cost of recruiting and training, and you just don't want to lose good people. Maybe you remember the jazz/blues song 'Makin'

Whoopee', which has been recorded by a number of artists, from Dinah Washington to Frank Sinatra to Cyndi Lauper. It's where the phrase, 'It's cheaper to keep her' comes from, and it's good advice for employers.

Remote promotes retention

This information is important when considering your own approach to a remote model and presenting this to key stakeholders because studies show that remote models promote retention. A 2017 FlexJobs survey of 5,551 respondents found that 79 per cent 'said they would be more loyal to their employers if they had flexible work options' (Reynolds, 2017). The sample included people from a variety of age groups, education levels and career levels. Another survey by AfterCollege, a career network for recent graduates, found that 68 per cent of millennial job seekers said an option to work remotely would increase their interest in employers (Bibby, 2015).

A big reason for this is one we've touted before: work–life balance. The 'boomer' generation (generally understood as anyone born between 1946 and 1964) have struggled with it just about all their lives, seeing it as a teeter-totter or see-saw, running back and forth to maintain balance. Millennials are more inclined to see work–life balance as a balance beam. According to Deloitte's 2016 Millennial Survey, good work–life balance is more important to this generation than career progression or amassing material goods. Given that, the teeter-totter approach won't work – instead of jumping from one side to the other, they believe they can stay in the sweet spot by taking advantage of technology.

Right now you may be thinking, 'I'm not a Millennial, but I want work–life balance.' We agree. A LinkedIn survey found that nearly half of all American workers – of any generation – would 'forgo the corner-office job and a high salary to gain more flexibility in their schedules' (Roth, 2016). When you go remote, you offer employees the number one reason to be loyal.

An inspired test

There are other reasons a robust remote model promotes retention. For example, a successful remote model requires a culture that encourages people to grow and realize their potential – a strong source of personal satisfaction. We'll discuss culture extensively in future chapters, but for now here's an anecdote of how Kim put this idea to the test.

David Harder is founder and president of Inspired Work, a workplace engagement, career and leadership development firm, as well as an author and speaker. His firm offers the Inspired Work Program, a two-day seminar that helps participants refine and redefine their relationship to work. The seminar is particularly useful for people at a crossroads in their careers, helping them clarify goals, explore different professional options and pursue the kind of work they most want to do. Kim and Chris both went through the seminar and, although they weren't at a crossroads at the time, both gained insight into their purpose and direction.

Kim had hired both Loren Miner and Nicole Cox at Decision Toolbox, and elevated them to executive roles, where they were successful and thriving. However, since they were both still in the early stages of their careers, Kim wanted them to be sure of their paths. She decided to pay for them to attend David's Inspired Work Program as well.

She knew it was risky, but felt confident that it would be productive for Loren and Nicole, while also helping prove that encouraging professional development also promotes retention. Kim's partner at DT, Jay Barnett, had reservations. He worried that the seminar would spark new insights in Loren and Nicole, leading them to pursue new paths, new utopias – away from DT. But he also felt it was worth the risk.

His worries were unfounded, however. Loren and Nicole had, in fact, explored several utopian visions during the Inspired Work Program, but the best fit for both was DT. Both reported that the seminar helped them see even more upside to DT, with its remote model and unique culture. It was the perfect place for each of them at that point in their careers, and both stayed with the company for years, even after it was acquired.

Self-forged golden handcuffs

Publishing this book is a two-edged sword. If remote truly goes mainstream, many of the things that set it apart from other work models will diminish. However, until that happens, remote effectively acts as golden handcuffs. A competitor can offer a $35,000 pay increase to one of your people to entice them to come over to their brick-and-mortar model. But that barely offsets the $700 per week savings your employee realizes by not paying for childcare.

It doesn't even offset the benefit of not commuting. We believe that the real cost of commuting is psychological, not only causing high stress levels, but also taking away time that could be spent with family, hobbies or even doing more work. But let's run the numbers based on the value of a person's time. Say this person makes $100,000 a year. That translates to about $50 an hour. To be conservative, imagine this person would drive 45 minutes each way to take advantage of the $35,000 raise. A typical year has 260 workdays, so that's 390 hours behind the wheel – getting to work, but not getting paid. Those 390 hours are worth $19,500 in lost pay. And this doesn't even factor in the cost of gas, vehicle maintenance, tolls or parking. That's less than $35,000, but do you really want to spend an hour and a half, every day, driving to and from work?

Kim used to ask her best people what it would take to keep them from leaving, and let them forge their own golden handcuffs. For one employee, it was as simple as providing dental insurance (which Kim extended to everyone). For another, it was the flexibility to start at 6 am, take off between noon and 3 pm to volunteer at her child's school, and then work again into the early evening. Remote enables you to offer talented employees autonomy, mastery and purpose, the key ingredients in employee engagement and retention.

The Me, Inc. spirit

The remote model promotes a spirit that Kim calls 'Me, Inc.' We touched on it earlier: it refers to running your life as a business – generating revenue, managing costs, developing strategy and working towards goals. We believe that everyone should be upwardly mobile in their life, building knowledge and skills and constantly striving to be better.

Your remote model can offer employees things that they, as the CEO of their own lives, value. Why do they value them? One reason is that these things help them be more productive, which is satisfying for them and a boon to your company. According to the FlexJobs survey (Reynolds, 2017), respondents provided the following reasons why working remotely promotes productivity:

- fewer interruptions from colleagues (76 per cent);
- fewer distractions (76 per cent);
- reduced stress from commuting (70 per cent);
- minimal office politics (69 per cent);
- quieter noise level (62 per cent);

- more comfortable clothes (54 per cent);
- more personalized office environment (51 per cent);
- less frequent meetings (46 per cent);
- more efficient meetings (31 per cent).

If you value employees who are entrepreneurial and driven to be productive, the remote model will help you attract and retain just that kind of professional.

Growing painlessly

You've probably seen opportunities that you had to pass on simply because you couldn't expand or adapt quickly or cost effectively. When you need to manoeuvre, a sticks-and-bricks model can be like an ocean liner – it takes time to change course by even a few degrees. In contrast, a remote model is like a speedboat, which can zig, zag and run circles around huge, lumbering competitors.

To give you an example, Kim's company was just making the transition to virtual when a client, Gate Gourmet, approached with a problem. Recall that Decision Toolbox went virtual shortly after 9/11. Gate Gourmet provides catering services to airlines, so you can imagine the impact they experienced at this time. Suddenly Gate Gourmet couldn't put any food on an aeroplane unless it was appropriately monitored and screened. Unfortunately, the monitoring services simply didn't exist.

Kim pulled her 'speedboat' alongside Gate Gourmet and said, 'Let's create a company to deliver that service.' Within a week she and the Gate Gourmet leadership team had invented an entirely new company called Gate Safe. While Gate Gourmet got the venture started, Decision Toolbox started recruiting for new crews in 300 airports around the country. For several years Gate Safe generated more revenue than Gate Gourmet, carrying the business until airline food service found a 'new normal'.

The agility and flexibility of a remote model allows you not only to ramp up quickly, but also to enter new markets that would be out of reach for an office-based organization. In addition, once you have proved your ability to deliver in a unique situation, you can package it up and sell it to other prospects. Call it mirror marketing or shrink wrapping a success story – a rose by any other name still smells as profitable.

PLUG-AND-PLAY FLEXIBILITY

At PeopleG2, Chris received an unusual request. A couple of entrepreneurs wanted to start up a company offering services 'adjacent' to background checks and then sell it in a couple of years. They asked Chris if PeopleG2 could act as their backend office. At the helm of his speedboat, Chris said 'yes' and hired and trained 35 people in a very short time. It was a different service and a somewhat different model, but Chris definitely knew how to scale.

Originally, the investors planned to terminate the 35 employees once the new company was sold. However, the model Chris had created was efficient, cost effective and well managed, so the employees and the model became part of the sale. The investors paid Chris an additional fee for the employees.

If Chris had been CEO of a brick-and-mortar business, none of this would have been possible. The remote model, however, made it possible for Chris to build a plug-and-play model that could change ownership seamlessly.

Increased productivity

We've already cited a few studies in this area, but to drive the point home, let's consider a few more:

- According to a Forbes.com article, Prodoscore is a firm dedicated to helping companies maximize the profit potential of their teams (Westfall, 2020). Prodoscore compiled data from some 30,000 users of their software, and found that 47 per cent were more productive when they switched to working from home.

- A nine-month Stanford study of 16,000 call centre employees found that working remotely increased productivity by 13 per cent (Bloom et al, 2013).

- A flexible work programme increased productivity among Best Buy employees by 35 per cent, according to another Forbes article by Kenneth Rapoza (2013).

- Another study, by ConnectSolutions in collaboration with SHRM, found that 77 per cent of workers reported greater productivity working off-site (Hopwood, 2019).

As mentioned, we'll share more about creating a culture that promotes engagement and productivity in a later chapter, but we'll outline some of the more basic reasons for doing so here. A 2013 Harris Interactive study of 2,060 American workers (PR Newswire, 2013) showed that:

- 61 per cent of respondents said noisy co-workers are the biggest distraction in offices;
- 86 per cent said they prefer to work alone to hit maximum productivity;
- 40 per cent consider impromptu meetings from co-workers stopping by their offices a major distraction.

To sum the chapter up, the remote model we're presenting here can help your company control costs, flex and adapt easily, and serve customers better across time zones. The company will be more resilient, and you'll be well positioned to attract top talent and keep them loyal. That talent will be more productive and engaged.

The following case study helps underscore why a remote model is best for your company. In this chapter as well as in Chapters 8 and 10, we're breaking down why a remote model is best for leaders, for companies and for employees. However, this case study reminds us that the benefits run across all three areas of focus in an interactive and synergistic way.

CASE STUDY
Business as (un)usual

Adam Miller and Cornerstone OnDemand

The thought of taking your entire organization remote can seem overwhelming, and it is no small endeavour. But what about taking the entire organization remote AND integrating 1,000 new employees from an acquisition at the same time? Adam Miller and Cornerstone OnDemand did it, and did it in some remarkable ways.

Adam founded Cornerstone in 1999, in his apartment, and today it has over 3,000 employees in more than 25 countries. Together they deliver a wide variety of professional development solutions for companies large and small across diverse industries. Under Adam's leadership, Cornerstone has become one of the world's largest cloud computing companies, and its products are used by more than 6,000 organizations, supporting more than 75 million people in 192 countries.

Before Covid-19, about a third of Cornerstone's employees worked in the company's headquarters in Santa Monica, California, another third in offices around the world, and a third worked from home. When the pandemic hit, they had an advantage: experience with both a distributed model and with a large group of employees working remotely. Cornerstone sent people home very early in the scenario, even before officials recommended doing that.

Cosmic irony?

On 24 February 2020, Cornerstone announced plans to acquire Saba, its largest competitor, on the same day that Wall Street woke up to the pandemic and the stock markets began a multi-week dive. Cornerstone completed the acquisition on 22 April, just nine days after President Trump declared a national emergency.

In spite of the pandemic, the wheels of the integration were in motion, and Adam and his team were faced with the task of growing their employee base by nearly 50 per cent while people were mandated to quarantine at home globally. There were three key challenges. First, they had to ensure that all employees were set up for success in the new remote model. Second, they needed to engage and onboard people who used to be competitors. Third, they had to do this remotely, on a global scale.

At this point we have to acknowledge that Adam is passionate about culture. Not only does he understand the importance of a supportive and motivating culture, but he is creative about implementing it. Kim and Chris have been to Cornerstone's headquarters many times, and on each visit it was evident how engaged the employees were, and how happy they were to work there. Adam, Chris and Kim huddled many times as members of an Adaptive Business Leaders roundtable think tank for over a decade.

Cornerstone does many of the culture-promoting things you might expect, like bringing breakfast and lunch in regularly, but they also do some unique things – from pet insurance to unlimited vacation, from amazing anniversary events to onboarding events replete with building bikes with kids from the Boys & Girls Club.

Fast-forward to the world of Covid-19. How do you communicate an over-the-top, tangible culture to 1,000 new employees virtually?

Onboarding by design

Adam worked with his leadership team (including leaders from Saba) to design a two-week onboarding and engagement programme. Many company onboarding programmes consist of filling out forms and getting trained on company history, products and processes. Those things were part of the Cornerstone programme, but they weren't at the centre of it.

Instead of focusing on company needs, Adam and team made sure the emphasis was on the employees. The overarching goal was to make sure everyone had a sense of belonging to the team. Employees of both companies participated, as there were new things to learn for everyone, not just the newbies.

First, they scheduled a specific Monday as Day One. Adam considered the announcement of the acquisition to be Day Zero, and he wanted the onboarding process to emphasize the new company, not the transaction. Leading up to that Monday his team started preparing, including generating buzz and excitement around the upcoming events.

Part of the preparation was to ensure that, on Monday, everyone had everything they needed to hit the ground running: equipment, login credentials, email accounts, access to Slack, etc. This was one of the biggest challenges, but Adam's IT team came through. He also recognized the great work of the human resources team, who had a LOT on their plate.

On Day One, Monday, there was a full schedule with a company-wide meeting in the morning, followed by divisional meetings and then department/team meetings. Over the next two weeks, they made sure no one went untouched. For example, every single new employee was assigned a buddy, a peer who could answer questions, share tribal knowledge and listen to concerns.

They took advantage of their own online platform to create an integration portal that provided information as well as welcome messaging, videos and training. Human resources established virtual office hours, when anyone could connect with an HR representative to get answers. The team organized and hosted virtual happy hours and other online social events to promote engagement.

This deliberately designed onboarding programme proved to be very successful. Adam and his team heard from many veterans of multiple acquisitions, and the message was consistent: it was the best onboarding experience they had ever had.

Tailoring remote to demographics

Adam found that employee success in the new remote model had more to do with demographics than with job function or pay grade. Overall people fell into one of four categories:

- living alone or in a household without children;
- living in a household with small children;
- living in a household with older children;
- living in a multigenerational household.

The Cornerstone leadership team adapted by managing to these characteristics.

As you might expect, the people without children put in the most hours and those with young children put in the fewest. Those in multigenerational households work at different times because they have to share equipment and/or space.

To connect with people in ways that were relevant to their different situations, the team took different approaches. Virtual happy hours went over well with those with no children and older children. For those with young children, they focused on childcare information, resources and activities for kids. They sent additional equipment to multigenerational households, such as Wi-Fi hotspots and furniture.

Adam firmly believes that companies need to adapt to individual employees, and not vice versa. In addition to adapting to the demographic groups, Cornerstone made adaptations across the board based on employee needs. For example, the use of videoconferencing increased significantly, as you might expect. However, it wasn't long before people were experiencing video burnout. Now the guideline is to use video for group meetings but not necessarily for one-on-one conversations.

They also asked managers to be more thoughtful about meeting times. This was important for teams made up of people in multiple time zones, but also helped with varying employee work schedules. While Cornerstone always has had flexible work options, they found that different employees' home situations meant that some had to work in the morning while others had to work in the evening. They also shortened meetings, such as cutting what used to be hour-long meetings to 45 minutes. In addition, they offered training to support remote issues, including managing anxiety and depression, time management skills and more.

Looking ahead

We asked Adam to speculate on what work dynamics will look like post-Covid-19. Like many, he does not think we'll return to some kind of pre-Covid-19 'normal'. For one thing, he believes that now that people have had a taste of working remotely, they will want to keep it – at least as an option. Cornerstone plans to offer that option once it is safe to return to the office. Adam feels that many will want to come back because they miss the camaraderie, but may still work from home one or two days a week. There will be others who would prefer to work from home, but because they don't have an ideal home office situation, will opt to work in the office.

He expects that most companies will see productivity levels stay the same, or improve. At Cornerstone they have seen levels of trust increase, partly out of necessity, but also because people have stepped up in a challenging situation. We may see employees choosing to work from home on Mondays or Fridays, since commute traffic is typically heaviest on those days. If that's the case, Mondays and Fridays may become low-traffic days. That is, we should expect things to continue to evolve.

One advantage Adam sees is that it will level the playing field for remote and non-remote employees. Before remote work became widespread, remote workers often felt like second-class citizens. They didn't have access to the in-office perks their peers enjoyed. Now employers will be challenged to come up with creative perks that are available to all. In addition, when a team had one remote member, that member was often excluded from meetings because of logistics. Now, however, people won't attend meetings in conference rooms, but from their desk, wherever that might be.

In fact, Adam predicts that many companies will reduce their real estate footprint. They won't feel an obligation to provide permanently assigned offices or cubicles to people who only use them part-time. That will trigger a shift to more flexible office arrangements, like hoteling, in which people come in and find an available spot for that day.

Flexibility is one of the important themes in Adam's story. The other is a focus on employees, and setting them up for success – including working with each person's unique situation. Both are necessary components for a remote model to thrive.

Hopefully you were inspired by the way Adam and his team responded to a double-barrel challenge. It certainly puts things in perspective for us, who both have experience with much smaller companies. A key point for us is the fact that culture played an important role in dealing with both challenges: setting everyone up for success in working from home, and also in planning and executing the integration. Another key to success was the deliberate approach Adam and his leadership team took to making it all happen.

We also agree with Adam that the company and its leaders have a responsibility to adapt to employee circumstances. Employees have to be adaptable too, but it's all too easy for leaders to think (but hopefully never say), 'That's just the way it is. Deal with it.' It may sound trite, but going remote truly calls for everyone to work together.

Like Julie Fletcher in the previous chapter's case study, Adam believes remote work is here to stay as a mainstream option. There will be hybrids and many variations, but working from home will not go back to being a rare exception. Pretty compelling stuff. But there's more – in the next chapter, as promised, we'll share why the remote model is best for the health and well-being of your people.

References

Bibby, A (2015) Why Millennials will help remote work grow, *Remote.co*, 1 September, https://remote.co/why-millennials-will-help-remote-work-grow (archived at https://perma.cc/4CW9-QZAK)

Bloom, N A et al (2013) Does working from home work? www.gsb.stanford.edu/faculty-research/working-papers/does-working-home-work-evidence-chinese-experiment (archived at https://perma.cc/5E6U-MHT8)

Deloitte (2016) The 2016 Deloitte Millennial Survey: Winning over the next generation of leaders, *Deloitte*, www2.deloitte.com/content/dam/Deloitte/global/Documents/About-Deloitte/gx-millenial-survey-2016-exec-summary.pdf (archived at https://perma.cc/MY67-4GJD)

Farooq, U (2018) What is competitive strategy, *Marketing Tutor*, 11 November, www.marketingtutor.net/what-is-competitive-strategy (archived at https://perma.cc/2GME-QHYW)

Fried, J and Hansson, D H (2013) *Remote: Office not required*, Currency, New York

Hopwood, S (2019) The benefits and challenges of working with remote employees, *Forbes*, 25 June, www.forbes.com/sites/forbesbusinessdevelopmentcouncil/2019/06/25/the-benefits-and-challenges-of-working-with-remote-employees/#35e9ea161cb6 (archived at https://perma.cc/8XXH-K2VJ)

McQuaid, D (2020) Employees willing to take a pay cut for remote working, *HR Review*, 23 June, www.hrreview.co.uk/hr-news/strategy-news/employees-willing-to-take-a-pay-cut-for-remote-working/126087 (archived at https://perma.cc/SP5C-JN8P)

PR Newswire (2013) New Ask.com study reveals workplace productivity killers, *PR Newswire Cision*, 7 May, www.prnewswire.com/news-releases/new-askcom-study-reveals-workplace-productivity-killers-206398681.html (archived at https://perma.cc/LG4U-SR64)

Rapoza, K (2013) One in five Americans work from home, numbers seen rising over 60%, *Forbes*, 18 February, http://www.forbes.com/sites/kenrapoza/2013/02/18/one-in-five-americans-work-from-home-numbers-seen-rising-over-60/#38ff8fe34768 (archived at https://perma.cc/QKE4-VPNX)

Reynolds, B (2017) 2017 annual survey finds workers are more productive at home, and more, *Flexjobs.com*, 21 August, www.flexjobs.com/blog/post/productive-working-remotely-top-companies-hiring (archived at https://perma.cc/KDZ6-PM9Z)

Roth, D (2016) Behind the top attractors: How we discovered the world's best hirers and keepers of talent, *LinkedIn Pulse*, 20 June, www.linkedin.com/pulse/behind-top-attractors-how-we-discovered-worlds-best-hirers-roth (archived at https://perma.cc/29J3-RRFP)

Search Solution Group (nd) Cost of a vacancy, www.searchsolutiongroup.com/wp-content/uploads/2018/11/Cost-of-a-Vacancy.pdf (archived at https://perma.cc/N6KB-AY8G)

Silver, C (2020) Study shows workers will take pay cut to work remote and live in Microsoft Teams, *Forbes.com*, 4 February, www.forbes.com/sites/curtissilver/2020/02/04/study-shows-workers-will-take-pay-cut-to-work-remote-and-live-in-microsoft-teams/#2fd6ce056372 (archived at https://perma.cc/NZR9-BAMT)

Stringfellow, A (2017) Importance of flexibility in business, *American Express*, 11 December, www.americanexpress.com/en-us/business/trends-and-insights/articles/why-flexibility-is-key-to-small-business-success (archived at https://perma.cc/95V7-BBEG)

Sullivan, J (2005) Cost of vacancy formulas for recruiting and retention managers, 25 July, *Ere.net*, www.ere.net/cost-of-vacancy-formulas-for-recruiting-and-retention-managers (archived at https://perma.cc/4QS5-KWFA)

Westfall, C (2020) New survey shows 47% increase in productivity: 3 things you must do when working from home, *Forbes.com*, 20 May, www.forbes.com/sites/chriswestfall/2020/05/20/new-survey-shows-47-increase-in-productivity-3-things-you-must-do-when-working-from-home/#d59218080dc8 (archived at https://perma.cc/KBB5-TMRU)

10

People health: why remote is best for your people

In the previous chapter, one topic was how happy employees are good for the bottom line of your business. Now we want to explain why being happy is good for your people. There will be some overlap in the discussion, but the difference in concepts is *not* subtle. We believe in a people-first approach, and a happy consequence of this is success in business, for you and your employees. Recall, from Chapter 8, the ideas around autonomy, mastery and purpose – if you provide these, your people will thrive. While good and motivated employees are great for your company, good employers are great for employees and their well-being.

IN THIS CHAPTER

We will cover:

- Bottom up instead of top down
- The world of personal excellence
- Great employees are born, not made
- Haloes and hamster wheels
- What is your personal utopia?
- Case study: Remote is in Buffer's DNA

Most people agree that a strong leader helps employees set and achieve goals, and that those goals should be tied to business objectives, etc. We're urging you to lean in even further and help your people achieve *life* goals. Do you need to be a personal life coach to every person? Not at all. But you need to let go of any notions about people living linear lives, and support them in any reasonable way as they navigate life's twists and turns.

This understanding and flexible approach will help develop strong loyalty. Not only do the twists and turns make them a stronger person, but they will never forget how you supported them. It's almost impossible to put a dollar value on that loyalty, but it is powerfully valuable. Both of us had more than one employee leave, only to come back – a returning employee gets up to speed faster, requiring less onboarding.

Great people are born, not made

The rest of the world can focus on finding and developing 'A-players'. These are people who are exceptional in a particular job. Instead, we look for Jedis. If you've just emerged from living in seclusion for 50 years, a Jedi is a member of a unique 'knighthood' in the Star Wars universe. They come in all shapes and sizes, but what they have in common is the ability to channel and leverage the power of the Force, the energy matrix that connects all living things.

For us, Jedis are different from A-players because they were Jedis when they were 12. They made more money on their paper route than all the other kids. In college they excelled in academics, sports *and* extracurriculars. They channel the Force – whatever it may be – into all they do. A-players can develop talents, but Jedis are gifted from the get-go. A-players achieve by overachieving – often to the detriment of their health or family life. Jedis work hard, but they do so with incredible proficiency – give them a job to do and they remove obstacles and cut through clutter with ease.

While A-players focus on competition, Jedis focus on values. That means A-players are prone to burnout, which also puts your company at risk. Jedis get the job done without the stress, and are thereby more dependable.

If you ask a prospective employee if they are a Jedi, and they hesitate, they probably aren't. Even if they never have been to a Comic Con, they will know what you mean. Kim often talks about Jedis in her presentations and the audience perks up. The sense of immediate understanding is palpable.

The remote model is ideal for Jedis. Create an environment that provides autonomy, mastery and purpose, and you'll attract and retain Jedis. You'll be offering an environment that they can't get anywhere else.

There may be a place for both Jedis and A-players in your company, although you'll need to pay a little more attention to the A-players, to help them avoid burnout. But put a Jedi into a key position and you can be assured that everything is on course. You'll want to monitor performance metrics and do regular check-ins, but Jedis will be your most autonomous employees.

The halo effect

In Chapter 3 we mentioned the halo effect. When someone scores a victory, they seem to be wearing a halo. Appearance alone can create the halo effect. If someone is dressed well, we often assume they are competent and reliable. That's why Brad Pitt features in ads for so many different products, from Rolex watches to Heineken beer to Toyota automobiles. He's *very* easy on the eyes, and advertisers know his halo will extend to the products with which he is pictured (Frey, 2020).

Remote eliminates the halo effect, which is good for your company, but it's also good for your people. Rather than being judged on their appearance, they are judged on their performance and results. They can analyse the monthly spend in their pyjamas or develop new products without ever applying a dram of mascara. It promotes inclusion and diversity by removing many of the things that can trigger bias.

Hamster wheels

Some jobs are hamster wheels. It's a negative image, but it's also reality, such as entering sales data, making outbound 'smile and dial' sales calls or helping yet another user create a new password. Every company has these kinds of jobs, and it's important that the work is done. But it can be tedious for the employee doing the work.

What can you do? Create the best hamster wheel possible. Kim created pods at DT to help with that, and for other reasons. A pod is a group of three or four employees who do similar jobs. They meet virtually once a week or so to share experiences, help one another solve problems and just vent.

It's a change of pace, a different virtual venue that breaks up the monotony. In cases where an employee was located near a client's offices, Kim encouraged them to suit up and visit that office. It helps cement relationships with clients, and gets the employee out of their routine.

What is your personal utopia?

You have an idea of your ideal world, your ideal job. So does each of your employees. Ask them about it. We bet you'll find that many people have similar goals, including you. As a CEO or other senior executive, you have the opportunity to create an environment that delivers what you and your employees want and the remote model can be particularly helpful for achieving that. Here, we outline some of the features that enable this.

Empowerment

Remote requires that you offer empowerment. Working from home requires a good deal of self-discipline and self-motivation. You want to hire people who demonstrate initiative and judgement, and then provide the environment in which they can thrive. The best way to flatten the hierarchy is to create more of it, and to use a military analogy, empowerment helps your people develop into tiers of colonels and generals.

In a traditional model you might have one general, two colonels and 20 soldiers. Instead, offer employees the empowerment and professional development opportunities to rise in the ranks. When you have five generals, eight colonels and 10 soldiers, you have more people who are qualified to make better decisions. And you have more employees who are enjoying the satisfaction and fulfilment that comes with autonomy.

Increased choices

We already explained how remote opens the talent pool for your company to choose from, but it also opens employment options available to top talent. One of Kim's Decision Toolbox employees was a blue-ribbon equestrian who keeps horses and competes in dressage competitions. If her only option was to work in a brick-and-mortar business, she probably couldn't live in the open spaces 35 miles outside Seattle. With a remote model, you can offer your employees a better quality of life, on their own terms, and so improve their personal and professional well-being.

Respect for their time

No one wants to sit through poorly organized meetings that take twice as long as they need to. In a remote model, it's essential that you stay on point. If you don't, you are sending a message that you don't respect your employees' time. Instead, by being efficient and engaging, you provide a much better environment for your team. In upcoming chapters we'll share some tips for doing this.

Like senior executives, employees at all levels need time to think and reflect. Chris discovered that his people prefer large blocks of time to work uninterrupted (talk about utopia), including working *on*, not *in*, their part of the business. With remote there is no one stopping by the cubicle, chatting loudly a few feet away or microwaving fish in the break room. He encourages his people to calendar time to reflect, not only about work, but about other aspects of their lives. He also teaches them how to manage their calendar to be more efficient while also preserving precious free time.

Personal excellence

Offer people the chance to focus on personal excellence: most employees will see this as a remarkable perk that they never thought could be part of a job. Chris and his team found two specific benefits to this. First, self-reflection resulted in everyone becoming more patient and so conflicts and disagreements are much less likely to escalate.

The second benefit is increased enthusiasm for going to professional conferences. With their time well managed and a healthy approach to professional development, Chris's employees look forward to these opportunities. After going remote, conference attendance increased from 20 per cent to 60 per cent at PeopleG2.

Attending professional conferences is a great learning and development opportunity for employees, and helps keep them motivated. It's also beneficial for your company, as the attendees can gather valuable information about emerging trends and competitors.

Promote learning and development

There are plenty of resources available for professional development, but the most valuable resource is the *time* to focus on it. By providing that, you are helping employees achieve their goals. You can also encourage people to explore personal interests.

Chris started a book club that meets monthly at PeopleG2. It is entirely optional, but employees are encouraged to calendar time in their workday to read. Chris chooses the books and, while most are about business and professional development, there are also novels. In addition to encouraging learning and getting the time to do it, the book club gives employees greater access to Chris and helps them build relationships that are not directly work-related.

Greater productivity = greater satisfaction

In the last chapter we talked about how working remotely allows employees to be more productive, which is great for your business. It's also great for your people, as most people take satisfaction in achieving goals and moving on to new ones. Amar Hussain (2019), an entrepreneur and consultant to startups, has identified several reasons remote employees enjoy greater productivity:

- no commute lowers stress and gives employees back 400 hours a year;
- flexibility to work when they want, take breaks when they want and finish work on their own time;
- no distractions by coworkers;
- schedule flexibility.

By offering these things, your remote model can help employees achieve new levels of productivity and, therefore, satisfaction. That is a great reason – helping others achieve their best. But at the same time you'll be promoting greater productivity for your company, and increasing loyalty and retention.

Mental and emotional health

Mark Murphy (2016), founder of www.LeadershipIQ.com and bestselling author, reports that:

- 24 per cent of people who work in traditional offices say they love their job;
- 45 per cent of people who work remotely say they love their job.

Scott Morris (nd) believes he knows why. Writing on Skillcrush.com, he lists 18 reasons why employees should work remotely. Among them is 'Naps are a serious option'. We couldn't agree more, and we both calendar short naps in our days. The Mayo Clinic (nd) says that napping offers adults a variety of benefits to well-being, including relaxation, reduced fatigue, increased alertness, improved mood and improved performance, from quicker reaction time to better memory. This is perhaps why Google has installed nap pods for those who work at their campus (Cassidy, 2017).

With a remote model, you can help your people better maintain optimal emotional and mental health. Morris (nd) also says it helps reduce major life stressors, like making it easier to be a working parent. Also, moving home and changing jobs are both major sources of stress and when they happen at the same time, it's a double whammy. However, remote employees can move wherever they want without having to change jobs.

Rhythm and no blues

We all have a circadian rhythm, although not everyone is synchronized to working during the day and sleeping at night. Consultant Daniel Pink (2019) calls people with this circadian pattern 'larks', after the songbirds of the morning. But there are also people who do their best work when most of the world is asleep, and Pink calls these people 'owls'.

When Chris discovered that he had two owls at PeopleG2, a light bulb lit. He had been expecting them to participate in meetings scheduled during regular business hours, but that is when they would normally sleep. One of these employees was grateful for the acknowledgement, but the other clung to his belief that he could burn the candle at both ends. As a result, he became irritable and a thorn in the sides of many coworkers. Chris finally helped him to realize, 'You have to be you. You can't be us and you at the same time.'

Chris has found alternative ways of sharing information that is inclusive of both larks and owls. One approach is to curate meetings, so that morning meetings cover tactical content, like team standups, and afternoon meetings cover more creative content. That makes it easier for owls to participate in the afternoon meetings, in which their insight will be valuable. If necessary, the owls can skip the morning meetings and get tactical updates through another channel, like a simple email, or a page on a collaboration platform.

In addition, Chris pays more attention to assembling teams, pairing the owls with each other, or with larks who are willing to be flexible. This helps match people with the same flow and energy. Whenever a team includes both owls and larks, they are required to flex both ways – sometimes the owls have to get up early, and sometimes the larks have to stay up late.

And that's really the gist of it, isn't it? For sanity and fulfilment, each of us needs to be true to ourselves. As a leader, you are uniquely positioned to create a work culture that helps each and every employee become the best human they can be. The case study that follows offers more insight into creating a culture that promotes employee well-being. You've heard from us – let's hear from someone new.

CASE STUDY
Remote is in Buffer's DNA

Buffer, a provider of tools for social media management, exemplifies many of the characteristics, philosophies and strategies we advocate. We talked with Courtney Seiter, Buffer's Director of People, to get more insight. Buffer has about 90 people in 40 cities in 15 countries, spanning 12 time zones.

Right there on the About Us page, they state, 'We've always aimed to do things a little differently at Buffer. Since the early days, we've had a focus on building one of the most unique and fulfilling workplaces by rethinking a lot of traditional practices.'

Courtney provided a little history. The two co-founders came from outside the United States but wanted to be part of the Silicon Valley scene. They took a few globetrotting detours on the way and realized that you can work from anywhere. At first they had a small office in San Francisco, but since people rarely went there, they let it go.

The move represented some significant savings in one of the world's most expensive real estate markets, but even more important was their desire to build remote into the company's DNA.

Now 10 years old, Buffer's journey has included experiments that worked and some that didn't. For example, in order to flatten the hierarchy, they eliminated job titles. However, this turned out to be confusing, so they brought the titles back. Experiments like these helped Buffer's leadership learn that remote requires a deliberate approach.

Seeing more without seeing

One thing they are deliberate about is asking people how they are doing. In a sticks-and-bricks model, you can see people's expressions and sense when there is an issue – but not always. Often you have to probe, and that becomes even more important when working remotely. Courtney says the leadership team has come up with different ways of asking, 'How are you doing?'

'A very important goal for us is to ensure people are engaged and fulfilled, and that they know they are valued,' Courtney explained. This allows everyone in the organization to grow and thrive.

In any meeting longer than 30 minutes, they use a check-in process they call 'traffic light'. Each meeting participant shares their current state of mind by identifying whether they feel most aligned with a red light, yellow light or green light that day. If the answer is 'yellow' or 'red', teammates can share more context if they like. While Buffer leaders emphasize that it's okay not to be okay, it still can be difficult to speak up about it. The traffic light exercise makes it a little easier.

Another way they encourage openness is for leaders to be open themselves. Sometimes just the act of talking about the issue makes people feel better, and Buffer also offers resources like Modern Health, a global resource for employee mental well-being.

Crossing cultures and time zones

Buffer values teamwork and togetherness, but they discovered that lots of online interactions weren't necessarily the answer. Many people grew tired of attending both business and social Zoom meetings. Buffer's leadership realized that different people have different needs and preferences with regard to social interaction, from the social butterfly who helps coordinate every event to the introvert who is happiest in productive tunnel vision, focusing on the task at hand.

On top of that, work style varies from culture to culture. With team members in 15 different countries, Courtney explains that they have learned to lean into dealing with it all. Leaders need to be culturally savvy and put a little extra time and effort into ensuring their message stays clear as it crosses all the boundaries.

Time zones are their own kind of boundary, and working globally can be a challenge. For example, US-based Courtney has a teammate in Singapore, so connecting live means one of them has to get up early or work during the evening.

One solution is asynchronous communication, or using tools that allow you to post notes and questions online. Then a teammate on another continent can review those at a different time. You may sacrifice personal interaction, but you get to maintain your circadian sanity. The team at Buffer uses Loom, a video messaging platform, which approximates real-time interactions in the sense that users' personalities and non-verbal communication come through. They use Threads for keeping track of context and decisions for longer-term projects, but you may want to try different options to find a good fit for your organization. Other platforms are Slack, Marco Polo and Mover.

Some activities need to be done together in real time, like brainstorming. Buffer takes a deliberate approach in these cases, including identifying the best people to participate and finding the best time for all. Inevitably one or two will be attending during their off hours, so if the same group reconvenes, the next meeting should be at a different time.

Actionable Values

Courtney shared that Buffer find their values very useful on a day-to-day basis. The six values serve as a North Star for all interactions, and the team made sure they were actionable for that reason:

- Default to transparency
- Cultivate positivity
- Show gratitude
- Practise reflection
- Improve consistently
- Act beyond yourself

These values are very similar to values we advocate. As an example, 'improve consistently' opens the door for feedback and discourages people from getting defensive. It helps ensure that everyone's opinion is heard, even when it runs counter to a leader's opinion. In addition, in most disagreements there is a nugget of truth on both sides, and voicing disagreement helps uncover all the nuggets.

According to Courtney, transparency has been very useful in the remote model, because it allows any employee to ask anything. The company fully discloses financial information, and employees are encouraged to provide input into any decisions.

Values have to be kept vital through constant alignment. For example, the salary of every employee at Buffer is available to the public on their website, in accordance with the company's focus on transparency. Although it's an unusual practice, Buffer views it as consistent with their values – and it's helped to attract like-minded talent. However, values can and should evolve as your team does. When some teammates shared that they felt unsafe having their name, city and salary on the website, Buffer listened. As a result, Buffer now offers options within the policy so that team members can choose to have their name or city kept private.

Not for everyone

Not everyone thrives in or enjoys working remotely. Courtney believes that even if they haven't tried it, most people know instinctively whether it is right for them or not. Just the same, their hiring process is a little longer than many because they screen for remote-worthiness. But they screen with a slightly different approach than you might expect.

'It's less about control and more about enthusiasm,' Courtney told us. They want to be sure they can provide an optimal experience, given the employee's time zone and other circumstances. They also look for very strong communication skills and a proactive approach.

Deliberate onboarding

Not many companies have good onboarding practices, but Buffer recognizes that it is essential to integrating new people and setting them up for success. This is particularly true in a remote model, in which just about all onboarding is done virtually. They make sure the new person's tools are set up *before* they start, to ensure day one is smooth. They follow this with a highly orchestrated programme that lasts six weeks for employees and three months for leaders. The programme includes the typical things, like enrolling in benefits, but also includes training about the six values. They make sure the employee understands their approach to making decisions, working with teammates and interacting with customers.

To support these and other onboarding efforts, each new employee is assigned a 'culture buddy' for the duration of onboarding. The buddy helps the new employee integrate and adapt smoothly.

Remote isn't immune to Covid-19

People often think that Covid-19 doesn't really impact a company that was remote before the pandemic broke out. For example, companies like Buffer didn't have to scramble in managing the logistics of sending everyone home. However, there is a psychological and emotional impact irrespective of whether a company is virtual or brick-and-mortar.

Courtney believes that the situation will accelerate attention on a workplace issue that is already being discussed: the effect of 24-hour news and social media on people's mental well-being. Pressure to 'stay informed' can be intense, and fear of missing out can keep people from getting the sleep they need. One way Buffer is helping employees deal with information anxiety is to be upfront and direct, and encouraging employees to be the same.

As with answering the question 'How are you entering this meeting?', Buffer is working to help people understand that it is okay to share negative feelings. Courtney feels that it is important, in a remote organization, to normalize things that may be seen as taboo. In the spirit of being deliberate about creating a healthy remote culture, she calls it 'making the implicit explicit'.

Deliberately supportive

One of the things that really stood out for us as we talked with Courtney is the fact that Buffer's approach to culture and work arrangements is very deliberate. They have been remote from the beginning, but rather than leaving anything to chance, they ensure that policies are aligned with their clearly stated values. In addition, they engage employees in the decision-making process, and remain flexible as things change.

Their methods exemplify many of the recommendations we made in this chapter, such as taking a bottom-up approach and encouraging personal excellence. They strive for a workplace utopia that empowers, respects and supports employees, accounting for both professional and personal goals.

Right now we'd like to encourage you to align yourself with us, as part of the Remote Work Movement. You'll find more great ideas and insights from many people, and you can share your own as well. Sign up at https://chrisdyer.com/remotework.

Next up: identifying the characteristics that help people excel in a remote model.

References

Cassidy, A (2017) Clocking off: The companies introducing nap time to the workplace, *Guardian*, 4 December, www.theguardian.com/business-to-business/2017/dec/04/clocking-off-the-companies-introducing-nap-time-to-the-workplace (archived at https://perma.cc/5DB2-KKU8)

Frey, K (2020) Brad Pitt makes the case for dressing up in sexy new Brioni campaign, *People*, 10 September, https://people.com/style/brad-pitt-brioni-fall-2020-campaign (archived at https://perma.cc/9NLH-K2LS)

Hughes, J (2016) Involved employees matter, 18 August, *Brand Learning*, www.brandlearning.com/views-ideas/latest-views-ideas/hr/involved-employees-matter (archived at https://perma.cc/H5BL-J23M)

Hussain, A (2019) 4 reasons why a remote workforce is better for business, *Forbes*, 29 March, www.forbes.com/sites/amarhussaineurope/2019/03/29/4-reasons-why-a-remote-workforce-is-better-for-business/#236b747c1a64 (archived at https://perma.cc/5C9H-9E22)

Mayo Clinic Staff (nd) Napping: Do's and don'ts for healthy adults, 20 November, www.mayoclinic.org/healthy-lifestyle/adult-health/in-depth/napping/art-20048319 (archived at https://perma.cc/XT4B-UG49)

Morris, S (nd) 18 reasons to start working remotely right away, *Skillcrush.com*, https://skillcrush.com/blog/reasons-to-work-remotely (archived at https://perma.cc/M52V-XPYS)

Murphy, M (2016) You're 87% more likely to love your job if you work from home, *Forbes*, 24 January, www.forbes.com/sites/markmurphy/2016/01/24/youre-87-more-likely-to-love-your-job-if-you-work-from-home-i-e-telecommuting/#d11fbf5463d6 (archived at https://perma.cc/3PRG-9CGB)

Pink, D (2019) *When: The scientific secrets of perfect timing*, Riverhead Books, New York

Scott, K (2017) *Radical Candor: Be a kick-ass boss without losing your humanity*, St Martin's Press, London

11

Who can work from home

Not everyone can work successfully from home. If your company had a large number of employees start working from home in response to the Covid-19 pandemic, you probably discovered that it was easier for some than for others.

IN THIS CHAPTER

We will cover:

- Goodness of fit
- Personalities that may be happier in an office
- Characteristics and skills for remote success
- Work ethic: good, bad and ugly
- Helping staff transition
- Screening new candidates for fit
- New talent pools

Kim had a similar experience when Decision Toolbox went remote. The company had 37 employees at the time. Though all said they were onboard with working from home, for some it wasn't ideal; it was a situation to accept partly because in the months immediately following the 9/11 attacks, jobs in the recruitment industry became scarce.

Kim had a conversation with each person, probing to find out whether each was prepared for the transition, and what the company could do to facilitate it. Some of the questions were, 'Do you need to be around people in order to be fulfilled?' and 'Do you have a quiet space at home where you can work undisturbed?' Following these conversations, four people chose to leave the company.

Both of us have worked with people who thrive working remotely, and with people who just aren't a good fit. There isn't a single formula for knowing which person is which, particularly as you are screening candidates. As Chris says, 'I can't tell you what poor candidate for remote work looks like, but I know one when I see them.' Still, there are some characteristics that seem to help people succeed. You can use this information to help existing employees develop their 'remoteability' or to evaluate candidates before hiring them.

Personality types

You probably know people who walk into a room and command it, whether through physical size or charisma. These individuals won't be able to do that in a remote model and, if their self-confidence relies heavily on that ability, they may become frustrated. Their charisma may come across in a Zoom meeting, but we're inclined to think that it won't, at least not to the same extent as it does in an in-person meeting.

Another type you may know is the person who takes pride in knowing all the gossip, from office politics to personal information. Perhaps they sit near the water cooler, or they're very good at the gossip game. The transition to remote will change the dynamic. We're not saying that remote employees don't 'dish the dirt'. In fact, writing in *Psychology Today*, Jennifer Haupt (2015) cites a study demonstrating that workplace gossip can be positive.

Gossip allows people to get things off their chest, instead of holding on to negative feelings. Haupt argues that it also encourages cooperation, relieves stress, fosters self-improvement and provides a valuable reality check.

A *Fast Company* article by Stephanie Vozza (2015) makes the same argument, drawing on a number of studies. She says that gossip accomplishes the same things as in Haupt's argument, and adds that it helps identify issues that need to be addressed.

Certainly office gossip requires different channels in a remote model, such as email or instant messaging. But more importantly, the performance-based culture we advocate is likely to attract people whose interest in gossip is minimal.

Some people thrive on being better than others. They dress better, eat at the best restaurants, drink the best wine or have the most amazing kids. This type also will be thwarted in a remote model. Again, it's possible to brag via instant messenger, but in the culture we promote, people stand out via results and performance, not designer clothes.

If you are going remote and your team includes these personality types, you should have a frank conversation with them. It may very well be that they will be happier in a brick-and-mortar office, which may mean leaving your company. If you want to retain them, you'll need to help them explore other ways of finding fulfilment in the new model. The office gossip might take a leadership role in organizing online social events. The wine connoisseur could start a monthly virtual tasting club. However, more important may be the 'soft skills' that enable some people to thrive in a remote model.

Characteristics and skills

Those who excel in a remote model share some skills and characteristics. By skills we mean things that can be learned, like communication, analysis and time management. Skills help people perform better. Characteristics, on the other hand, come from values and personality, and include things like accountability, thoroughness and compassion. Characteristics can be negative, but the positive ones enable a person to add value beyond pure performance.

When we started to brainstorm a list of those qualities, we realized it was a lot of the same qualities that help people thrive in an office setting. The difference, however, is that these qualities need to be heightened or well honed in order to drive remote success. For example, a sense of responsibility is valuable in any setting, but absolutely essential in a remote model, in which people work independently.

We interviewed consultant Jackson Lynch, who has worked at and with a number of companies (including PepsiCo and Nestlé) in various capacities, including forming and leading remote teams. He shared some of the characteristics that he believes are essential for remote employees. They include:

- **very strong critical thinking skills**. You want that in just about any employee, but Jackson explained that prioritization is different in remote work;
- **collaboration** and, because collaboration is harder in a remote model, those who are thoughtful and deliberate collaborators will stand out;

- **professional drive**, or the motivation to build one's talents, both horizontally and vertically;
- a **results orientation** and **sense of urgency**. These are also important, and a remote model will reveal those who lack these traits faster than a sticks-and-bricks model will.

Another important skill Jackson emphasized is **clear communication**. Just about every job posting you'll see asks for 'excellent communication skills', but they become indispensable in remote work. One reason is that, in a remote model, you often lose body language, facial expressions and intonation in most communication channels. You may have heard of the work of Dr Albert Mehrabian (2007), who concluded that communication is 7 per cent verbal, 38 per cent vocal and 55 per cent visual. By 'vocal' he means intonation, volume, etc. That means that 93 per cent of communication is nonverbal.

The remote model allows for some nonverbal communication, such as intonation over the phone and facial expression in video meetings. However, according to Jackson, letters, emails and even instant messages require excellent writing, grammar and spelling skills. Some jobs don't require mastery in this area, but any job that requires a good deal of collaboration will require pretty strong communication skills.

Within the context of communication, good writing is a skill that can be learned. One important point is that in good writing, clarity is the primary goal, and style is a secondary one. Some resources you can share with your team to help them write more effectively:

- *On Writing Well: The classic guide to writing nonfiction*, by William Vinsser (1998)
- *Revising Business Prose*, by Richard Lanham (1999)
- *The Elements of Style*, by William Strunk Jr and E B White (1999).

More characteristics and skills

Additional insight comes from Lisette Sutherland's 2018 book, *Work Together Anywhere*. She argues that, to excel in a remote model, employees should have:

- technical savvy;
- problem solving and troubleshooting skills;

- a proactive mindset;
- the ability to work independently and be a team player;
- reliability;
- high responsiveness;
- a pleasant and positive attitude;
- a supportive attitude towards others;
- receptivity to feedback.

Work ethic

This is another characteristic of a good employee in any setting, but there are unique aspects to work ethic when working remotely. For one thing, assuming you follow our model and implement performance metrics, poor performers are revealed pretty quickly. We will go into more detail about measuring performance in Chapter 15. Regarding work ethic, however, we suggest that, when you go remote, you set expectations and clarify just how you will measure performance. When a low performer is revealed, you can act quickly to find out what the problem is and address it.

Self-discipline is non-negotiable in remote. Working from home is fraught with multiple demands for attention, including children, pets, television and chores. In Chapter 8 we said that one of the reasons that remote is great for leaders is that it gives you time for quiet reflection. And that's good for everyone else as well. However, as many people discovered during the peak of Covid-19, having family members of different generations at home when you are working there is both a blessing and a challenge.

Work ethics gone wild

Another interesting take on work ethic in remote settings comes from Leigh Thompson, professor at the Kellogg School of Business. While a strong work ethic is desirable, she argues, too much of a good thing can be a problem. In 2014, she and Sarah Townsend conducted a study to determine how high levels of the Protestant work ethic (PWE) influence individuals and teams. Building on the early 20-century work of Max Weber (2010; originally published 1905), they simplified the concept of PWE into 'The belief that hard work and the delay of gratification will lead to success' (Townsend and Thompson, 2014).

Based on that study, Thompson believes that people with very high PWE may be at risk in four ways in a remote model (Thompson, 2020). First, these people work harder, putting in long hours. They have a hard time letting go, and may work on a problem long after others would have escalated it or accepted it as unsolvable. Control is important, but they may feel that they have less control in the remote scenario. All of this is a recipe for burnout and frustration.

If you have someone like this on your team, you should help them create boundaries around work hours, such as setting a timer or alarm to remind them to stop working and do something else. You can also help them adopt new ways to control the things that need to be controlled. For example, if they lead a team, they may feel a loss of control because they are not able to directly supervise them. Help them understand that, in the remote model, 'control' will come from monitoring their team's performance metrics rather than observing their work habits or micromanaging them.

Second, those with high PWE typically eschew socializing and dive right into work. However, some socializing is important and necessary to a healthy culture. Thompson believes that this all-work-no-play approach can be damaging to morale and lead to unrealistic expectations. One way to help your high-PWE employees with this is to create social and/or team-building events – like Chris's book club – and make it clear that you expect this person to participate. In this way, your high-PWE colleagues are encouraged to not focus solely on work and the team itself becomes more cohesive through different forms of communication.

Third, this type of person usually sees challenges and crises as competition – the unhealthy kind: a sort of workplace Darwinism in which only the strong will survive. Thompson's research with Townsend (2014) leads her to believe that high-PWE people thrive on being able to set themselves apart. Recognition is an essential part of any healthy culture, but high-PWE employees may crave it more than others. Make a point of sharing this person's successes without giving them more attention than you give others – sometimes a comment like 'great job' can make a big difference. On the other hand, guard against letting these employees set themselves *too far* apart by promoting collaboration as a key value in the culture.

Fourth, high-PWE people become frustrated when others don't seem to want to work as hard as they do. This can be particularly problematic if the high-PWE person is a supervisor or manager, constantly checking up on team members. Remote workers have enough distractions without being micromanaged. You'll need this person to buy in on the use of performance-based metrics. One way you might do this is to set this expectation and hold the person accountable. You can also encourage them to use the metrics in their weekly team stand-ups – that will help them own the metric-based approach to supervision. In addition, they will have to come to terms with the new reality: as long as a team member hits the target metrics, it doesn't matter how hard they worked, how many hours they put in or when they did the work.

Helping existing staff through the transition

Setting your existing employees up for success as you go remote will require a fair amount of training. We've shared several tactics for doing this, such as ensuring each team member has good time management skills. If you have been conceiving of your role as 'boss', it's time to reinvent yourself as a mentor and coach. You are a facilitator who helps team members solve problems and achieve goals. Coaches may be tough at times and encouraging at others, but they should always focus on helping their team members and teams succeed.

Most importantly, ask your people what they need. It's great to encourage input, but don't just sit and wait for it. First of all, it shows that you care about your employees' well-being, and that can be motivating in and of itself. Find out what challenges they are facing and help them overcome those challenges. At the same time – and this is something of a balancing act – respect their autonomy and encourage them to be resourceful and self-sufficient. In Chapter 17 we'll go into more detail about helping employees in general.

Screening for remote success

When you are bringing on new employees, there are ways to help predict whether or not they will be effective in a remote model. One way is to determine whether or not they can follow easy-to-understand instructions. This can be embedded in the recruiting/onboarding process, such as asking them to go online to schedule an interview or take and submit a personality assessment. Good remote employees are self-reliant, and if simple instructions are a challenge, it might be a red flag.

Chris has a clever assessment tool. He asks candidates to state the difference between Louis Armstrong, Neil Armstrong and Lance Armstrong. It's a virtual test and the answer is written. Obviously if someone gets the answers wrong, that's a very bad sign. But the way a candidate answers the question can be insightful.

For example, if concise communication is important in the open position, the ideal answer is something like, 'trumpeter, astronaut, cyclist'. If research is an important skill for the position, you want to see evidence that the candidate did some digging. On the other hand, if the answer is clearly copied and pasted, that's a red flag.

With any kind of assigned task, you want to see that a candidate can work independently and resourcefully. At the same time, it can be a good sign when a candidate 'raises their hand' to ask for help. This person is showing that their ego doesn't get in the way of achieving goals. In fact, it takes some courage for a candidate to admit to a prospective employer that they need help with an assignment.

Your process will probably involve a video interview with candidates. If someone struggles with the technology to get into that interview, it may be a bad sign. Someone with high 'remoteability' will take time in advance of the interview to make sure everything is good to go.

We do advise against using any single weak spot as the lone deciding factor. For example, suppose you have a video interview and notice, in the background, that the candidate's bed isn't made or the living room is a mess. You might be tempted to think, 'Well, they didn't make much effort to put their best foot forward.' That may be true, but it also may be that they dealt with an emergency earlier that day, and making the bed was simply pushed off the to-do list.

Another way to identify potential remote talent is to consider candidate pools made up of people who often are overlooked or rejected by brick-and-mortar employers. Remote work can provide opportunities that are otherwise unavailable to some, and one would expect that these candidates are highly motivated to make it work. Who are we talking about?

Fishing in new talent pools

We're talking about military spouses, people with physical disabilities and 'non-traditional' employees. Many companies shy away from military spouses because there is a good chance they will be transferred. As a remote employer, you don't have to worry about this. Even if an employee is transferred to another country, you can make it work with much less effort than it would take to replace that employee.

From our experience they may need a couple of personal days to make the move and settle in, but that's barely a bump in the road. In *Get Scrappy*, which Kim co-wrote with Dave Berkus (2015), she relates the story of two very talented but non-traditional employees. One was a military spouse who was director of recruitment quality and client engagement. While this individual's family lived in Dallas, her husband, a naval officer, was posted to Hawaii for several months. She packed up the kids to be right there with him and didn't miss a beat with her work.

The other was an accounting/HR assistant who worked six months of the year from on board a clipper ship in Connecticut, and the other six months from the jungles of Costa Rica. She also spent time, including working, on a Coboat excursion – an 82-foot sailing catamaran with satellite connectivity designed for 'digital nomads and entrepreneurs'.

Another underutilized talent pool is people with physical disabilities. Not every brick-and-mortar facility has the accommodations, and even if they do, transportation may be challenging. Not only can you engage talent that your competitors miss out on, but you also might develop a reputation for being a disability-friendly employer. Talented people with disabilities might seek you out.

Writing on 101Mobility.com, Brian Havens (2016) lists top companies hiring people with disabilities, including IBM, Procter & Gamble, Cisco and others. Monster.com's list (Martis, 2019) includes Accenture, Boeing, Disney, KPMG, Wells Fargo and many others. Good company to keep! However, Havens (2016) states that people with disabilities are employed at about half the rate that non-disabled people are. There are, no doubt, many reasons for this, but one of them may be that these well-meaning employers don't offer remote options.

It certainly is possible that neurodiverse people can succeed in a remote model. According to Disabled-world.com (2020), neurodiversity is 'an approach to learning and disability that argues diverse neurological conditions are the result of normal variations in the human genome'. Such conditions include autism, ADHD and dyslexia.

In the spirit of full disclosure, this is not an area in which we have deep expertise. These conditions vary widely from individual to individual – one reason that people often speak of autism as a spectrum rather than a single condition. For that reason, you will have to assess neurodiverse candidates on a case-by-case basis.

For example, AutismSpeaks.org (2018) says that many employers don't realize that people with autism can have 'intense attention to detail, commitment to quality and consistency, creative and "out of the box" thinking, the ability to excel on repetitive tasks, lower turnover rates, honesty and loyalty'. On the other hand, those with autism are often challenged in the areas of interpersonal interactions and communication. We've already emphasized the importance of these characteristics in the remote model, so there is your challenge as an employer.

There are things you can do, as an employer, to support neurodiverse employees, and it can depend on specific individual needs. Writing on SHRM.org, Taryn Oesch (2019) says that support can range from on-the-job training in communication and interpersonal skills to engaging help from organizations that specialize in helping neurodiverse individuals succeed at work. The article also recommends pairing neurodiverse individuals with neurotypical 'buddies' who can help them. This topic is broader than we can cover in this book, but if you want more information, we suggest starting with the articles cited here.

Determining which employees can and can't work from home is not as simple as it seems. There are a lot of factors at play, and a person may have one skill set that outweighs a drawback. We're inclined to believe that almost anyone can do it, but it falls to you, as the leader and mentor, to help them be successful. In fact, that sets us up to move to the next chapter, which is about which leaders can thrive in a remote model.

References

AutismSpeaks.org (2018) Changing the spectrum: Autism in the workplace, www.autismspeaks.org/blog/changing-spectrum-autism-workplace (archived at https://perma.cc/42A9-YDJM)

Berkus, D and Shepherd, K (2015) *Get Scrappy! Business insights to make your company more agile*, Berkus Press, Los Angeles

Disabled-world.com (2020) What is: Neurodiversity, neurodivergent, neurotypical, 4 September, www.disabled-world.com/disability/awareness/neurodiversity (archived at https://perma.cc/9973-6BDY)

Haupt, J (2015) 5 benefits of gossip (even negative gossip), *Psychology Today*, 22 June, www.psychologytoday.com/us/blog/one-true-thing/201506/5-benefits-gossip-even-negative-gossip (archived at https://perma.cc/J5FX-BL6C)

Havens, B (2016) Top 6 companies that hire people with disabilities, 101Mobility.com, 1 March, https://101mobility.com/blog/top-6-companies-that-hire-people-with-disabilities (archived at https://perma.cc/U2WK-Z9US)

Lanham, R (1999) *Revising Business Prose*, Pearson, New York

Martis, L (2019) These are the leading disability employers in 2019, Monster.com, www.monster.com/career-advice/article/disability-friendly-companies (archived at https://perma.cc/7242-JRAZ)

Mehrabian, A (2007) *Nonverbal Communication*, Routledge, Oxfordshire

Oesch, T (2019) Autism at work: Hiring and training employees on the spectrum, SHRM.org, 19 August, www.shrm.org/resourcesandtools/hr-topics/behavioral-competencies/global-and-cultural-effectiveness/pages/autism-at-work-hiring-and-training-employees-on-the-spectrum.aspx (archived at https://perma.cc/ES9Q-78ZB)

Strunk, W and White, E B (1999) *The Elements of Style*, Pearson, New York

Sutherland, L and Janene-Nelson, K (2018) *Work Together Anywhere: A handbook on working remotely–successfully–for individuals, teams, and managers*, Collaboration Superpowers, The Hague

Thompson, L (2020) A Kellogg professor says high-performing employees have these 4 traits, *Business Insider*, 24 August, www.businessinsider.com/kellogg-mba-professor-high-performing-employees-possess-4-traits-2020-8 (archived at https://perma.cc/44CB-JWMJ)

Townsend, S M and Thompson, L (2014) Implications of the Protestant work ethic for cooperative and mixed-motive teams, *Organizational Psychology Review*, 4 (1), pp 4–26 (February)

Vinsser, W (1998) *On Writing Well: The classic guide to writing nonfiction*, Harper Reference, New York

Vozza, S (2015) Five hidden benefits of gossip, *Fast Company*, 5 March, www.fastcompany.com/3043161/five-hidden-benefits-of-gossip (archived at https://perma.cc/6XN3-AMNZ)

Weber, M (1905) *The Protestant Ethic and the Spirit of Capitalism*, 2010 reprint, Oxford University Press, Oxford

12

Who can lead from home

Some 2,500 years ago, Lao Tzu wrote, 'The wicked leader is he who the people despise. The good leader is he who the people revere. The great leader is he who the people say, "We did it ourselves"' (Lao Tzu, 2006; originally written as early as the 6th century BC). The best leaders empower their people and then step into the background. They create a culture in which employees enjoy the satisfaction of knowing that they were responsible for results and success. This chapter is a discussion of the attitudes, practices and characteristics of strong remote leaders.

IN THIS CHAPTER

We will cover:

- Leading from the background
- What leaders should be worried about
- Characteristics of strong remote leaders
- Attracting strong remote employees
- Keeping strong remote leaders

Leading from the background

Empowering employees to work independently is especially important in a remote model. Roles need to be clearly defined, up and down the stream, and KPIs need to be in place. At the same time, there are many intangibles in leadership which we will cover later in the chapter. It's a little like watering an invisible garden.

You may recall from Chapter 3 that a CEO can be compared to the conductor of an orchestra, and the analogy extends to empowering others. In a concert, the orchestra conductor is in the foreground and, like a CEO, often serves as the 'face' of the orchestra to the public. But the best conductors and CEOs know they have highly accomplished 'first chairs' placed strategically among the musicians. In the business world these first chairs are C-suite executives and vice presidents. Like a conductor, the CEO trusts that the first chairs are alert and always thinking. There is strong respect between the conductor and the first chairs. In a real orchestra, the first chair violin often steps in when the conductor is absent, just as a COO or CFO may step in to cover for a CEO.

Two things make first chair executives valuable. First, they have more direct knowledge of their area (finance, marketing, etc) than the CEO. Second, they have the experience to recognize what may be missing, what their teams need. Today the team may need 'Kumbaya' support and encouragement, but tomorrow they may need a firm hand to meet deadlines. Seeing what's missing is always challenging, but even more difficult in a remote model, so leadership is important at multiple levels.

In Chapter 4 we differentiated between infinite and finite teams. Infinite teams are constant, tasked with ongoing functions, like sales, IT or accounting. Finite teams are temporary, formed to address a specific issue or project. First chairs lead your infinite teams, and it can be easy to assume that, because someone is a leader on the organization chart, they also should lead finite project teams. However, this isn't always the case, as we'll see in a moment, and finite teams represent a great opportunity for others to get experience in leadership roles.

Legos® deliver insight

Kim has a great exercise to demonstrate that organizational charts and arbitrary hierarchies are not the best way to select a project team leader. First, organize people in groups of five and explain that they need to choose an observer, a communicator and a building team. Give each group a small LEGO® kit, but without the box or instructions – just the jumbled pieces. The process is for the observer to go behind a curtain and look at the manufacturer's instructions to see a picture of the completed toy. They describe the toy to the communicator, who gives the team directions on assembling it.

Kim has done this exercise more than once, with different groups, and what typically ensues is a lot of back-and-forth, trial and error and even tension and frustration. No team has ever successfully assembled the toy, but that's not the point.

The real winners are those who realize how easily the chain of communication can be broken. Teams often assume that the observer or communicator is the leader, and so they put the most senior person in that role. But why should a chief financial officer be good at observing and describing a toy? Why assume that a software development manager will be good in the communicator role? Being good in those roles has nothing to do with titles or authority.

As a CEO or other senior executive, you can contribute your skills and knowledge to project teams without having to assume a lead role. Instead, ensure that the leader is chosen by a thoughtful, deliberate process. This is a great opportunity for you to delegate responsibilities, which is important for several reasons. First, it helps ensure that your plate doesn't overflow. Second, it helps you empower others to engage at a higher level than they might otherwise – and engagement promotes productivity and retention. Third, it lets you 'audition' people for potential promotion to a leadership role.

Show up and shut up

The same is true for meetings. Just because you attend a meeting doesn't mean you have to be the shining star, the one who talks most or the one who takes over. There will be meetings where you should be the leader, but in many cases a meeting is an opportunity for you to let others shine.

To give you an example, Chris's organization includes a research team led by a very effective manager. Chris didn't attend every department meeting of course, but when he did, all he had to do was show up and wait for questions. If he were to take over simply by virtue of being 'the boss', it would degrade the leadership dynamic. The manager has worked hard to create a solid, tight-knit team. If Chris started giving direction to that team, there would be confusion, leading to frustration – eventually, people might stop listening to either leader.

Another advantage to showing up and shutting up is that you listen to others. The founder of Toyota, Sakichi Toyoda, was famous for standing in a circle and simply observing what was happening at the point where value was created (on the line by employees). Toyota to this day believes that you cannot lead from an office and professes every leader needs to be out of the office more than in (Liker, 2004). In a department meeting you might listen for the cultural dynamic or for signs that a particular employee might be a candidate for development into leadership roles. In meetings with peers or clients, listening helps you refine your opinion.

GOOD LEADERS DON'T NEED CREDIT

When Chris first started participating in CEO roundtables and other peer events, it often happened that he would share ideas or insight, only to have someone else share the same thing 10 or 15 minutes later. It was frustrating because the second person usually got credit for the idea. That promotes competition where there should be collaboration. However, he realized that these people weren't stealing ideas, they were building on them. Now Chris bides his time, listens to what others have to say, and cultivates an opinion that is informed by what others have said. Then, when he does share an opinion, it is more impactful and memorable.

Balanced scorecard

If showing up and shutting up sounds good to you, angel investor Dave Berkus (Shepherd and Berkus, 2015) describes a great tool for setting expectations and holding managers accountable. It promotes transparency, empowerment and autonomy, which will help your managers become less and less dependent on you. According to Dave, it also will discourage managers from trying to game the system – trying to present a scenario that looks better than it is.

A balanced scorecard is a single location to track the performance of the manager or department. Dave recommends using the four most important measures of success, such as:

- **financial perspective**, or a dashboard summary of key performance indicators like revenue, expense, net income, etc;
- **customer perspective**, possibly including customer satisfaction survey results, customer retention rates, market share, etc;
- **internal process perspective**, which could monitor cycle times, response times, waste, improvement, innovations, etc;
- **learning and growth perspective**, such as employee satisfaction survey results, employee turnover, professional development efforts for department employees and the manager, etc.

When you and your manager have this information in front of you, you can focus on solutions, identify strengths and weaknesses and minimize surprises. These reviews should be collaborative to help eliminate the performance pressure that might lead a manager to fudge information.

Scrum of Scrums

Another way to promote transparency, collaboration and autonomy is to eliminate traditional hierarchies and replace them with a concept from Scrum. Global or whole-company leadership is important, but you also need solid local leadership where the rubber meets the road. In Scrum, the global leadership is provided by the 'Scrum of Scrums', the team assembled to oversee local Scrums or teams. You've probably already realized that the Scrum of Scrums would be made up of your first chairs, or senior leaders.

So what differentiates Scrum teams from traditional organizational structure?

It's an emphasis on cross-functional dynamics. A good Scrum is made up of people with different areas of expertise. Even in IT, a Scrum might include architects, developers, quality professionals and business analysts. By gathering representatives of different functional areas, you minimize time spent going back and forth, while also ensuring diversity of input.

A senior leadership team is, by definition, cross-functional, including leaders representing operations, sales, accounting and other areas. However, some senior leadership meetings consist of going around the table so each leader can report on their area. On the other hand, if your senior leadership meetings involve a good deal of cross-functional brainstorming and collaboration, you've already got the essential spirit of Scrum.

Kim called her Scrum of Scrums the Leadership Pod and Chris calls his the Tiger's Den, as we mentioned in Chapter 3. Whatever you call yours, the mission of the Scrum of Scrums is to monitor the well-being and performance of the other teams. That's really what remote leaders should be focused on.

What leaders worry about

There are times when senior leaders need to pay attention to production or operations, but their real job is to focus on the intangibles that surround the work being done. This is what we mean by working *on* the business rather than working *in* it. In an effective remote model, leaders ensure that production and operations run smoothly, NOT by worrying about them, but by worrying about the following characteristics – and taking action, of course:

- **Communication:** How robust is the information network or matrix that runs around and through your organization? Where might the ball be dropped?

- **Productivity:** Not the number of widgets produced, but how they are produced, and how they might be produced better.

- **Culture:** The shared values that are at once the glue that holds your organization together and also the grease that minimizes friction and promotes teamwork.

- **Teamwork and individual participation:** What do teams need to thrive? How can the company help individuals succeed? How do we ensure everyone is involved?

- **Mission and vision:** You articulate and evangelize these, but even more importantly, you ensure that they are embedded and/or instilled in everything done by you and your team, from developing strategy to responding to a client email.

- **Mental health:** Who is getting burned out? Who needs a pep talk and who needs a break?

- **Work–life balance:** Whatever you choose to call it, it is essential both for you and your people. You need to model it as well as set and reinforce boundaries. No one should be on a conference call at 8:30 pm when they should be reading their child a bedtime story.

- **Loneliness:** As we shared in Chapter 3, it's lonely at the top. The higher your employees rise, the lonelier it becomes. To combat this, encourage each member of your management team to be active in a roundtable-type group or work with a career coach. Otherwise the loneliness can fester and create toxicity.

As you can see, these items are intangibles and weighted much more towards culture than operations. This may be a big change from what you're used to. However, we believe that, if you focus on these things, your company will meet its financial and operational targets.

The 80/20 rule

We have found that about 20 per cent of our leaders create 80 per cent of the momentum in the organization. Also known as the Pareto rule (Lavinsky, 2014), this is something we have observed in our own companies and in others. That means the 20 per cent are at risk of burning out. The ideal situation is a leadership team that flies like snow geese. Muna and Mansour (2005) describe three important lessons to be learned from snow geese.

LEARNING FROM SNOW GEESE

Work as a team: Snow geese regularly migrate as far as 3,000 miles one way, and they use a V formation that minimizes wind resistance. This allows the flock, as a team, to fly 70 per cent farther than any one bird could on its own.

Selfless leadership: The goose at the apex of the V grows tired, it falls back and another takes its place. Being at the apex is harder, as wind resistance is at its greatest there. You don't see any flock members trying to be 'SuperGoose' and staying in the lead all the time.

Humane behaviour: If a goose becomes hurt or sick and has to land, two others go along. They stay until the first one either recovers or dies.

The main message is that you should pay attention to your own well-being as well as that of your employees. You can apply these 'learnings' in your own organization in a couple of ways. For example, you might encourage team members to keep an eye on one another's well-being. This could be incorporated in the pod groups we discussed in Chapter 3. Alternatively, you could set up a buddy system. Sometimes we each need an objective opinion to remind us to take care of ourselves. In a remote model, these tactics can help alleviate isolation and loneliness as well.

We've also found that 20 per cent of our leaders cause 80 per cent of issues and headaches. Again, this is based on our own observations of both our own and other companies. If you're using balanced scorecards, you may be able to identify what is causing the issues. However, a leader's issues may be more personal. A leader's performance may suffer because a spouse is recovering from surgery or a parent is moving into long-term care. In these cases, a compassionate response will help promote loyalty. People break. You can't expect a leadership of clones, and each person is unique. This is one of the situations in which leadership is less science and more art form.

As you know, there may be a time when the only choice is to cut your losses and make a change. Often, however, issues are temporary.

To excel as a remote leader you need to monitor the mental health of your first chairs and know when someone is wearing out – when they need to drop from the apex and draft with the rest of the flock. This applies to you, too, and that can be an opportunity to model snow goose behaviour for your leaders. If you're experiencing burnout it's okay to say so, and let another member of the team take the apex role for a while. The point is, everyone on your team should know when they are broken or exhausted, and feel safe and comfortable asking for help.

You can help promote leadership well-being by creating formal and informal programmes. Your people should see leadership as a profession, and be motivated to become better at it on a continuous basis. Chris sends new leaders to a couple of leadership courses in order to reinforce this. It has the added benefit of providing his leadership team common concepts and vocabulary. In addition, as we've already mentioned, he has organized a book-a-month club, and gives people time at work to read. Kim made sure that each leader belonged to an active roundtable type of group, and asked them to bring at least one takeaway from each meeting. They shared the takeaways on the Leadership Pod calls.

Characteristics of strong remote leaders

In the previous chapter we discussed those traits and work habits that set people up to succeed as employees in remote work. Many of those characteristics apply to leaders as well. In addition, Wade Foster, CEO of Zapier, has created a useful checklist that they use when considering potential leadership hires (2019). Founded in 2011, Zapier is entirely remote, with employees in more than 20 countries. When hiring, they look for:

- an action orientation and the initiative to be productive even without a specific task list;
- prioritization skills, knowing what to focus on and what to let go;
- proficient writing skills, given that most communication on remote teams uses writing. They also stress the importance of being tactful in writing, so that a message won't be taken the wrong way;
- a local support system, which means that an employee won't depend entirely on work for their social needs;
- trustworthiness – this is essential, since you don't see or interact with everyone every day. In addition to hiring who you trust, they advocate trusting who you hire.

We see the two aspects of the trustworthiness item – hire who you trust and trust who you hire – as an example of respect. Remote leaders should recognize that respect is a powerful ingredient in culture, and essential to promoting the autonomy necessary in a remote model. Trader Joe's culture serves as a great example of the importance of mutual respect. Of course, Trader Joe's isn't remote, but the example is still compelling. Here's an excerpt from a piece Kim wrote for *Get Scrappy* (2015):

> If you shop at Trader Joe's, you've probably noticed how upbeat their people are. They're bagging my groceries and they're smiling and having fun... not like the baggers at some other places. That enthusiasm makes us respect them, don't you think? It's because Trader Joe's culture is unique and goes deeper than Hawaiian shirts. It helps their people respect themselves by helping them feel they are part of something that's bigger than themselves and something that's unique.

Attracting strong remote leaders

In Chapter 9 we shared results from the FlexJobs annual survey of employees (Reynolds, 2017). A quick revisit to those results gives you a good idea of what you need to get the attention of top candidates for any position, but especially for leadership roles. FlexJobs asked more than 5,500 respondents to rank what they desire most when considering a new job and we have outlined the results here:

- work–life balance (72 per cent);
- flexible salary and schedule (69 per cent);
- telecommuting (60 per cent);
- professional challenge (36 per cent);
- company culture (34 per cent).

The FlexJobs survey doesn't indicate whether executives were among the respondents. However, these attraction factors are valued by people at all levels. Writing on Glassdoor.com, Jacqui Barrett-Poindexter (2019) describes what executives look for in a job, and the list is very similar:

- They want to be heard by the CEO and the board of directors.
- They want the opportunity to move the needle, as opposed to simply maintaining the status quo – similar to 'professional challenge' above.

- They want work–life balance, including schedule flexibility, both of which are on the FlexJobs list.

- They want a positive, motivating culture that promotes learning and is also fun. The FlexJobs report only indicates that culture is important, but Barrett-Poindexter's description of a desirable culture is altogether consistent with our opinion.

In fact, when you think about it, the executives you want to recruit probably want what *you* want in a job. In Chapter 7 we encouraged you to create a utopia for yourself and your employees. The ability to offer utopia will give you a decided advantage in recruiting top executive talent. If you build it (a great remote model), they will come.

Keeping strong remote leaders

We figure that a leadership approach that is designed to support employees in high-stress jobs during an unprecedented crisis should be effective in just about any situation. Sarah McVanel is an author, consultant, speaker and coach whose work is intended to bring out the greatness in individuals, teams and organizations. It's based on 15 years of experience in hospital leadership, and many consider hospitals to be among the most complex organizations to manage. Healthcare workers in the best of times are vulnerable to the impact of stress, and this has been magnified during the Covid-19 pandemic. No doubt you have seen videos posted by these frontline heroes, in which their stress is all too clear. On the other hand, we doubt you have seen videos thanking the leaders. There is a reason why they say it's loneliest at the top, and Covid-19 was no exception: making tough calls with incomplete information and hundreds or thousands affected by your call during the biggest health crisis of our generation. Not easy.

McVanel published a guide specifically for this scenario called *ROCKSTAR: Magnify your greatness in times of change* (2020).

First, McVanel identifies four leadership behaviours that enable one to be the ROCK that this kind of situation calls for: Recognize, Organize, Communicate and Kindness. Second, she argues that using these behaviours will help you and your people deliver STAR results: Satisfaction, Teamwork, Accomplishment and Retention. The ROCK behaviours may seem simple, McVanel argues, but they can set you and your organization up not only to survive a crisis, but also to thrive through it and beyond.

Without a framework like ROCKSTAR, leaders can flounder in crises. You've probably experienced that yourself at some point, and it's very likely that your leaders have as well. By sharing this approach with your leadership team, you will not only help them deal with crises and challenges, but you also will earn loyalty points.

KINDNESS VS STRESS

McVanel's approach can also have a positive effect on health and well-being for you and your employees. Stress is a major issue in our society, causing both emotional and physical health problems. Several studies have confirmed that stress can impact brain function, including memory and cognition; weaken the immune system; contribute to cardiovascular disease; cause gastrointestinal issues; and overload the endocrine system (Yaribeygi et al, 2017). The dangers are real for all of us. According to psychiatrist Bessel van der Kolk (2014), 'Today's stress is imprinting upon the body of the future.'

Passion lives in the why

Passion motivates people to be exceptional and promotes retention. In Chapter 8 we talked about Simon Sinek and the power of why, and this is the perfect time to expand on this potent concept. Sinek argues that too many organizations start with the more tangible things, like the WHAT (products or services) or the HOW (logistics, business models, etc). But those that excel, those that defy expectations, start with the WHY. One example is Apple. There are other computer companies that have access to the same resources, but Apple continues to innovate in ways that others don't. Apple doesn't just lead markets, it creates them. That's because its business model puts the WHY at the core and then develops the HOW and WHAT out of the WHY.

The WHY is not to make a profit. That's a result, Sinek says. The WHY is deeper. Think about your own situation. WHY do you work where you do? WHY did you bring your passion to your current company? Do they start with the WHY? Is their WHY aligned with yours? If so, you're probably very happy with your job, and your cohort is very happy with your performance.

Passion is a lot of things and, for us, money isn't all that high on the list. More important are things like enjoying what we do. We don't *have* to do it — we *get* to do it. Another reason: both of our companies allow us to give back to the community. As we've said, we don't believe in work–life balance, but in life balance that integrates all our interests. Working with community groups allows us to help people improve the quality of their lives, and it's also a great way to network.

Kim shared Sinek's WHY presentation at a nationwide all-staff gathering, and then asked all her people to write down their WHYs. Here's a sampling (Shepherd and Berkus, 2015):

- A recruiter: 'Love our culture, flexibility and support.'
- A director: 'I want to feel like I am part of something that makes a difference.'
- Recruiter: 'I'm in control.'
- Media specialist: 'It is very important for me to spend time with my children, and the company allows me the flexibility to attend football, basketball and other activities.'
- Recruiter: 'Recruiting with a conscience.'
- Writer: 'I get to partner with the company, not be an employee.'
- Recruiter: 'I'm a single parent... this company changed our lives. I'm never leaving.'

If that last one didn't move you, you probably should have an electrocardiogram (EKG). Not one of them wrote, 'It pays the bills.' If you can help your leaders understand their WHY, it's very likely they will stay with you for years. For one thing, you will have helped them gain great insight, but you also will connect their passion to their role. Knowing the WHY is also a strong motivation to help keep you and your team looking for solutions and opportunities in the holes versus the cheese.

Tour of duty

There's a flip side to retaining great remote leaders, and that's knowing when to let go. The Tour of Duty approach will enable you to let go in ways that support employees even as they are leaving and ensure a smooth transition for your company. Paradoxically, it will also promote retention of other leaders by demonstrating that you have their interests at heart.

The concept was developed by Reid Hoffman, Ben Casnocha and Chris Yeh in their book, *The Alliance: Managing talent in the networked age* (Hoffman, Casnocha and Yeh, 2014). They believe that the relationship between employee and employer has changed significantly. To be successful, employees and employers need to see the relationship as an alliance. In a later blog post, Hoffman (2014) explains that, in this alliance, 'employees invest in the company's adaptability while the company invests in employees' employability by commissioning them on finite yet transformative mission assignments or "tours of duty".'

Here's how it works: first, dismiss the old-school notion that leaders will stay forever. Instead, come to an agreement with each one in which you both commit for a certain time period. For example, you might agree to a three-year tour of duty in which the leader commits to increasing revenue by 20 per cent. In turn, you agree to provide professional development opportunities that will help the leader achieve that goal. You're actually helping the leader be more attractive to other employers, but that happens anyway.

What's different is that six months before the tour of duty ends, you sit down with that leader and discuss next steps. Does the leader want to re-up for another tour? Do they want to keep doing the same thing, or explore other opportunities in your company? Or are they considering moving on and leaving your company?

Whatever the answer is, you support them. If they are re-upping, define a new alliance, a new tour with new goals and end dates. If they are planning to leave, help them as much as you can, such as writing recommendation letters and leveraging your network. In addition, you now have six months to find a replacement in a manner that is far healthier and more intentional than you would have with a two-week notice scenario. In addition, the leader can use that time to tie off loose ends, get everything in order for the transition, and possibly help recruit, onboard and train their own replacement.

The Tour of Duty idea works well in both remote and brick-and-mortar models. We feel it is particularly relevant to remote because it embodies an entrepreneurial spirit. The remote model requires, thrives on and encourages an entrepreneurial spirit. In Chapter 8 we talked about the Me, Inc. mentality, an entrepreneurial approach to life, not just business. Tour of Duty will appeal to those with the entrepreneurial Me, Inc. mentality.

Chris used the Tour of Duty approach when he lost a great vice president of sales at PeopleG2, resulting in a transition that was no more disruptive than a bump in the road. Of course he didn't want the VP to leave, but since it was going to happen, the approach helped get the replacement up to speed more quickly.

Kim used a similar approach when Decision Toolbox's brilliant IT director, Michael Bearding, wanted to leave in order to start his own consulting firm. One of the big issues was that Michael had a treasure trove of information in his head. Kim and Michael reached an agreement in which Michael stayed long enough to download and document that information, and also hire and train his replacement. In return, DT 'leased' Michael as a consultant, essentially helping him fund his startup. Interestingly, Sarah McVanel, who we mentioned earlier in this chapter, transitioned from hospital administration to a full-time speaker in a similar way. A work-from-home mentality primes the whole organization to look at the holes in the Swiss cheese as opportunities rather than as evidence of problems.

Brave new world

We hope by now that you agree: the world of work is changing in many ways. The companies that will excel in this brave new world will have leaders that empower employees while keeping a low profile, and create the kind of collaborative, positive and non-hierarchical relationships between and among employees and leaders that you find in Scrum. These leaders will work *on*, not *in* their business, and ensure that their teams are driven by the passion that comes from having a clear *why*. They will embrace and promote workplace flexibility as well as the entrepreneurial spirit of the Tour of Duty concept.

Our remote model will help you do all of these things which, in turn, will help you attract and retain top leadership talent. At the core of our model is culture, and that's the topic for the next chapter.

References

Barrett-Poindexter, J (2019) What do executives really want in their next job? Glassdoor, 2 Jul, www.glassdoor.com/employers/blog/what-do-executives-really-want-in-their-next-job (archived at https://perma.cc/SKH6-DHE5)

Berkus, D and Shepherd, K (2015) *Get Scrappy: Business insights to make your company more agile*, Berkus Press, Los Angeles

Foster, W (2019) *The Ultimate Guide to Remote Work: How to grow, manage, and work with remote teams*, LeanPub, Victoria, British Columbia

Hoffman, R (2014) Use the Tours of Duty concept to attract and retain entrepreneurial employees, *LinkedIn Talent Blog*, 6 August, https://business.linkedin.com/talent-solutions/blog/2014/08/use-the-tours-of-duty-concept-to-attract-and-retain-entrepreneurial-employees (archived at https://perma.cc/WQ2M-8Y8W)

Hoffman, R, Casnocha, B and Yeh, C (2014) The alliance: Managing talent in the networked age, *Harvard Business Review Press*, Boston

Lao Tzu (2006) *Tao Te Ching: A new English version*, Harper Perennial Modern Classics, New York City

Lavinsky, D (2014) Pareto Principle: How to use it to dramatically grow your business, *Forbes*, 20 January, www.forbes.com/sites/davelavinsky/2014/01/20/pareto-principle-how-to-use-it-to-dramatically-grow-your-business/?sh=3226479a3901 (archived at https://perma.cc/RE3B-G3ZJ)

Liker, J (2004) *The Toyota Way: 14 management principles from the world's greatest manufacturer*, McGraw-Hill Education, New York

McVanel, S (2020) *ROCKSTAR: Magnify your greatness in times of change*, GO Publishing, Toronto

Muna, F A and Mansour, N (2005) Leadership lessons from Canada geese, *Team Performance Management*, **11** (7/8), pp 316–26 (October)

Reynolds, B (2017) 2017 annual survey finds workers are more productive at home, and more, *Flexjobs.com*, 21 August, www.flexjobs.com/blog/post/productive-working-remotely-top-companies-hiring (archived at https://perma.cc/6BTN-4KJV)

Sinek, S (2009) *Start With Why: How great leaders inspire everyone to take action*, Portfolio, New York

Van der Kolk, B (2014)*The Body Keeps the Score: Brain, mind, and body in the healing of trauma*, Viking Press, New York

Yaribeygi, H et al (2017) The impact of stress on body function: A review, *EXCLI Journal 2017* (16) pp 1057–72

13

Who are you as a company?

This is the final chapter before we really dive into the *how*, and you need to answer this seemingly simple question before going on: what is your culture?

Every company has a culture. Ideally you designed it with intention. But even if you didn't, you still have a culture. It has a life of its own. If you tend it well, it can grow like a lush garden. If untended, it could grow in any number of ways, from a lifeless patch of dying weeds to an uncontrolled infestation of poison ivy. We can't say it often enough: design what you want or deal with what you get.

IN THIS CHAPTER

We will cover:

- Defining culture
- 7 pillars of great company culture
  - o Why you need them
  - o How to implement them
- Marine Corps: the world's strongest culture

We'd like to share some high-level insights into culture to help you be crystal clear on what your culture is, and what you may want it to become. If you haven't used Simon Sinek's process for discovering your *why*, this is a good time to do it. You can use his original book, *Start with Why* (2009), the follow-up workbook, *Find Your Why* (2017), or even start with the TEDx Talk that started it all (Sinek, 2009). We're not the only ones who are big fans of Sinek and *Why*. The TED video has been viewed over 51 million times, and the transcript has been translated into 48 languages.

Culture defined (sort of)

So what is culture, anyway? Well, it depends on whom you ask. Kim believes it boils down to a single question: how do the employees feel? Anxious? Gratified? Fulfilled? Chris's definition is a little more complex: 'Company culture is the combination of the easily seen ideals, like vision statements and values, combined with the harder-to-see norms, behaviours, languages, beliefs and systems.' For Chris, how employees feel is an outcome of the culture – if the culture is healthy and focused, they will feel fulfilled. For Kim, culture IS feeling.

How did these two approaches look in action? At Decision Toolbox, the culture was performance-driven. The employees were like joyful samurai warriors, highly skilled, dancing, brandishing swords, and stopping every so often to show their love and admiration for each other. Their emphasis was internal: since there are too many variables to guarantee a specific outcome in recruiting, they focused on developing and implementing great processes, and on trying harder than the competition.

At PeopleG2, the employees are like highly trained rock climbers, using specialized equipment – ropes, pitons, carabiners – and dogged determination to scale sheer rock faces. The emphasis here is external: their customers expect a background report, and they focus on a tangible deliverable.

There is no one right answer to what culture is or should be. Our point is that you need to be clear on what your culture is, and ensure that all your employees understand it and are on board with it.

Zappos, Apple and performance

Even two high-performing cultures can be very different. Both Zappos, the online shoe retailer, and Apple, the tech innovator, have well-defined cultures with an emphasis on performance. According to Warrick et al (2016), Zappos CEO Tony Hsieh believed that the right culture drives the desired outcomes. He made sure they recruited and trained with the culture in mind, and encouraged everyone to have fun and work hard in a family-like atmosphere. The company offers free lunch and snacks, along with parades and other celebrations. A more well-known aspect of the culture is that Zappos empowers employees to 'wow' customers by going above and beyond.

It works. The company's revenues went from $8 million to over $1 billion in eight years (Warrick et al, 2016). Further proof of their positive culture came in 2010, when a Zappos sister site, 6pm.com, made a pricing mistake that cost the company $1.6 million (Engleman, 2010). Their pricing engine accidentally capped all prices at $49.95, in spite of the fact that the site offers items that normally cost much more – in some cases, thousands of dollars more. Staying true to their positive culture, Zappos leadership effectively shrugged their shoulders, said 'Oops – our bad' and took the loss.

In contrast, Apple has a highly focused, results-oriented culture that would sooner cut the fat than host a parade. The company holds employees to strict secrecy guidelines to protect intellectual property, so what goes on within the circle of Apple Park is shrouded in mystery. However, Jim Edwards (2016) pulled information from various online sources, particularly the question-and-answer platform Quora, to put together an insider's view.

> One Apple intern posted the message that she and other interns received upon starting with the company: 'There's work and there's your life's work. The kind of work that has your fingerprints all over it. The kind of work that you'd never compromise on. That you'd sacrifice a weekend for. You can do that kind of work at Apple. People don't come here to play it safe. They come here to swim in the deep end. They want their work to add up to something. Something big. Something that couldn't happen anywhere else. Welcome to Apple'
> (Edwards, 2016).

It's an extreme culture with very high expectations: if you work at Apple, you'd better bring your A game every day. Some of the posts also cited:

- Trash bins are monitored by security.
- Some people had to show up at 4 am every day to meet with coworkers in other time zones.
- Apple even provides guidelines about what employees can discuss with their spouses – but the person who posted this comment said he understood and embraced it.

- Teams often decide that pulling an all-nighter is necessary. No one says, 'Ok, let me call home first.' They just nod in agreement.
- No one works from home.
- One former employee received emails while in the hospital, insisting that he complete a report.

And yet jobs at Apple are highly coveted. Many of the posts praise Apple's practices. The company is very upfront about the expectations, and it seems that employees are willing to make sacrifices in order to meet those expectations. The result is a series of market-disrupting products and innovations.

Trader Joe's 'accidental' culture

Well, it wasn't accidental once it was implemented, but Trader Joe's CEO John Shields fell into changing the culture somewhat by accident. In the last chapter we described the culture briefly. Kim met John once, and he told her how he gathered the input that would become the foundation of a fun and very successful culture.

John went to several Trader Joe's stores around the country and, at random, chose a group of employees to participate in a retreat. It was a three-day event, with all expenses paid, and the group had one mission: come up with a list of four things about working here that will make your jobs better. He expected to hear things like 'more money', 'better benefits' or 'longer breaks'. Instead, this is the list they presented:

- We want to wear Hawaiian shirts.
- We want to wear jeans.
- We want to give boxes to people who need them to carry things like wine and booze.
- We want to be allowed to socialize with customers on a personal level.

Trader Joe's implemented those ideas and is regularly recognized for high employee engagement in an industry that generally suffers from high turno-ver. According to David Harder (2018), the average tenure of Trader Joe's cashiers is 19 years. Though it's not the highest-paid job, and stocking shelves, ringing up customers or bagging groceries isn't for everyone, the general outcome is staff who are very engaged and happy in their jobs. The chain has appeared on Glassdoor's list of 100 Best Places to Work each year since 2017, reaching #14 in 2020.

Seven pillars of culture

All these examples demonstrate that, while culture varies from company to company, it plays a crucial role in company success. And even though your own culture may be completely different than the ones we've described, we believe that there are common characteristics to a strong, effective culture.

In his book *The Power of Company Culture*, Chris studied the cultures of many successful companies and identified seven key characteristics of culture. The characteristics may be manifested in different ways, and drive different specific results, but they make up the framework, or the pillars that rise up from the foundational mission and vision. As you read through these descriptions and examples, think about how strong each pillar is in your own company.

1. Transparency

Efficient, accountable organizations promote transparency – open communication and information sharing across the company, in the form of candid feedback from staff all the way up to internally posting the company's financial numbers. Jack Stack, author and CEO of SRC Holdings Corporation, provides several compelling reasons to practise transparency (Stack, 2014). The first is that it helps employees to think and act like owners. He not only provides the company financials to his employees, but he also ensures they are able to understand and interpret them. The result: more people come up with more great ideas.

In addition, Stack believes that transparency promotes team cohesiveness, leadership development, critical inquiry, knowledge sharing and employee retention. Remember the case study about Buffer in Chapter 10? Courtney Seiter told us they feel so strongly about transparency that they post everyone's salary publicly. Over time Buffer has evolved the policy to provide more privacy for those who need it, but they kept the policy in place.

Some other ways to promote and practise transparency include:

- Clarify roles and goals. You want all employees to know who to go to for what, but they also should understand other people's goals. That way they have a context for every interaction.

- Adjust communication styles to different people's personalities – this is a great use for DiSC profiles.

- Ensure your company has forums or channels for employees to raise concerns and share ideas freely.

2. Positivity

In most companies, employees have a problem-solving mindset. However, leading companies promote positivity, encouraging employees to frame challenges as opportunities to optimize strengths rather than to fix weaknesses. A 2015 study published in the *Journal of Applied Psychology* showed that positive and optimistic interactions elevated team effectiveness (Knight and Eisenkraft, 2015).

The power of this approach is demonstrated by the efforts of Save the Children, an international non-governmental organization, in addressing malnourishment in Vietnam. In the wake of the Vietnam War, in villages across the country, 64 per cent of children were seriously malnourished and many were facing starvation. In 1990 Save the Children sent Jerry Sternin, along with his wife Monique and their young son Sam, to assess the situation and develop a solution (Dyer, 2018).

At the time, the US was still enforcing an embargo on Vietnam, and the Sternins were among a small handful of Americans allowed in the country. They were given six months, and they met with significant resistance from the locals, for whom the war was still a living memory. Previous efforts, which focused on bringing supplies in from outside the country, had failed.

Sternin chose a different approach, known as positive deviance. Instead of focusing on why 64 per cent of the children were malnourished, he focused on why 36 per cent were doing well. It seems deceptively simple, but Sternin's team researched what families were doing differently for the 36 per cent. It turns out the families would go to the rice paddies every day to collect shrimp and crabs, along with certain wild plants, all high in protein. In addition, since young children can't process large amounts of food at once, these families fed their children smaller meals several times a day. They also made a point of washing the children's hands frequently. The solution was there all along, but it took a different mindset to see past the assumptions and the failed focus on the problems (Sternin and Choo, 2000).

Positive deviance is related to another useful concept, appreciative inquiry. This was developed in the 1980s by graduate student David Cooperrider and Professor Suresh Srivastva of Case Western University (1987). The basic concept is that group systems tend to advance in the direction set by their main areas of focus, study and discussion. For instance, if they concentrate on struggles, they will struggle. If they concentrate on achievement, they will achieve. We'll explore appreciative inquiry more deeply in the next chapter, but it underscores the point we want to make here: in your company, when it is evident that something needs to change, instead of fixing a problem, build on strengths and success.

3. Measurement

If you want to improve performance, you must begin with measurement, the process of compiling relevant data and analysing it to identify trends, make forecasts and chart a course. Using objective measurement helps promote accountability and avoid blame – and that promotes team cohesion.

We advocate the Scrum dictum, measure what matters and avoid over-measuring. Focus tightly on KPIs known to affect the success and failure of your business. Assessments can record performance after the fact, as with customer satisfaction surveys or employee reviews, or they can track in-progress activities such as website hits measured by computer analytics. Frequent, periodic evaluation affords comparative and ongoing insights.

Make data collection and analysis an integral part of your operational framework by using short weekly surveys or a project-management system such as Scrum. You can use whatever system or process you like; the important thing is that you measure, analyse and respond.

4. Recognition

Great companies routinely celebrate successes through recognition, a system of monetary or symbolic rewards that build team cohesion and cultural awareness. Acknowledging employees publicly fills basic human needs, such as improving self-esteem, promoting trust and demonstrating respect. This gives employees the motivation to perform well – individually and as a team – and to unite with co-workers behind the company's mission, values and vision.

Recognition can take a lot of different forms, from a thank you at a standup meeting to formal programmes. At Decision Toolbox, Kim implemented the concept of green flag emails, a way to highlight landing a new project or filling a position. Chris and his team use the water cooler channel in Slack to share kudos. One more example to demonstrate the diversity: Caesar's Palace uses a recognition platform that allows *guests* to acknowledge employees for going above and beyond. The employees earn points for kudos, and can cash those points in for a variety of products from an online catalogue.

In their book *RESPECT*, Jack Wiley and Brenda Kowske (2011) share research demonstrating that recognition is the second most important thing employees want from an employer, after pay. They also argue that, while tangible rewards are important, sometimes the simple act of acknowledging service or success goes a long way in promoting employee engagement.

Tangible rewards can come in the form of cash, personalized gifts, service plaques or redeemable gift certificates or credits. Preferred treatment, such as first crack at the most desirable accounts, represents a non-monetary reward that still holds great value for employees. At the same time, monitor rewards like preferred treatment to make sure you don't get a lopsided distribution of work and rewards. If this seems to be happening, you might find out what the top performers are doing differently, and then share it with the lower performers. In addition, be aware that low performance can be caused by issues outside of work, such as illness or family problems.

5. Uniqueness

Brands are immortalized when companies articulate their uniqueness – those elements that distinguish a business's people, operations and products or services from those of their competitors. Differentiating your company in the marketplace is an essential step in being competitive, of course. You can gauge your company's uniqueness by identifying the distinct selling points of your products or services. Selecting and defining a particular target clientele can also help businesses to set themselves apart.

Uniqueness goes beyond brand, however. For example, developing a unique culture has advantages that include providing shared experiences and attitudes that bring employees together. Most people want to feel that they are part of something special, and you want everyone pulling together towards shared goals. That unique culture gives you an edge in recruiting and retaining top talent.

One way to promote a unique culture is to develop and encourage unique terms and phrases, a kind of company dialect. For example, we both use the term 'cockroach meeting' to refer to a brief meeting to deal with an issue that is not major but nonetheless requires attention. A unique term that Chris uses is 'ostrich meeting', one intended to help everyone pull their heads out of the sand and understand an issue or concept clearly. He finds that the simple act of admitting you don't know something and requesting assistance is usually enough to get anyone talking.

A company vocabulary fosters teamwork and gives people a kind of insider knowledge. That, in turn, promotes trust between and among individuals, and in the company itself. We believe that, as trust grows internally, your clients and customers will sense this dynamic and place their trust in you.

6. Listening

Listening well is an art form, particularly when we're all faced with so many distractions like mobile phones, pinging computers and background noise. In the office, background noise can be co-workers joking around, and at home it can be children clamouring for attention. Other barriers to active listening include HALT – being hungry, angry, lonely or tired. In addition, we all have cognitive biases that make it difficult to hear and accept what others are trying to say.

On the other hand, active listening frees people to empathize, understand and innovate, which all drive business identity, visibility and performance. To improve your listening skills, you can schedule time specifically to listen to someone else, putting aside all other distractions. You can also try repeating someone's message, in your own words, to confirm that you understand them.

On a broader level, you can implement 'listening' processes for teams, departments or the entire company. A common practice is an annual employee survey, although Chris prefers to pose a weekly question. That way he keeps a finger on the pulse of the company. He also feels people are more likely to respond to a single question once a week than to a long series of questions once a year. Anonymity usually helps ensure more direct and honest answers, so you might use a platform like SurveyMonkey. An essential point here is that you respond to input and put it to use to make your company better. Otherwise, employees will feel it is a waste of time.

7. Mistakes

The best companies view mistakes not as failings, but as valuable opportunities to change direction or gain inspiration. We want to distinguish between mistakes and errors here. Honest mistakes happen despite someone's best intentions and judgement, and often lead to corporate benefits that might not otherwise have occurred. Maybe an employee took a calculated risk and tried something new, but it simply didn't work. Errors, however, show careless practices that typically violate correct procedures and have few positive consequences. For example, when processing payroll, it's simply an error to try to do the maths in one's head.

A famous mistake that turned into a windfall is the glue used on Post-it® Notes from 3M. While trying to develop very strong adhesives, 3M scientist Dr Spencer Silver discovered an adhesive that was just the opposite: it stuck lightly to surfaces and could be removed and reapplied (3M, 2017). Silver tried for years to find an application for the product. Finally, another 3M scientist, Art Fry, shared that he had a frustrating problem. As part of a church choir, he liked to mark the week's selections in his hymnal at Wednesday night practices. However, by Sunday the marks had all fallen out. The two collaborated and created a product that today is an office essential. In fact, 3M maintains a detailed database of R&D efforts, successful or not (yet), in case information becomes relevant to a future problem. Former 3M CEO said, 'Management that is destructively critical when mistakes are made kills initiative. And it's essential that we have many people with initiative if we are to continue to grow' (Lockheart and Hicken, 2012).

Individuals who are comfortable facing mistakes can find opportunities in what went wrong for new techniques or solutions. That means you need to make it safe for people to own up and share both mistakes and errors. Mistakes can provide insight, and errors should be addressed in a constructive manner.

One of the best ways to create a safe environment is to celebrate mistakes. Kim instituted a Boo-Boo of the Month award, giving a Starbucks gift card for the biggest mistake. Her thinking is that if you tell everyone what they did right, they may not remember it. But if you tell everyone what someone did wrong, no one else will do it.

Chris created an 'Oops – my bad' room on Slack where people can post mistakes. He knows that people don't want to disappoint him, but if he's not aware of a mistake, the company may keep stepping in it down the road. The Oops room is stigma-free. The team will joke about a mistake and call a meeting to deal with it if necessary. Another key point: to promote trust and the feeling of safety, leaders should admit their own mistakes. Chris has posted more than one mistake in the Oops room, and Kim has received her share of Boo-Boo gift cards.

We'll wrap up this chapter with a look at what many believe to be the world's strongest culture: that of the United States Marine Corps.

DEFENDING LIBERTY WITH CULTURE

The culture we advocate is intended to make you and your employees feel good about what you're all doing. What about a culture that motivates people to put their life on the line for their country? Marine Corps culture is extremely powerful, and perhaps the most powerful culture in the world with regard to uniting people in driving to a common goal. To find out more about that kind of culture power, we talked with Melvin Spiese, Major General, United States Marine Corps, Retired. You may recall from Chapter 1 that while he was serving at Camp Pendleton, he had asked Kim to address his officers.

One of Mel's many assignments over his lifelong career was to oversee education programmes, from bootcamp for new recruits to ongoing officer training. Mel believes that education and training are essential to culture in any organization, and we agree.

According to Mel, the Marine Corps education programmes are designed to ensure that people are inculcated into the culture while also learning the nuts and bolts of operations. That's why they do things a little differently than the other branches of the armed forces. While other military services make their biggest educational investments in people who have completed a tour of duty, the Marines put their biggest push up front.

Missions can be very complex and intense, and the consequences of either success or failure can be significant. The Corps' approach to education is to ensure that every Marine, at every level, has:

- a common understanding of terminology and procedures;
- the ability to understand the outcome or objective of any mission or manoeuvre;
- a strong sense of ownership, both individual and shared, for that outcome.

A foot soldier may not know much about an operation beyond their own tactical objectives, but they know how their performance contributes to the overall outcome.

As an individual advances in rank, the scope of knowledge they require grows geometrically. For example, a lieutenant has to know how to call in air support, but a captain has to know how the plane is fuelled, how pilots are assigned, how the unit is deployed, and more. Without a strong foundation – a shared understanding of both operations and culture – it would be almost impossible for individuals to build to the next level. Every new rank is a title that people earn by overcoming a series of challenges and obstacles, starting with the private right out of boot camp. That makes everyone who has earned a title a stakeholder with ownership.

Even if your culture doesn't involve putting employees in harm's way, there are learnings to draw from General Spiese's story. One of the most important points is that, in order to create the culture you want, you have to provide training and education deliberately designed to convey and reinforce the values of that culture. In addition, you should do that early in any employee's tenure – it's not enough to teach someone the ropes. You also have to communicate the cultural values that give context to the ropes. This is important in the remote model because you can't count on people just 'absorbing' your culture and values across the virtual divide. Teaching culture is an essential part of building the bridge that connects your team across the divide.

Three other points that resonate with our model: you need a common language that promotes bonding (we'll explore that more in Chapter 19), a clearly communicated understanding of goals and outcomes (more on that in Chapter 16), and the sense of shared ownership of the outcomes. This last point is an example of Simon Sinek's *why* – it's important for everyone to know the goals, but it's even more powerful when everyone *owns* the goals, driven by a shared passion and mission.

With these and other learnings in hand, it's time to get hands-on and start building your remote company. Before we do, however, we want to check in and see if you have joined the Remote Work Movement yet. It only takes 30 seconds to sign up, at https://chrisdyer.com/remotework, but those 30 seconds will give you access to lots more great ideas – and enable you to share your own ideas.

References

3M (2017) History timeline: Post-it® Notes, www.post-it.com/3M/en_US/post-it/contact-us/about-us (archived at https://perma.cc/S2JW-Q36W)

Cooperrider, D L and Srivastva, S (1987) Appreciative inquiry in organizational life. In W Passmore and R Woodman (eds), *Research in Organization Change and Development* (Vol 1, pp 129–69), JAI Press, Greenwich, CT

Dyer, C (2018) *The Power of Company Culture: How any business can build a culture that improves productivity, performance and profits*, Kogan Page, London

Edwards, J (2016) Apple employees break their vow of secrecy to describe the best– and worst–things about working for Apple, *Business Insider*, 14 December, www.businessinsider.com/apple-employees-best-worst-working-for-apple-2016-12 (archived at https://perma.cc/DPT4-ZF75)

Engleman, E (2010) Pricing mistake costs Zappos more than $1.6 million, *Puget Sound Business Journal*, 23 May, www.bizjournals.com/seattle/blog/techflash/2010/05/pricing_mistake_costs_zappos_more_than_16_million.html (archived at https://perma.cc/J5B2-DZ57)

Glassdoor (2020) Best places to work 2020, employees' choice, www.glassdoor.com/Award/Best-Places-to-Work-LST_KQ0,19.htm (archived at https://perma.cc/CZ22-DNU7)

Harder, D (2018) Why is the average tenure of Trader Joe's cashiers 19 years? *LinkedIn*, 14 August, www.linkedin.com/pulse/why-average-tenure-trader-joes-cashiers-19-years-david-harder (archived at https://perma.cc/VG2N-WX9Y)

Knight, A P and Eisenkraft, N (2015) Positive is usually good, negative is not always bad: The effects of group affect on social integration and task performance, *Journal of Applied Psychology*, www.ncbi.nlm.nih.gov/pubmed/25495091?dopt=Abstract (archived at https://perma.cc/2BLM-RK24)

Lockheart, J and Hicken, M (2012) 14 executives who swear by meditation, *Business Insider*, 9 May, www.businessinsider.com/ceos-who-meditate-2012-5?op=1/#lesforcecoms-marc-benioff-started-to-meditate-because-his-job-at-oracle-was-so-stressful-2 (archived at https://perma.cc/V8BE-H8AU)

Sinek, S (2009) *Start With Why: How great leaders inspire everyone to take action*, Portfolio, New York

Sinek, S (2009) How great leaders inspire action (online video) www.ted.com/talks/simon_sinek_how_great_leaders_inspire_action (archived at https://perma.cc/5VJX-CV4Y)

Sinek, S (2017) *Find Your Why: A practical guide for discovering purpose for you and your team*, Portfolio, New York

Stack, J (2014) *The Great Game of Business: The only sensible way to run a company*, Profile Books, New York

Sternin, J and Choo, R (2000) The power of positive deviancy, *Harvard Business Review*, January/February, https://hbr.org/2000/01/the-power-of-positive-deviancy (archived at https://perma.cc/7Z58-XNDS)

Warrick, D D, Milliman, J F and Ferguson, J M (2016) Lessons learned from Zappos on what it takes to build high performance cultures, *Organizational Dynamics*, http://iranarze.ir/wp-content/uploads/2017/01/E3354.pdf (archived at https://perma.cc/59E7-K4MY)

Wiley, J and Kowske, B (2011) *RESPECT: Delivering results by giving employees what they really want*, Pfeiffer, Hoboken, New Jersey

14

Getting started

Throughout the previous chapters we've been sharing the theory behind our approach. We've shared some examples that you can put to work, but it's now time to get into the step-by-step of how to do it.

IN THIS CHAPTER

We will cover:

- How to break it down to build it up
- Four elements of remote success
- Four Ds of appreciative inquiry
- Five Is of appreciative leadership
- People, process, tools and technology
- Finding your champions
- Case Study: Girls Inc. adapts without missing a beat

Break it down to build it up

As we've discussed throughout, success in taking your company remote requires much more than sending people home to work. You need a different model and a different way of thinking about work. Not only do you *need* to rethink your company's structure and culture, but it's also a great opportunity to do so. You need to deconstruct your organization and then reconstruct it in new and better ways. We'll outline the key steps to help you undertake this journey.

First step: get in the zone

Clarity is of the essence, and distraction is the enemy of clarity. You need to block out a significant chunk of time and go to a space where you know you won't be disturbed. Turn off your phone. Seriously. Think of it as a meditation, focused on where you are and what you have, what the future state looks like and what you need to do to get to that future state. You've heard of the cone of silence, or the cone of uncertainty? Well, now you need to create a cone... of zone.

When Chris did this step, he stayed in his office for two days, eating cardboard-like pizza. He wouldn't allow himself to leave or think about anything else until he had a clear vision. No multitasking, no juggling. Kim did this on a bicycle, during a 600-mile AIDS ride from San Francisco to Los Angeles. With nothing but traffic lines zipping past her field of vision, she settled deep in her own head. She missed two pit stops and others remarked how 'absent' she looked. You don't have to do exactly what we did, but it's important that you find a space where you can sequester yourself for a good period of time.

However you choose to do this, you need to break your company down and build it back up. Remember Lincoln Logs®, the toy set of notched logs you could use to build things like cabins? Imagine your company is made up of Lincoln Logs. If you're not familiar with Lincoln Logs, you can imagine your company as a Lego® structure. Now take it all apart and reassemble it. Try new ways to fit the pieces together. You'll find pieces that are redundant as well as spaces where pieces are missing.

Second step: invert the pyramid

It may be tempting just to start making changes in your organization before you have cone-of-zone clarity, but resist. Earlier in the book, in Chapters 7 and 8, we mentioned the inverted pyramid way of thinking, and this step calls for it. As you can see in Figure 7.1, the pyramid is made up of steps, with the broadest layers at the base representing the foundational step of understanding your goals, and the narrow point representing the ultimate goal. The layers in between represent the steps needed to get to the point or goal.

In the graphic, time is represented from the top down. Often people start with the narrowest point, the ultimate goal, and then work down. The result? They don't invest enough time at the outset, and then have to spend even more time down the road, fixing things and even starting over. When you invert the pyramid, you invest the biggest chunk of time in clarifying goals and planning, and then you follow the steps until you reach the goal.

To illustrate the point, Kim and her partner in Decision Toolbox, Jay Barnett, created a hypothetical scenario. Imagine that your chief financial officer quits. Many companies focus immediately on the point of the pyramid: filling the seat. They rush to post the job description and start reviewing a pile of résumés.

However, if you were to invert the pyramid, you would stop and give this some thought – invest more time up front to make sure you get things right from the outset. Why did the CFO quit? Is there something about the job you need to change? Do you need to reconsider the profile of the person you're looking for? Or is it possible that there is something about your remote model that needs rethinking? Once you've defined your ideal candidate, you can update the description and give thought to the best places to post it. You'll get a handful of well-targeted, highly qualified candidates. Overall, this process is faster and more efficient than sorting through 30 résumés of candidates who may or may not be a fit. And it burns a lot less hair.

Right brain/left brain

There is both art and science to this process; you should use both your right brain (creativity) and your left brain (analytical thinking). It's a good idea to start with a little cerebral spring cleaning – clearing out the little ideas and assorted junk that keep you from getting to the bigger concepts. Chris learned this from songwriting, and many artists do it. For example, Mumford & Sons are a folk/alternative rock group from Britain who have a unique way of clearing the cobwebs from their craniums. They call it '10 songs in 10 hours in 10 pubs'. As the name suggests, they visit a new pub every hour and write a song on each visit. By the eighth pub, they have got all the small ideas out of the way so the big, album-worthy ideas can start to emerge.

FOUR ELEMENTS OF REMOTE SUCCESS

Jackson Lynch is Founder and President of 90Consulting, a human capital firm providing strategic support for companies experiencing changes in leadership, by both ownership and leadership. The experts at 90Consulting view your business strategy through a talent lens and help improve execution of the business strategy. Jackson has served as a business leader with some of the country's most iconic brands, including PepsiCo Frito-Lay and Nestlé S.A.

After joining Nestlé in 2007, Jackson spearheaded human capital efforts around the merger of Nestlé Dreyer's and Kraft Pizza. First he built the sales HR team from scratch, and then led the development and execution of all people strategies, HR process design and change efforts. He also took point on integrating both organizations into Nestlé USA.

At that time, large portions of the organization were distributed in multiple locations around the country. During the integrations, Jackson had to learn what makes remote models work. Since the onset of Covid-19, he has refined his ideas into four key elements:

Rituals and rhythm

Before working remotely, Jackson's weekday ritual was like many people's: getting ready, climbing into the car and making the commute. Once he started working remotely, however, he was ready to work right after a shower (and sometimes earlier). It's convenient, but here is a need to create at least a sense that work is separate from other aspects of life. He consciously makes time and space for family, friends, personal pursuits and more. He even puts 'walk the dog' on his calendar. For Jackson, it is creating a social contract around his daily schedule.

When you go remote, the signposts that used to structure your day change. If you don't create new structures, you risk falling into unhealthy behaviours. For example, for many people, the commute home used to signal the end of the business day and the beginning of family time. Without that signal, many people continue to work, such as holding conference calls at 10 pm when they should be paying attention to other parts of their lives. They risk burnout. Structures and signposts help us to be mindful about a healthy, well-rounded life.

Group and individual check-ins

When you are working, you should take a deliberate approach to staying in touch with team members. Working remotely requires *more* check-in time than working together in an office. You have to recreate the 'drop in', where a surprising amount of alignment takes place. It allows you to stay in touch and reinforce priorities. It also enables redundant communication, a great reinforcer. For example, you may announce a new priority at a meeting of the full staff. Following that, in individual check-ins, be sure to discuss the new priority and each person's role in supporting it. Check-ins also allow team members to have a voice and share their ideas.

Focus on effectiveness

Jackson says it is important to pay attention to how you and your team work in the absence of face-to-face interactions. There are new rules of engagement and you need to be sure everyone is on the same page. In a sticks-and-bricks model, for example, things like communication, time management and problem solving are almost taken for granted – everyone is familiar with those skills and processes in an office. However, these processes will be different once you go remote. To be effective, your team will need to understand how they are different, and even learn new communication, time management and problem-solving skills.

By clarifying the new norms and helping your team adapt to and incorporate them, you'll build trust and confidence and promote effectiveness. Jackson also points out that you'll be better able to plan ahead in uncertain times.

Manage distractions

Trying to create a sales plan, for example, while sitting in front of the TV is going to result in a poor sales plan and anxiety over the hours wasted. Instead, create as much of an office environment as you can at home. Establish a quiet space where you aren't likely to be disturbed. Since you'll be on videoconferences from this space, keep it neat, but don't be afraid to humanize it.

Your team also is susceptible to distractions. As you interact with them, learn how to spot symptoms that someone may be struggling. Symptoms may include missing deadlines, not following the conversation, failing to participate, running late with deliverables, irritability, lack of healthy disagreements and dissent, turning off the camera at random times and meetings going too fast due to lack of participation. Struggles may be due to distractions or to a lack of structures and signposts. If necessary, help them establish a structure that works for them, and set healthy boundaries to know when enough is enough.

Appreciative inquiry in 4-D

In the previous chapter we introduced the concept of appreciative inquiry, a way of approaching issues and change with a positive and open mind. The power of appreciative inquiry is unleashed through what is called the 4-D process: discovery, dream, design and destiny. Our description is based on information provided by the Corporation for Positive Change (nd), a consulting firm that specializes in applying appreciative inquiry.

We'll start by describing the discovery step, but the process is cyclical overall, and you may find yourself moving through the cycle several times, or moving back and forth between two steps before moving to the next. As you cycle through the steps, we recommend that you take a piece of paper, divide it into quadrants – one for each step – and take notes.

Discovery

In this step you identify and appreciate what works. Look at people, goals, processes, locations and schedules. When you know what is working very well, you can use that as a model for changing other things. This might include:

- creating the profile of a top performer, based on the characteristics that enable your best people to stand out;
- understanding which goals your organization achieves readily;
- identifying processes that always run smoothly and rarely run into problems;
- exploring what works best as people collaborate from different locations and across multiple time zones.

Dream

In this step you imagine what might be, what the perfect world should look like. This includes the same areas of attention as in the discovery step (people, goals, processes, locations and schedules). In addition, you should clarify what kind of organization you want; for example, do you want to be a business that provides employees with the chance to live a particular life-style? Do you want to build a $100 million company and sell it in five years?

Design

Now it's time to create the systems and structures that will facilitate making those dreams come true. Apply the insights about what works well from the discovery step. Appreciative inquiry is all about focusing on positives, so as you identify what you used to call a weakness or a problem, remember to think of them as areas of potential change. In addition to developing a clear picture of what success looks like, pay attention to the things that might cause you to fail. Your design will include things like:

- key performance indicators (KPIs);
- return on investment (ROI) analyses;
- team structure;
- systems and frameworks, such as Scrum or Lean.

We also recommend you include at least one BHAG. Jim Collins, in his book *Built to Last* (1994), says that a Big, Hairy, Audacious Goal (BHAG, pronounced be-hag) is a clear, compelling goal that can jumpstart motivation and drive progress. It should be clear and simple, but ambitious. Collins refers to President Kennedy's goal of putting a man on the moon as an example. KPIs and ROIs don't make good rallying cries, but a BHAG should help you get people excited about all the changes.

Destiny

This is the implementation step. Break design into steps and assign responsibilities, most likely by department. However, ensure that people and departments with different responsibilities collaborate in bringing the design to life. We like that the Corporation for Positive Change calls this step 'destiny', as it conveys the potential for positive change. At the same time, implementation can be approached with standard best practices in project management. One additional consideration is who might help in this effort. It might be a consultant, mentor, vendor, partner or even a strategic addition to your staff.

ASPIRIN OR VITAMIN?

As you identify issues and changes, classify them as aspirin or vitamin. Chris developed this concept in *The Power of Company Culture* (2018). Aspirin solutions target specific issues that are causing acute pain right now. Vitamin solutions help nurture the overall health of your company, promoting long-term growth and well-being. Implement the aspirin issues first, but recognize the importance of the bigger-picture view and vitamin solutions.

Five Is of appreciative leadership

Diana Whitney, PhD, is president of the Corporation for Positive Change and one of the authors of *Appreciative Leadership* (2010). In the book, Whitney and her collaborators recommend using five strategies to keep your approach positive: inquiry, illumination, inclusion, inspiration and integrity.

These strategies should be part of the foundation of your company, and everything you and your company do should connect to them. As CEO, you need to live and implement them – model them – to start integrating them. Help your leaders live and implement them and pass them on to their teams. Employing these strategies, and the values they embrace, will help promote personal excellence and a robust culture:

- **Inquiry:** When you or anyone in your organization asks questions in a positive way, it can lead to valuable knowledge, information and ideas. For example, instead of asking, 'Why aren't we hitting sales targets?' you might ask, 'What did we do in Q3 last year that helped us exceed sales targets?' In addition, asking people for their input lets them know that their opinions are valued.

- **Illumination** helps you reveal strengths and capabilities in people that may not be known. Not only is this helpful for your company, but it also helps employees recognize their own strengths and understand how they can make their best contributions. When coworkers understand one another's strengths, they find collaboration easier and more productive.

- **Inclusion** is a deliberate approach to engaging people in working together towards the company's destiny. By including people from diverse backgrounds, you create the opportunity for a richer and broader pool of viewpoints and ideas. In addition, you promote a sense of belonging and ownership, both powerful elements of engagement.

- **Inspiration**, in the context of appreciative inquiry, goes beyond motivating others. It is about helping people connect with a vital positive energy that drives not only performance and innovation, but also personal affirmation. It provides direction and purpose, and keeps your culture upbeat and hopeful. A BHAG, with its clear, simple goal, can be a source of inspiration.

- **Integrity** is about honouring core values, but also about promoting a wholeness to business and life. Values should be integrated into every strategy and action in order to build processes and habits that are affirming and sustainable. Leaders who demonstrate integrity build trust and set a standard that others are willing to follow.

As you can see, appreciative inquiry and appreciative leadership are positive, constructive, collaborative and supportive. They sound 'squishy' or soft, but they don't exclude more technical tactics like setting and monitoring performance metrics. Instead, we would argue that they help you and your team reach the more tangible, 'hard' goals around both individual and company performance. In fact, what follows is some structure for applying appreciative inquiry and leadership.

People, processes, tools and technology

This exercise will help ensure that, as you go through the 4-D process, you address all the key functional areas of your business. Take the page with the 4-D quadrant notes, flip it over and create a new quadrant for notes. We provide some suggestions for thinking about each area, and you can build on them or create new ones to tailor the exercise to your organization.

People

Some things to consider when taking your company remote are:

- Do we have the talent we need? If not, how will we fill in the gaps?
- Are there current employees who might take on new responsibilities or even new roles?
- How will we measure performance?

Some ways to assess and address these items:

- Do StrengthsFinder and DiSC assessments to help you and your team get to know one another's strengths and styles.
- Conduct 360-degree reviews for each employee. This type of review includes getting feedback not only from a supervisor, but also from coworkers and possibly vendors and clients.
- Ask each employee to set personal goals for excellence.
- Host an all-staff meeting to promote collaboration and team spirit.

Processes

This is an opportunity to reinvent processes. We suggest you start with a comparison grid that shows what you have now and what you want it to be. Considerations might include:

- What is each process intended to accomplish?
- Is each new process as streamlined as possible?
- How will we work together as a team?
- Do we want a flat organization, a top-down one or some other configuration?

Some potential activities to help assess process:

- Revisit and possibly revise your organization chart.
- Review and revise quotas and KPIs.
- Develop communication plans, including 'rules' for different types of online meetings.

Tools

Working remotely requires some unique tools. Some may be virtual versions of tools you have used, and some will be completely new. As many companies are finding out, not every employee has a computer or a stable internet connection at home. You may need to determine who needs what and provide it. Some tools to consider include:

- video conferencing platforms like Zoom, GoogleMeet, Skype, etc;
- document sharing applications like Microsoft SharePoint, Google Drive, goCanvas, etc;
- communication/collaboration/chat tools like Slack, Microsoft Teams, Chatwork, etc.

Technology

These days there is significant overlap between tools and technology, as you can see from the list above. In fact, as we talked about in Chapter 7, it is internet-based technology that makes it possible for entire companies to work remotely. If you are taking an established company remote, the enterprise resource planning (ERP) and other systems you already use can probably be accessed from anywhere. Of course, that doesn't prevent you from rethinking your current technology.

If you are creating an entirely new remote company, or just rethinking your technology, your company probably will benefit from the following:

- A **customer relationship management** platform (CRM), which helps you keep track of the who, when and what of interactions with customers. Salesforce.com is one of the most popular CRM systems. Your CRM should help you track orders, preferences and even personal notes about contacts, like birthdays.

- **Human resources** platforms, or HR information systems (HRIS) are invaluable for tracking essential information about employees. They should also help you comply with local, state and federal employment and payroll laws. Popular HR platforms include Paychex, Ceridian, ADP and PeopleSoft.

- **Collaboration/chat** platforms. We mentioned this on the tools list, but it is so important in a virtual model that it bears repeating. Slack, Monday and Microsoft Teams are examples. A good collaboration platform will help your team stay in close touch in spite of geographic separation. Most platforms are customizable so you can create 'rooms' for specific purposes.

- **Project management** software can be useful if your company model is strongly project-driven, such as with software development, process implementation or equipment installation. Popular choices are Basecamp, Asana and Microsoft Project.

- **Video hosting** platforms may be useful for sales efforts, enabling you to create and share videos about products and services. You also can use them to create a video blog to establish your subject matter expertise. Make sure your video platform integrates easily with your social media channels. Examples include Vidyard, Vimeo, Wistia and, of course, YouTube.

- **Social media management** platforms are helpful for managing social media campaigns across multiple channels. We love Buffer, as you might expect, but other available ones include Hootsuite and Zoho.

- **Online or digital marketing** platforms make it easy to track, manage and deploy multimedia marketing campaigns, including email, text, social media and more. Mailchimp, Acoustic and Pega are among the offerings.

- **Web hosting platforms** enable you to design, deploy and manage web pages, including both your main website and e-commerce sites. Typically these platforms also host your email. Examples include GoDaddy, 1&1 Ionos and HostGator.

Security protocols are essential in technology, and as more people work from home, more points of vulnerability are created. In *Remote: Office not required* (2013), Fried and Hansson recommend that you make sure:

- all computer hard drives are encrypted;
- encryption is turned on for frequently visited sites – you should see a small padlock next to a site's URL;
- all tablets and smartphones are password protected and can be wiped clean remotely if lost;
- everyone uses unique, long-form passwords for each device and site – passwords should include upper- and lower-case letters, numbers and symbols;
- everyone uses two-factor authentication where appropriate.

Details about cybersecurity are outside the scope of this book, but your IT resources should help fill in gaps.

Find your champions

Now that you have discovered, dreamed and designed, you should find champions in your organization to support your destiny – the implementation. Possibly the hardest part of implementing change is getting people to buy in and embrace it. That's where champions come in.

A person needs strong enthusiasm to be a champion, but they also need deep knowledge about the initiative or effort. For example, if you are implementing Slack, your champion is the person who has dug into Slack and found ways to make optimal use of it. They would qualify to be an administrator or

FIGURE 14.1   Levels of understanding

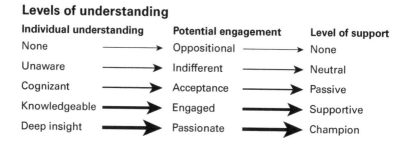

'super user'. In addition, they think Slack is the coolest thing *ever*. The table here gives you an idea of how understanding and engagement indicate the level of support an individual is likely to provide.

Employees whose engagement level is 'oppositional' or 'indifferent' will be roadblocks to implementation. Set up an informal meeting between the roadblockers and your champion. Peer-to-peer influence is much stronger than authority, and your champion's enthusiasm should be contagious. The champion can take different approaches, but one way is to give people a *why*, such as helping roadblockers understand how the new change will help them to be more productive or efficient. Since you will probably have multiple initiatives underway, you'll want to find multiple champions. As the champions raise people's level of understanding, they also raise people's engagement and support.

BANISHING DEMONS

Change, such as the implementation of new designs and destinies, can be as frightening as demons, and frightened employees can put up resistance. Champions can help those who are frightened, making the demons – and resistance – disappear. Chris related this experience in *The Power of Company Culture* (2018):

'Back when PeopleG2 was poised to move from an office-based business to a virtual model, we started implementing new processes. I immediately saw three group responses. The first were my champions. They loved the idea. The second group was in the middle, and were going to do whatever the company ended up asking them to do. The last group was afraid. They did not understand how this would work, or how it might affect their performance, job security and the company's stability.

'Over the next few days, I noticed the champions having deep conversations with people in the other two groups. I pulled a few of the champions aside and asked what they were hearing – not to name names, but to gauge the overall responses. They related fears, theories and all sorts of wild conjecture I never expected to hear. This allowed me to adjust my message to meet the needs that they were expressing. Their fears were demons representing the unknown. So, we set up additional meetings to do two things.

'First, we addressed concerns where we could and dispelled any misinformation that was being repeated. Second, I asked the champions to tell us what they were excited about. Little by little, as they spread the word through the entire company about all of the positive things they anticipated from the change, the afraid group dwindled. In fact, one of them later became a champion. The majority of the rest ended up in the middle group, willing to proceed and see what would happen. A few stragglers remained. I had the choice of ending our working relationship or converting them. Guess what: everyone stayed.'

From that experience, Chris learned that using champions is most successful when certain conditions are met:

- The idea is a good one. In fact, if no champions emerge, an idea may not be as great as you thought it was. You may need to go back to your two quadrants and rethink some things.
- There is a high level of transparency, to promote trust and open dialogue.
- You are willing to pivot or change course if the idea is not good, or your team comes up with a better one.

Up next is a case study about how one leader not only faced going remote, but also turned it into a great opportunity for a non-profit in Orange County, California.

CASE STUDY

Without missing a beat

Girls Inc. is a national not-for-profit organization that provides girls between the ages of 5 and 18 with a combination of long-lasting mentoring relationships, a pro-girl environment and research-based programmes. These programmes focus on the development of the whole girl, and equip them to lead fulfilling and productive lives, break the cycle of poverty and become role models in their community.

Before the Covid-19 pandemic, the majority of these programmes were delivered in person. Once the stay-at-home orders went into place, however, leaders at Girls Inc. scrambled to find ways to keep the girls engaged and learning. At the Orange County chapter, that's where Jessica Hubbard stepped in.

As Chief Programme Officer, Jessica oversees a variety of programmes, including elementary and teen, college-bound, externships and STEM. Prior to Covid-19 these were in-person programmes, although Jessica's background is in online education, including a master's degree in the subject from Columbia University. She had been working on online programmes for the chapter, but in the non-profit world, pet projects are often slowed by lack of funding.

Covid-19 turned the agency's priorities on their ear, however – without the face-to-face programmes, the organization's impact on the next generation of women leaders would diminish significantly. Jessica went into action immediately, had online resources available within days, and went on to create highly successful programmes. Here's how she did it.

Start with stopgap

Starting with first things first, Jessica assessed her team to discover what skills and strengths were available for online development. A few had basic video editing experience. They decided to start with YouTube, figuring that most girls have access at least to a smartphone. Her team started creating content right away, and what they may have lacked in video skills they made up for in being creative and nimble. Within a week of the stay-at-home orders, they had a YouTube channel with multiple videos.

As of early September, the Orange County chapter had more than 90 videos on the channel, 300 subscribers and thousands of views. However, even as they were expanding the YouTube offering, Jessica knew that was just the beginning. For one thing, an essential component of the Girls Inc. experience is interaction.

Sustainability and quality

In order to transition the entire programme online, Jessica knew she needed a robust learning management system, and researched the options. She chose Canvas because she felt it had everything they needed now, as well as the ability to scale. She wasn't looking for a quick fix, but a sustainable platform that could help the chapter continue to reach girls, even after resuming the in-person programmes.

Funding the investment in Canvas wasn't easy. Jessica moved some items around in her budget, such as money earmarked for materials and snacks for in-person programmes. This wasn't enough, however. Knowing she would have to build a case for a long-term investment, she met with the Canvas team to get even more insight.

Jessica presented her case to chapter CEO Lucy Santana-Ornelas and Chief Development Officer (CDO) Ann Duncan Levy. She presented options, including some less expensive ones, but she pushed Canvas, believing it was the one viable option that would keep the organization impactful. Other organizations in the space had a few YouTube videos and other resources, but Girls Inc. is committed to providing comprehensive, in-depth education. The focus is on the girls, and they need to reach them quickly and easily. The CEO and CDO agreed and, with their help, Jessica was able to get full support of Board Chair Bailey Weinberg and the rest of the board of directors.

Reframing and rethinking

Now that Jessica and her team were on Canvas, she knew that they all needed to change just about everything. She told her team that they had to enter into the project with the understanding that, whatever you did before, this was going to be different. On top of that, she was determined that they had to produce best-in-class virtual programmes.

One thing that she knew would be the same is the Girls Inc. DNA, the vibe, the characteristics that make their programmes attractive to girls while also promoting educational goals. She knew that many online teachers were struggling to be more than just babysitters, and knew her biggest challenges would be to promote engagement and retention.

One way Jessica and her team promoted engagement was to offer diverse programmes and channels. Before Covid-19, many programmes were carried out in partnership with schools. Now that schools were also online, she wanted to make sure that the Girls Inc. programming was distinctive.

Another challenge was getting the girls to adapt. At first they assumed that the girls were 'digital natives' and would take to the programmes like fish take to water. But it turned out there was a learning curve. However, Jessica figured that, if Girls Inc. can teach girls how to build a robot (and they do), teaching them to log on and participate in the programmes wasn't impossible. Other considerations in this area included determining which age groups needed which technologies, and how to help the girls get what they needed. They also developed programmes specific to different needs, including English as a second language (ESL) learners, and girls with disabilities.

Strong, smart and bold

The mission of Girls Inc. is to inspire girls to be strong, smart and bold, and Jessica knew her programmes had to be the same. She made sure that every offering has both synchronous (online together at the same time) and asynchronous (viewing content alone) parts. They discovered that, even after they sign off from a session, the girls want to continue. Therefore they put as much planning into asynchronous learning as they did the synchronous sessions. In synchronous sessions, the leader gauges if the girls are understanding by seeing them nod. But with asynchronous content, she made sure her team provided clear activities and assignments, as well as ways for the girls to get help.

Girls Inc. of Orange County provides six summer camp sessions, and Jessica and team recreated those for online delivery. To give you an idea of the innovative nature of the sessions, here are some descriptions:

- **Girls Inc. Smart-ups** help girls in grades 3 to 6 learn business concepts and leadership skills by taking over failing businesses, transforming them and presenting their new business plan to a team of investors, as in Shark Tank

- **Eureka!** is for grades 7 to 12 and engages girls in crime investigations, cybersecurity and social media, including creating an advocacy-based social media campaign for themselves and their community.

- **Girls Inc. She-roes** focuses on leadership, character education and fun for grades 3 to 6.

Jessica believes strongly in the importance of rethinking and reframing as you transition from in-person to online. It isn't enough to take what you used to do and just do it virtually. This approach proved very successful, as demonstrated by the numbers from the summer programme. The Girls Inc. team tempered their expectations, not knowing how the new format was received. However, it turned out better than the in-person sessions from the previous year. In 2019 they served 219 girls, while this year they served 230.

Even more important to Jessica are retention numbers. In every programme, more girls start than finish. However, retention for the summer 2020 sessions hit 80 per cent, higher than any previous summer. The takeaway here? If you're going to go remote, it pays to do it with thoughtful intention.

Looking ahead

Speaking of changing course, in this chapter we've covered some bigger concepts, ideas that will help you set sail for a brave new world. But, as you know, it's one thing to chart a course, and another thing to unfurl the mainsail and tie the right kinds of knots in the rigging. In the next chapters, we'll get into the nitty-gritty.

References

Collins, J (1994) *Built to Last: Successful habits of visionary companies*, Harper Business, New York

Corporation for Positive Change (nd) How the 4-D process works, *positivechange.com*, https://positivechange.org/how-the-4-d-process-works (archived at https://perma.cc/C3WQ-EUVF)

Dyer, C (2018) *The Power of Company Culture: How any business can build a culture that improves productivity, performance and profits*, Kogan Page, London

Fried, J and Hansson, D H (2013) *Remote: Office not required*, Currency, New York

Whitney, D, Trosten-Bloom, A and Rader, K (2010) *Appreciative Leadership: Focus on what works to drive winning performance and build a thriving organization*, McGraw-Hill Education, New York

15

Meetings and measurement

Now that you have a clear vision, plans and champions, there are some key elements to incorporate into the implementation. The ideas are based on our own experience and what others have published. We encourage you to take the ideas that resonate with you and your company, tailor them to fit and make them even better.

IN THIS CHAPTER

We will cover:

- How meetings drive culture...
- ... and many different types of meetings
- Ideas for measuring performance
- Optimizing decision-making
- Off-the-chart organization

Meetings: communication and culture

Meetings are essential for communication in all organizations, but in remote models they are also a great tool for driving culture and reinforcing your company's vision. How often you meet depends on your organization, but one thing applies to all organizations: if you do meetings poorly, your company will suffer.

We're going to talk about different kinds of meetings later in the chapter, but let's start with three rules that apply to any and all meetings.

Fundamental meeting rules

1 **Start on time.** This promotes efficiency, of course, but even more importantly, you make a cultural statement that no one's time is more valuable than anyone else's. We both use a fun but impactful punishment for those who are late. At Decision Toolbox, Kim made those people sing in front of everyone else. At PeopleG2, Chris makes them recite bad poetry. If you or any of your senior leaders are habitually late in starting meetings, you're sending the wrong message.

2 **Always end meetings early.** You may have heard of Parkinson's law (1957), which states that work expands to fill the time allotted. Logically, then, if you shorten the time, you will tend to be more efficient. You can schedule the meeting for an hour, but finish five minutes early. It's an act of goodwill that requires no effort on your part. It allows you to give the gift of time to your people while also letting them know you respect their time.

3 **Keep it small.** In the online world, a videoconference with more than seven participants isn't a meeting, it's a webinar. Essentially you will have one or two people presenting to everyone else. Those kinds of events can be useful, but when we say 'meeting' here, we are referring to a brainstorming or update session in which everyone has the opportunity to engage.

Two more best practices come from an Inc.com article about Chris, 'What 1 Founder Learned Running 100,000 Virtual Meetings' (Downes, 2020). First, in a virtual model, you need to find the right balance between having enough meetings to get the work done and limiting the number of meetings so that people don't experience what has come to be called 'Zoom burnout' (Martins, 2020). To be fair to Zoom, of course, it can happen on any platform. Second, keep your meetings professional, but also recognize that many participants are dealing with caregiving responsibilities, varying levels of connectivity and their own well-being. Recall the tactics in Chapter 10 for checking in to make sure everyone is doing well.

Types of meetings

Between the two of us, we've defined a few meeting types that are extremely useful and effective. We've been sharing and building on one another's ideas for years, and in some cases we use the same name but do things a little differently.

Cockroach: Imagine you have a cockroach in your bathroom. It's not a serious issue, but it needs to be addressed quickly, and you can't do it alone. The business equivalent might be that you find out a product won't arrive by the time you promised the customer. To solve it, reach out to a handful of people who are in a position to help, keep the cockroach meeting to 15 minutes, and keep it focused on the one problem. Attendance should be optional – if someone has something more pressing, it's okay for them not to participate.

Ostrich meetings help team members get their heads out of the sand. Maybe someone needs help with an Excel formula, or someone wants to get an update on a project or issue. Ostrich meetings follow the same guidelines as cockroach meetings: small group, 15 minutes, single topic, optional attendance.

Tiger team: Imagine there is a tiger in your bathroom. The stakes are exponentially greater than with a cockroach problem. You need animal control, a dart gun sharpshooter and others. For your company, a comparable problem may be that a client wants to double the size of the engagement next month. A tiger team meeting will have a large agenda, such as hiring new staff, scaling up processes, procuring additional equipment, etc. It may last an hour or all day. If you're the meeting leader, you need to do a fair amount of preparation and come to the meeting prepared to work hard. Attendance is not optional, but you should choose the participants strategically. Activities may include brainstorming and whiteboarding, and a tiger team meeting should result in specific action items and assigned responsibilities.

Tiger's den is a variation on the tiger team that Chris holds once a month with his senior leaders. Rather than focusing on a particular problem, the team looks at overall company performance, the health and well-being of all teams, processes that might be improved and so on. It's strategic rather than tactical. When necessary, Chris will call a mini tiger's den to check in on progress.

Tsunami: Kim and Chris each have a unique version of tsunami meetings, but the basic idea is that you gather a team and solve a hypothetical problem on the scale of a tsunami. Topics might include: What if the CEO was hit by a bus? What if half of our clients disappeared tomorrow? We touched on tsunami planning in Chapter 4 and mentioned that the topics don't have to be negative; for example, you might posit that the company is hitting 100 per cent of targets consistently – where do we go from here?

At Decision Toolbox, Kim would take her senior leadership team through tsunami meetings every quarter, and the meetings would last from one to three hours. The result was a five- to seven-page blueprint that went into a binder for future reference. She also had a version for all-staff meetings that regularly resulted in great ideas, many of which could be implemented for free. Chris holds tsunami meetings once a month with the leaders of finite teams (department heads) and he also keeps the ideas that are produced, and both have referred back to the ideas and made use of them.

However you organize tsunami meetings, they should provide the following key benefits to your team:

- They create a psychologically safe space where your employees can practise delivering bad news and speaking frankly. Recall the Google study (Rozovsky, 2017) we cited in Chapter 3 showing that one characteristic of effective teams is that team members feel safe about taking risks.

- They allow your team to practise collaborating on solving big, big problems, making it easier for them to collaborate on small and medium ones.

- They compel people to look beyond the current situation and, in some cases, step outside their comfort zone.

- They result in action steps that can be kept for future reference.

Stand-up meetings are short meetings among finite teams (sales, customer service, etc) to make sure everyone is on the same page and up to speed. You decide on the frequency, but these meetings often get the day or week started. These should be no longer than 15 minutes, and the leader should stick to a defined agenda.

Ongoing meetings help leaders stay in touch with teams and individuals. Annual performance reviews and annual surveys simply don't allow you to course correct in a timely manner. Think back to the Tour of Duty idea, which is based on the recognition that you can't expect anyone to stay in a job forever. You enter into a relationship that is more like a partnership, in which both the employee and you have commitments and expectations.

Combine the transience of the relationship with the emphasis on a partnership, and you will see the downside of waiting a year or even six months to check in with one another. Chris has all his managers meet with each direct report for 15 minutes once a month, and this replaces the annual review. For one thing, an annual review is a one-way street, with the employer telling the employee how they're doing. With a Tour of Duty approach and more frequent partnering, you create a two-way street that allows both sides to express how things are going, needs they may have and things that may need to be changed.

There are alternatives to holding a lot of ongoing meetings. For example, Chris sends a 'question of the week' email to everyone. This replaces the annual employee survey and, while some responses may prompt him to call a meeting, it keeps one-on-ones to a minimum. The frequency allows him to identify problems, trends and potential issues quickly.

There is a cause-and-effect dynamic at work, in which the more thought the CEO puts into creating the questions, the more valuable will be the information in the responses. Chris estimates that he spends two to three minutes creating the questions, and 20 to 30 minutes reading them. He gets a 95 per cent response rate, so he keeps his finger on the pulse without holding a lot of one-on-one meetings.

Most questions are business related, but he also peppers in some funny ones. Examples include:

- What do you need right now to make your job easier?
- Which clients are creating the most work for you and why?
- How is the CEO getting in your way?
- Which coworker is doing an amazing job?
- What is the best thing that happened to you this month at work?

He also breaks things up in other ways. For three months, he will keep the responses completely confidential, and then for the next three months the responses will be shared with the whole company. In either case, respondents' identities are always confidential. Chris uses SurveyMonkey, but there are other survey platforms available.

Ensuring focus

In the case study about Buffer in Chapter 10, Courtney Seiter recommended that meeting leaders check in to make sure no participant is suffering from HALT – hunger, anger, loneliness or tiredness. A great example of this comes from *Thinking, Fast and Slow*, by Daniel Kahneman (2011), a psychology professor at Princeton and the only non-economist to win a Nobel prize in economics.

Kahneman cites a study of eight judges in Israel who spent entire days reviewing a high volume of applications for parole. Parole was denied in 65 per cent of the cases overall, making it the default decision. However, in the study, they compared the timing of the decisions, which are recorded, with the timing of the judges' three daily snack/meal breaks. They found that the number of paroles *granted* spiked right after each break, to as high as 65 per cent. The percentage of approvals then dropped steadily over the next few hours, to almost zero right before the next snack/meal. Study authors took care to eliminate other possible explanations, but finally concluded that when the judges were tired and hungry, they went to their default decision.

The great thing about working remotely is that people have control over their environment, including their eating schedule and the thermostat. However, when planning meetings, consider the time of day. If Chris has to schedule a meeting at 10:30 am, right between breakfast and lunch, he'll make it a coffee-and-bagel meeting. He's even sent bagels to clients. The more important the meeting, the more important it is that you ensure people are able to focus.

We both believe it is important to have face-to-face meetings periodically. With your leadership team, it might be once a quarter. Once a year, you should gather all your employees for an in-person, all-staff meeting. This really doesn't have to deal with business issues, assuming you have other, more frequent meetings for that. Instead, your annual all-staff meeting should drive culture and engagement. It also provides an opportunity for employees to step out of their routine. We've mentioned a few activities you might conduct during the meetings, such as StrengthsFinder and/or DiSC assessments (Chapter 5) and tsunami planning (above), and you might also invite a motivational speaker.

Chris schedules all-staff meetings in December, and the schedule includes the meeting followed by a holiday party. The next day, employees meet as teams. The idea is that the group can plan together, eat and drink together and then debrief together. At Decision Toolbox, Kim would usually schedule all-staffs in spring or summer. People would arrive on Sunday for a cocktail party, the meeting was on Monday and on Tuesday the leadership team would debrief.

Measuring performance

We've already told you why measuring is important. There are many different ways to do it, and you can get as detailed as you want to. Remember to measure what matters. For example, Kim developed a unique set of KPIs to use in assigning jobs to recruiters. Each recruiter was assigned an index score based on six KPIs, including days to find the candidate hired, days to fill the position, customer satisfaction, repeat business and others.

Her team also created technology to track these scores, including a dashboard that showed the score, the number of new jobs the recruiter wanted, and the recruiter's area of expertise. When a new project came in, let's say a search for a Process Engineer, the recruiting manager would select all recruiters with engineering expertise, and the one with the highest score would have first dibs.

This system not only eliminated anything arbitrary in the process of assigning jobs, but it also helped recruiters manage their own workloads. Most importantly, it rewarded top performers. The recruiters earned a small base salary, with variable incentives per project. With talent and drive, a recruiter would enjoy a steady stream of projects and revenue. Note that the score included two customer-based components – no one fills 100 per cent of their open positions, but everyone can deliver a great customer experience.

What happened to the weak performers? They wouldn't get much work, and eventually they would leave – and go to competitors. This system allowed Kim to attract and retain strong performers, and feed the weak ones to the competition.

Chris's KPIs are a little less complex, but they also work to reward strong performance. For his sales team, there are the kinds of targets you would expect. For everyone else, their target is based 100 per cent on Net Promoter Score (NPS). If you're not familiar with NPS, it is based on customer feedback. Since customer satisfaction drives their business, Chris's employees ask each customer: how likely are you to recommend PeopleG2 to others? Customers respond using a scale of 0 (not at all likely) to 10 (extremely likely).

Chris was somewhat influenced by Jeff Bezos of Amazon, who describes himself as 'congenitally customer focused' (Kirby and Stewart, 2007). Amazon focuses on customers rather than on the competition. This approach works well for PeopleG2, as they currently have an NPS of 94 in an industry where 40 is typical.

Another way to approach KPIs is by using scorecards, as described by Gino Wickman and Tom Bouwer in *What the Heck is EOS?* (2017). EOS stands for Entrepreneurial Operating System®, which Gino developed to help leaders run more effective businesses, gain better control and enjoy better life balance. Similar to a dashboard, a scorecard provides a few key numbers measuring KPIs. You can create scorecards for individuals, teams, departments or your whole company. The advantage of scorecards is that they eliminate guesswork and promote transparency – the numbers show that either you're achieving goals or you're not. In addition, as Wickman and Bouwer put it, 'What gets measured gets done.'

The key takeaway here is that it doesn't matter what system you use, but your system should drive performance.

Decision-making

You want your employees to be part of the decision-making process, and also feel empowered to make decisions independently. There are a few things you can do to promote both.

Establish trust

One of the most important things is to establish trust. Colleen Barret, now President Emeritus of Southwest Airlines, says that trust is an essential component in employee engagement (Marchica, 2004). As an example, Southwest employees are empowered to make decisions on the spot. If an employee makes a well-intentioned decision that turns out to be a mistake, Southwest will back them up publicly. They may correct the employee in private, but in a constructive way. You can't say, 'You're empowered to make decisions' and then punish people for making them.

The scourge of groupthink

Another consideration in decision-making is to avoid groupthink, which happens when people are more concerned about fitting into the group than about making the best decisions. Perhaps the culture puts too strong an emphasis on the infallibility of the CEO or the company, or perhaps peer pressure discourages people from rocking the boat.

A couple of famous examples of the dangers of groupthink come from Kodak and Blockbuster. Kodak remained doggedly committed to film as the rest of the world went digital. This was in spite of an internal market research report that concluded that digital photography had the potential to supplant film (Mui, 2012). Once one of the most powerful companies in the world, Kodak eventually filed for bankruptcy and had to sell off patents in order to pay debts (Anthony, 2016).

In the early 2000s, Blockbuster held a commanding chunk of the video rental market, including rental rights to a massive portfolio of movies. At that time, a young upstart company, Netflix, wanted to get access to that portfolio (Walker, 2015). Netflix made several offers for Blockbuster to buy them for $50 million, but Blockbuster refused each time. Jonathan Salem Baskin (2013) worked in the corporate office at Blockbuster at the time, and 'had a small speaking role in the unfolding drama'. He claims that internal stubbornness killed Blockbuster. While a handful of internal players argued that the company needed to shift its focus on optimizing the retail customer experience – including exploring the streaming option – the majority insisted that the best approach was to be a convenience store with movies. By 2010 Blockbuster had lost over $1 billion and filed for bankruptcy, while Netflix's value at that time was $13 billion (Walker, 2015).

AVOIDING GROUPTHINK

There are a few things you can do to help your team avoid groupthink:

Draw your own conclusions before considering the opinions of others. We're not recommending that people be closed-minded. Instead, each person needs a sense of what the right answer might be – it serves as a baseline to assess other ideas against. In addition, if someone has no opinion, they are at risk of going along with whoever is the loudest – and that person may be wrong.

Designate the devil is a kind of game that ensures at least one person will push back. In the in-person version, you would hand out a playing card to each meeting participant, making sure that two of the cards are queens (or whatever – jokers may be ironically apropos). Whoever draws the queen is required to question the ideas of others in a constructive way. In the virtual version, you can use any random process for designating the devil and then letting those people know prior to the meeting. The idea is that when at least one participant challenges or pushes back, it signals to the others that it's okay to disagree. Chris designates the devil without revealing it to the larger group and, at the end of the meeting, asks the group to guess. They almost always identify one devil correctly, usually the one who first pushed back. However, they rarely guess the second one, because once the first devil voices disagreement, many others follow suit.

Ask key questions. When the overall group wants to go one way and one person has doubts, key questions help the lone dissenter voice an opinion. The questions should be non-confrontational, such as 'What else could we do?' or 'Is it alright if I disagree?' Remember that you are creating a psychologically safe place for people to share ideas, so how questions are asked can be as important as what is asked.

Organization charts and beyond

In a sticks-and-bricks model it's easy to get by without being highly organized. When you go remote, however, organization is essential. The good news is that going remote gives you many opportunities to get more and more organized.

For example, in the last chapter you deconstructed and reconstructed your company (like Lincoln Logs®, if you recall). The next step from there is to ensure your organization chart reflects the new structure. The org chart supports transparency, so there are no mysteries around who is responsible for what and who reports to whom. A great org chart will link the structure to the goals of the company, each leader and each department, and it should be available to every employee.

If you think of yourself as messy and disorganized, it may be challenging to create a strong org chart. However, there is hope for you. Chris believed the same thing until he found Dan Charnas's book, *Work Clean* (2016). In it, Charnas recommends the technique used by French chefs, *mise-en-place*, which translates to 'setting in place' or 'everything in its place'. He chose *mise-en-place* not because he is a fan of food, per se, but because the method is used by chefs to achieve excellence.

Think about a busy professional kitchen. *Mise-en-place* means that, before the dinner rush starts, the chef has prepared and assembled ingredients, tools, pans, plates and everything else necessary to quickly and efficiently prepare any dish on the menu. Charnas also says that, as taught in culinary schools, *mise-en-place* includes the direction to keep your kitchen workstation clean.

Charnas details the experience of students at the Culinary Institute of America, in New York, and explains that *mise-en-place* doesn't tell them how to cook, but how to *work*. By extension, he says it can apply to any aspect of life. To apply it, you have to invest some time up front (think inverted pyramid) and almost reverse engineer what it is you need to reach a particular goal. Once he started applying *mise-en-place*, Chris realized that he wasn't, by nature, a messy person. He just hadn't learned a system.

Clearly taking your company remote is a significant undertaking, and it requires a good deal of organization and planning. Taking advantage of an organization system will make it easier, and help keep you from feeling overwhelmed. The process can also help you identify conflicting goals, or a situation in which a win by one group causes another group to lose.

Mise-en-place saves a top performer

Everyone in your company benefits from your being organized, and from being organized themselves. Structure can be a huge help for first-time remote workers, and *mise-en-place* can help them set up their home office. As an example, Chris used *mise-en-place* to help a new employee who was clearly talented, but still struggling. Chris had lured this person away from his competition, so she knew the industry. Still, she was having a very hard time getting up to speed. Several people tried to help her, and Chris was even considering letting her go.

As a last effort, Chris went back to basics, starting with assessing her *mise-en-place*, her home office setup. He quickly realized that she had only one computer monitor, trying to do complex work that requires two monitors. Chris got her a second monitor and her performance quickly improved. In fact, she is now one of his top performers.

Mise-en-place in onboarding

Onboarding is an essential part of the new hire process, but many companies miss the opportunity to use it to promote employee engagement. Your onboarding process sends a message, whether you intend it to or not. However, if you design what you want in an onboarding programme, you won't have to deal with what you get. To underscore the importance of this point, a survey of 1,500 job seekers (Engage2Excel, 2017) found that 71 per cent of respondents said that their onboarding experience was either likely or highly likely to influence their decision to stay with the company. Gallup's State of the American Workplace Report (2017) found that only 12 per cent of workers surveyed feel that their company did a good job of onboarding.

If your onboarding programme consists of having the new employee spend all day filling out HR forms, you're not sending the right message. Here's where *mise-en-place* can help. Make sure that everything is ready before the employee's first day, including phone lines, business cards, access to online systems, email and more. This lets the employee know that you have it together, and sets an expectation that they should be on their toes as well.

Chris also sends all the paperwork (including online forms) in advance, so that on day one the employee is free to meet the team. He makes a point of talking about the company's culture with every new employee right from the start. This lets him emphasize that in the PeopleG2 culture, *how* you do things is just as important as the things you do.

Kim used to send each new employee a giant fortune cookie, with a fortune that read, 'We predict a long and prosperous future together.' The cookie was giant because she didn't want them to eat it, but to keep it on their desk to remind them that they are part of something unique and special.

Staying on point

Another element of implementation and operations is keeping people focused on what's most important, whether that is the customer, sales, products or something else. We feel this topic deserves its own chapter, so grab a bagel and a cup of coffee and get ready to read on.

References

Anthony, S D (2016) Kodak's downfall wasn't about technology, *Harvard Business Review*, 15 July, https://hbr.org/2016/07/kodaks-downfall-wasnt-about-technology (archived at https://perma.cc/AMT8-2GXN)

Baskin, J S (2013) The internet didn't kill Blockbuster, the company did it to itself, *Forbes*, 8 November, www.forbes.com/sites/jonathansalembaskin/2013/11/08/the-internet-didnt-kill-blockbuster-the-company-did-it-to-itself (archived at https://perma.cc/A4YJ-GJX9)

Charnas, D (2016) *Work Clean: The life-changing power of mise-en-place to organize your life, work and mind*, Penguin, New York

Downes, S (2020) What 1 founder learned running 100,000 virtual meetings, *Inc.com*, 12 May, www.inc.com/sophie-downes/virtual-meeting-remote-work-from-home-zoom-productivity-empathy.html (archived at https://perma.cc/RFH6-TS7G)

Engage2Excel (2017) Trendicators Report: The role of recognition in recruiting, onboarding & retaining employees, https://www.engage2excel.com/resource_type/articles (archived at https://perma.cc/TF98-SNYR)

Gallup (2017) State of the American Workplace, https://www.gallup.com/workplace/238085/state-american-workplace-report-2017.aspx (archived at https://perma.cc/3PLN-ZAX7)

Kahneman, D (2011) *Thinking, Fast and Slow*, Farrar, Straus and Giroux, New York

Kirby, J and Stewart, T (2007) The institutional Yes, *Harvard Business Review*, October, https://hbr.org/2007/10/the-institutional-yes (archived at https://perma.cc/F356-BFEG)

Marchica, J (2004) *The Accountable Organization: Reclaiming integrity, restoring trust*, Black Davies Publishing, Palo Alto, California

Martins, A (2020) Tips on how to avoid 'Zoom burnout', *Business News Daily*, 3 June, www.businessnewsdaily.com/15728-zoom-burnout.html (archived at https://perma.cc/7BHK-UMMP)

Mui, C (2012) How Kodak failed, *Forbes*, 18 January, www.forbes.com/sites/chunkamui/2012/01/18/how-kodak-failed/#78b39a3d6f27 (archived at https://perma.cc/P2KE-PZ2Z)

Parkinson, C N (1957) *Parkinson's Law and Other Studies in Administration*, Ballantine Books, New York

Rozovsky, J (2017) The five keys to a successful Google team, re:Work, https://rework.withgoogle.com/blog/five-keys-to-a-successful-google-team (archived at https://perma.cc/ZK2F-JNLJ)

Walker, B (2015) How to remove bias from your decision-making, Duke Corporate Education, www.dukece.com/insights/how-remove-bias-from-your-decision-making (archived at https://perma.cc/W7U3-WVUZ)

Wickman, G and Bouwer, T J (2017) *What the Heck is EOS? A complete guide for employees in companies running on EOS*, BenBella Books, Dallas

16

People, processes, tools, technology... and momentum

The concepts and recommendations in this chapter apply to any business, remote or brick-and-mortar. If you're not planning on taking your company remote, but you've stuck with us this far, you may find this the most insightful chapter yet. We're going to take a deep dive into people, processes, tools and technology (PPTT), with an emphasis on how to set up and leverage KPIs (Lexico, nd) in each area, making this chapter a solid course in Business 101 for any model. In each area, apply an 80 per cent rule – to be effective, you should be scoring at least 80 per cent, and hopefully more. Along with some stories and examples, this chapter will provide tips for building and maintaining momentum.

IN THIS CHAPTER

We will cover:

- Defining your strategic advantage
- More cognitive biases to avoid
- Great decision-making strategies
- KPIs for People
- KPIs for Process
- KPIs for Tools
- KPIs for Technology

How you use and apply PPTT will depend on who and what you are as a business. Are you customer focused or sales focused? Do you provide a service or manufacture a product? If you haven't narrowed this down, refer to Chapter 13. This would include identifying and leveraging your strategic advantage. Here are three examples of strategic advantages.

Being the **low-cost leader** gives you a competitive edge, but it can work for you in other ways. For example, Decision Toolbox was a smaller company, so Kim took a cost-based approach to cutting the knees out of bigger competitors. While other recruiting firms charged high fees, Kim charged 8 per cent of the open position's salary. This compelled clients to be active partners in the recruiting process. Decision Toolbox did the heavy lifting, but expected the client to participate in a discovery call session, provide timely feedback on candidates and more. As long as clients would partner in searches, Decision Toolbox could leverage processes and technology to keep costs low.

High-touch service allows you to attract clients who expect 5-diamond service. Chris considers this to be a key strategic advantage at PeopleG2. His clients want a concierge experience. In the background check space, customers jump from one low-cost provider to another at the drop of a hat. However, the high-touch approach promotes strong client loyalty.

Blue ocean strategy was developed by W Chan Kim and Renée Mauborgne (2015) in their book of the same name. It refers to entering unexplored new markets – blue ocean – in contrast to waters red with the blood of competition. An excellent example is Uber. Instead of competing with taxicabs, they created a whole new model. With Lyft and other competitors following suit, the waters were not long blue, but when Uber launched, they were the only ones in the market. That has also made it easier for them to maintain market leadership.

We believe that blue ocean is a variation on Swiss cheese. Instead of starting a business to make more cheese, Uber looked at the holes in the transportation market and created a game-changer. Airbnb and Angie's lists are two more examples. Perhaps the biggest challenge in creating something new is to gain traction and educate prospective customers, which can take time and money. However, as these examples show, the extra effort pays off.

More on cognitive bias

As you lead your team through the significant changes involved in going remote, one of the challenges can be overcoming cognitive biases. You should be aware of these three ideas as you help people – and yourself – think in new ways.

Reluctance theory

This theory states something that most of us know: people don't like to be told what to do. We often associate this with teenagers, but it can be true of any age group. To give you an example, if you post a sign that says 'Please don't write on the walls', it's likely that the incidence of wall-writing will increase. Some people feel that such rules threaten their freedom or autonomy, and they may respond with defiance, including breaking the rule. With children or teenagers, reverse psychology may be useful: 'Whatever you do, don't clean your room!'

With adult employees, however, you need a more subtle approach. The ideal approach is to persuade people, showing them how a particular choice benefits them personally, so that they accept it on their own terms. If that doesn't work, you can try offering choices that they may not be thrilled about, but can live with. Get the person involved in exploring the options, so they have a sense of control. The same applies to you as you make decisions. If you feel like your freedom of choice is taken away, pause and reflect – someone may be trying to manipulate you.

Just-for-me effect

This bit of cognitive bias can happen when a person is presented with vague, generalized information and they accept it as being specific to them. A great example is a published daily horoscope. It can include very broad statements like, 'You're bright enough to understand that life can deal you some tough cards once in a while. Maintain your perspective and find the right balance between being down-to-earth and being a dreamer.' These statements could apply to just about anybody, but the Barnum-Forer effect kicks in when someone is certain that it was written just for them.

Named after famous hype man P T Barnum (Meehl, 1956), the effect was further confirmed by psychologist Bertram Forer (1949) in a classroom experiment. He asked his students to take a personality test, promising to provide an individualized personality evaluation to each student, based on their responses. Instead, he provided the same evaluation to each student, which he had cobbled together from newspaper horoscopes. He then asked each student to rate how accurately the evaluation captured their individual personality. On a scale of 1 to 5, with 5 being 'very accurate', the class returned an average rating of 4.6.

To help your employees avoid the Barnum-Forer effect, encourage them to think critically about what they read and hear. If the technique can be used by fortune tellers to make money, you can assume that there are people who will try to use it to manipulate others. A better approach may be to follow the advice of Edgar Allen Poe: 'Believe nothing you hear, and only one half that you see' (1844).

Availability heuristic

This cognitive bias occurs when you jump to a conclusion based on the most recent, or available, information or experience. For example, if you go to the beach a few days after hearing several news stories about shark sightings, you might be afraid to go on the water. It doesn't matter that the sightings were far from your beach; with the availability heuristic, what matters is that the information is fresh in your mind. In other words, people unconsciously assume that because information is readily available, it must be accurate.

The availability heuristic, developed by psychologists Amos Tversky and Daniel Kahneman (Kahneman, Slovic and Tversky, 1982), can be problematic in decision-making. For example, a marketing team may be brainstorming on how to reach a wider audience for a personal security product like mace. One member of the team may recently have seen a documentary about Jack the Ripper. That may influence the team member's contributions to the brainstorm, in spite of the fact that Jack the Ripper was active some 130 years ago.

To avoid the availability heuristic, you and your employees should make a point of considering several options, not just the first one that comes to mind. In addition, research may be helpful or even necessary. Market research certainly would be more useful than anecdotal information about something that happened decades ago.

Decision-making revisited

In the last chapter we talked about ways to optimize decision-making, and here is another one. Many CEOs compare decision-making to chess, and in chess there is a mathematically optimal choice for every move. If you have a computer-like mind, you may rank with the great masters like Bobby Fischer and Garry Kasparov. However, for those of us with standard-issue brains, Annie Duke has a different recommendation.

Duke was a champion poker player for years, and since then has turned to business consulting, with an emphasis on decision-making. Prior to becoming a poker professional, she studied cognitive psychology at the University of Pennsylvania, backed by a National Science Foundation Fellowship. She says life and business aren't like chess, but like poker. In her book *Thinking in Bets: Making smarter decisions when you don't have all the facts* (2018), she argues that there is no formula for arriving at the best decision every time. Instead, you should approach decision-making as if you are playing the odds.

Her approach puts the emphasis not on the decision itself, but on the decision-making process. For example, if you consider the odds and determine that a new sales strategy has a 70 per cent chance of succeeding, you should go for it. The odds are in your favour. It is entirely possible that the 30 per cent will kick in and the strategy fails, but that doesn't mean the decision was wrong. Instead of kicking yourself for making a bad decision, focus on the quality of your decision-making process. You should be able to improve your odds, but there always will be a chance of losing.

Chris and Kim both shifted their decision-making processes in ways consistent with Duke's philosophy. Chris used to try to make the perfect decisions around growing sales, focusing on increasing the percentage of business actually won. Regardless of different tactics he tried, the wins remained right around 40 per cent. He realized that it probably wasn't realistic to think PeopleG2 would ever win more than 40 per cent of prospects in the pipeline. To grow sales, then, he and his team focused on expanding the number of prospects in the pipeline.

Kim also realized that there were no 'perfect decisions' in the sales process. Recall that her model was to offer a lower price, but in actual practice it wasn't that simple. Prospective customers wanted different things, and not all of those things fit into Decision Toolbox's cost structure. To increase her odds of winning new business, she stopped leading with price and instead asked prospects to tell her about their goals, challenges and needs. Then she could talk price, letting the prospect know what Decision Toolbox could do for the basic rate, and how much it might cost to add some of the service the prospect wanted.

People, processes, tools and technology

Now that you have defined your business model, have decision-making strategies at hand and are on the alert for cognitive bias, let's get into PPTT and some of the KPIs you can use to monitor performance and drive improvements. To make sure we're all on the same page, we'll define key performance indicators as quantifiable metrics used to monitor and assess success in achieving established goals. We want to stress the word 'quantifiable' in the definition – KPIs must be measurable.

People

As Figure 16.1 shows, and as we've mentioned before, it all starts with your people. We've already talked about hiring for success and helping existing employees develop skills. So right now we'll assume you have your staff – including your champions – in place. Here are some KPIs you can implement to monitor their performance and well-being, as well as your performance in engaging and retaining top talent:

- **Internal surveys.** Think of your employees as your customers, and gauge their customer satisfaction. Are 80 per cent of your employees satisfied with their jobs?

- **Sales targets** are among the most common KPIs used.

- **External surveys,** such as customer satisfaction ratings, help you and your team understand what's working and what they can change. Net Promoter Scores (NPS), mentioned in the previous chapter, are one example.

- **Relative market share** data provides insight about overall business performance, but it can also suggest what individual employees can do to move the needle in this area.

- **Mental health status scores** are important indicators of employee well-being. Workplace stress and anxiety is a major contributor to mental health issues (Jeon and Kim, 2018), and these issues are responsible for up to $500 billion of lost productivity every year (Mental Health America, 2017). A resource that you can encourage employees to use for self-assessment is Check Up from the Neck Up (https://checkupfromtheneckup.us/quiz), developed by the Mood Disorders Association of Ontario.

- **Employee turnover rate** (ETR) gives you a glimpse into how well your culture engages and retains people. For larger companies, you should

FIGURE 16.1 People-processes-tools-technology

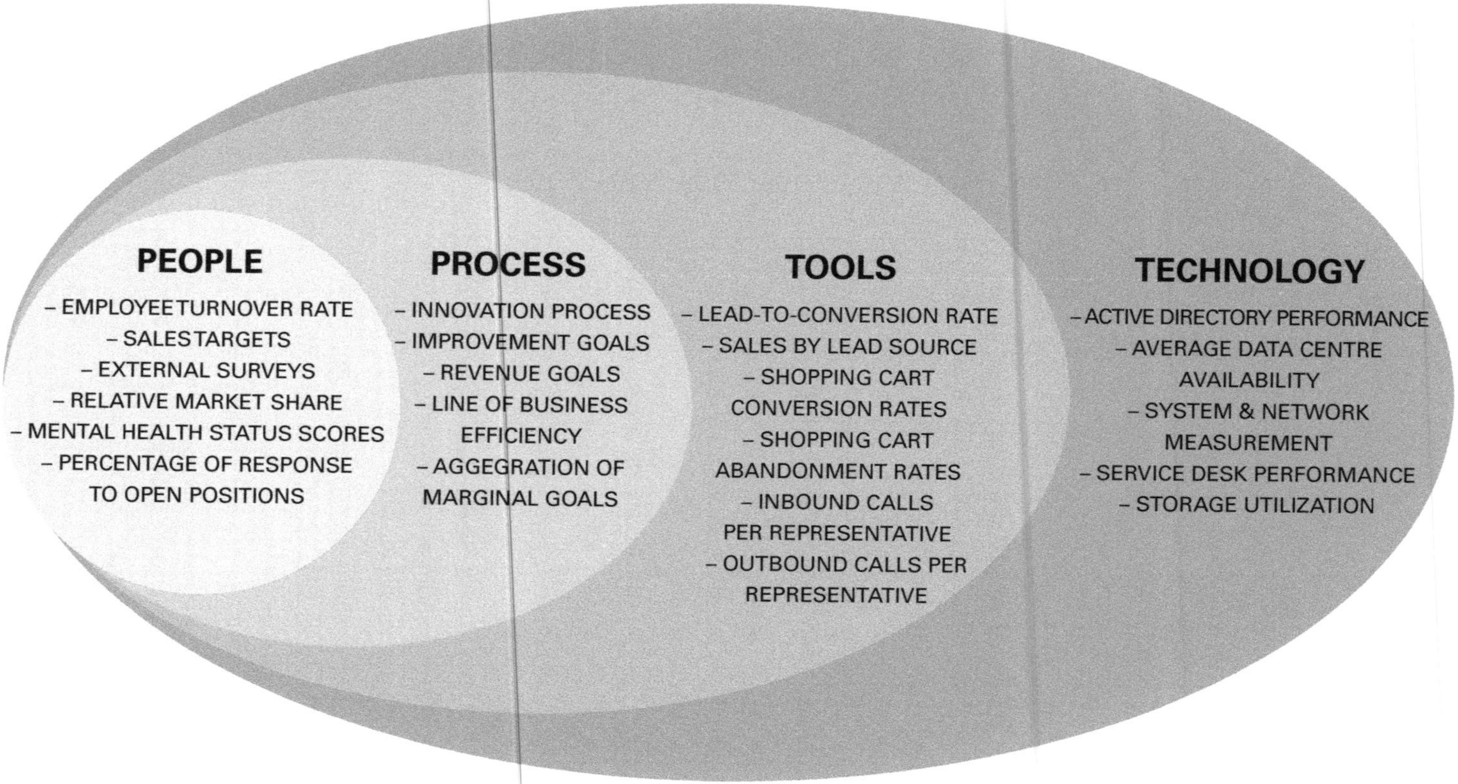

PEOPLE
– EMPLOYEE TURNOVER RATE
– SALES TARGETS
– EXTERNAL SURVEYS
– RELATIVE MARKET SHARE
– MENTAL HEALTH STATUS SCORES
– PERCENTAGE OF RESPONSE TO OPEN POSITIONS

PROCESS
– INNOVATION PROCESS
– IMPROVEMENT GOALS
– REVENUE GOALS
– LINE OF BUSINESS EFFICIENCY
– AGGEGRATION OF MARGINAL GOALS

TOOLS
– LEAD-TO-CONVERSION RATE
– SALES BY LEAD SOURCE
– SHOPPING CART CONVERSION RATES
– SHOPPING CART ABANDONMENT RATES
– INBOUND CALLS PER REPRESENTATIVE
– OUTBOUND CALLS PER REPRESENTATIVE

TECHNOLOGY
– ACTIVE DIRECTORY PERFORMANCE
– AVERAGE DATA CENTRE AVAILABILITY
– SYSTEM & NETWORK MEASUREMENT
– SERVICE DESK PERFORMANCE
– STORAGE UTILIZATION

calculate ETR for different departments or divisions – it's not unusual to see higher ETRs in different areas. It's tempting to assume that certain jobs will always be associated with high ETRs, but as we saw with Trader Joe's, you can take steps to keep ETR to a minimum.

- **Percentage of response to open positions** can provide information about a number of factors, and suggest action. For example, if response to your postings is low, consider changing up your postings to highlight the value propositions from the candidate's view. If response rates are high for accounting roles but low for sales roles, that gives you some clues as to what to investigate. Worst case scenario: response rates are low because your company has a poor reputation, such as negative reviews on Glassdoor. You may need to make some major changes to become an employer of choice.

LEVERAGING EXPONENTIAL ENERGY

You're probably aware of many ways to motivate your people to meet and exceed KPIs, but exponential energy may be new to you. It's a way of making a positive move that impacts as many people as possible, in the tradition of 'more bang for your buck'. Here's an example.

As Decision Toolbox was making the transition from sticks-and-bricks to remote, they would have in-person holiday parties to get everyone together. One year, many of the recruiters requested business cards. At the time, Kim felt that the cards would serve a dual purpose: to promote business development, but also to give reassurance to the newly remote employees that they were, in fact, an important part of the company.

Then it occurred to her that those cards could serve a third purpose. At the party, Kim played Santa Claus and passed all the cards out, including giving a box to Nicole Cox, Director of Recruitment, and Loren Miner, Vice President of Finance. Nicole and Loren both responded to the effect that, 'I don't need these – I have plenty.' Kim replied, 'Open the box.'

Inside were the business cards of the new Chief Recruitment Officer and Chief Financial Officer. Kim used the occasion to let the two know they had been promoted. The box also included an individual note about increased salaries.

The entire team saw the look of surprise and joy on the faces of Nicole and Loren, and they got to be part of the surprise. This is where the exponential energy kicks in. Kim promoted only two people, but made an impact on the entire team. Not only did the team get to see how their leadership team recognized and rewarded performance, but they also saw how it was done in a fun and creative way, consistent with the Decision Toolbox culture.

If you've ever seen the movie *Finding Forrester*, you may recall the scene where William Forrester (played by Sean Connery) gives a piece of advice to Jamal Wallace (Rob Brown): 'The key to a woman's heart is an unexpected gift at an unexpected time' (Movieclips, 2012). We feel that it works for anyone, irrespective of gender.

The examples show that by taking an extra five minutes to be creative, leaders can create exponential positive energy. You should have lots of opportunities to do this, assuming you celebrate *everything*: new sales wins, exceeding targets, exceptional praise from customers – and even boo-boos.

Processes

When designed well, processes help you stay focused, keep things from falling through the cracks and ensure accountability. Every process should support a deliverable or set of deliverables, and each should help you deliver at a targeted level 80 per cent of the time. The data you gather as you assess processes can help you identify and solve specific issues (such as in root cause analysis) and also help you identify and address long-term trends. Some key processes to assess include:

- **Innovation goals,** which involve doing or creating something new that drives business value. Significant or major innovative goals include things such as designing a new product from the ground up or targeting a new market sector. Less ambitious – but still potentially valuable – goals might include incremental product enhancements. For example, Coca-Cola regularly releases variations on its key product, like Coca-Cola® Cherry or Coca-Cola® Zero Sugar, helping to keep a 130-year-old brand fresh and relevant. Either way, innovation goals can typically be broken down into sub-goals.

- **Improvement goals** focus on existing resources and processes, and making them better. There are a variety of continuous improvement methodologies available, such as lean manufacturing, Six Sigma, Kaizen, 5S and others. Most emerged from manufacturing, but can be applied to other business processes. Note that all such methodologies involve establishing and monitoring metrics. Leaders, employees and teams can – and should – establish and pursue improvement goals as well. This can involve, among

unlikely that there is a single change that can be made in order to jump to that goal overnight. If the leader simply tells the team, 'Here's your goal, make it happen', the team is likely to experience the same performance-disabling anxiety as the fifth graders in Jody's class.

Instead, the leader can identify multiple areas in which to make small adjustments. These might include increasing customer retention, discovering new ways to leverage their CRM and other tools, revising the value proposition based on customer data and others.

You can even break metrics into smaller components. For example, most sales teams monitor win rates, but if you look more closely, you might discover that the wins frequently drop off just before the deal closes. What is happening at that point? What can you and the team do differently to minimize that drop-off?

Tools

Your people use tools to help them achieve goals, and any tool should help your people be more efficient and effective. A particular tool should enhance the performance of at least 80 per cent of the people who use it. Here are some examples of ways to monitor and measure the efficacy of tools:

- **Lead-to-conversion rates** help you assess lead generation tools like HubSpot, Unbounce and Lucky Orange. There are many lead gen tools out there, and you should be using several – but you need to know which ones are working for you and which ones aren't. These tools come with analytics built in, allowing you to measure lead-to-conversion and other metrics.

- **Sales by lead source** is another metric for assessing the tools mentioned above, as well as other lead sources, such as referrals and social media marketing. This information is helpful in knowing where to focus your efforts, whether that is increased attention to your most fruitful sources or strategizing to increase leads from lower-performing sources.

- **Shopping cart conversion rates** help you compare the number of orders actually placed by online customers compared to the number of orders started but not placed. Your suite of e-commerce tools should include this metric. If the rate is low, it could be that the tool you're using isn't the best one for you, but it can also suggest some tactical responses, like offering free shipping or free returns, or making your forms easier to fill out.

- **Shopping cart abandonment rates** provide insight into the flip side of conversion rates. If abandonment rate is high, it might be an indication that your checkout process is complicated or untrustworthy.

- **Inbound or outbound calls per representative** are among many metrics to assess your telephony tools, such as an interactive voice response (IVR) or auto-dialler system.

Of course, you can create tools to suit your purposes, and if you don't have the tool-building talent on your team, you can work with a contractor. For example, at Decision Toolbox, Kim's email signature would include a link to schedule time on her calendar. You may have that now, from applications like ScheduleOnce and Calendly. However, back in the early 2000s, there weren't any commercial versions available.

Fortunately for Kim, her Decision Toolbox partner Jay Barnett was a tech whizz. He and his small IT team created the calendaring tool for Kim years before the commercial ones came out. In fact, Jay and team created Recruiting Machine, an ERP/CRM/HRIS platform still used by the company. It started as an internal tool – Jay and Kim didn't feel the commercially available ones were right for their needs – and today the owners, Engage2Excel Recruitment Solutions, lease Recruiting Machine in a software-as-a-service (SaaS) model.

Technology

Most aspects of business are transacted using technology, so it is essential that you monitor how well your technology is working for you:

- **Active Directory performance.** Microsoft's Active Directory (AD) is at the heart of many organizations' IT infrastructure, and some estimate that 95 per cent of Fortune 500 companies use it (Delmonico, 2016). Even small businesses using this ubiquitous technology should be monitoring KPIs such as service outages, mission-critical processes and more.

- **Average data centre availability** is a way of knowing how well your data centre is performing. Whether you have a small 'server farm' on-site or you contract with an external provider, availability impacts all your digital processes. KPIs should include quality, quantity and responsiveness measures.

- **Availability** is a metric that can be applied to most aspects of your IT infrastructure, including servers, networks, hardware, applications and others. Often it is calculated as uptime divided by (uptime plus downtime). An uptime rating of five 9s, or 99.999 per cent, is considered an excellent measure.

- **System and network administration measures** help ensure that the IT team is keeping things up to date, secure and optimized. Such measures include percentage of data back-up success and percentage of patches/ updates completed.

- **Service or support desk performance** is important, and measures include client satisfaction, time to resolve issues, issue resolution rate and others.

- **Storage utilization** measures how efficiently your organization uses your data storage resources. These may include the percentage of storage used in periods of peak demand, average time to store or retrieve files, average size of files stored and retrieved and more.

GETTING THE MOST OUT OF TECHNOLOGY

PeopleG2 has always taken an aggressive approach to technology. According to Chris, 'As a company we will try just about anything in the hopes of finding a new cool feature, an advantage in the marketplace or just an efficiency to be more productive. We were one of the first companies to use a system called HipChat, later purchased by Slack. Although we now use and love Slack (a foundational part of our technology), early adoption of this platform allowed us to communicate faster, asynchronously, and document along the way. This was the first time that the Quora or Reddit style of communication was brought into a format for business. In Quora or Reddit a question is asked, and people reply to create a thread. This allows someone else to come along and read that thread and even see the most popular answer.

'At PeopleG2, HipChat allowed us to create the threads in advance by topic, such as customer service, sales and accounting – not to mention our famous water cooler channel, where we send thank you notes and green flags. Not everyone can or wants to be on a call or video chat. Sometimes just reading and responding, in writing, can get us far enough without disrupting productivity or performance.

'Today, HipChat has been absorbed into Slack. The power of collaboration technology to help us run a business is not only important, but transformative. In Slack we can connect and access Google, OneDrive, thousands of integrations with Zapier, and social media. Employees can display emojis and funny gifs, track and create their timecards, ask FAQs to a knowledge-based internal bot, schedule out-of-(home)-office time, display their active status and search for past conversations and documents. The platform also helps us host weekly trivia games for the whole company.'

We believe these tips will help you and your company get up to speed and maintain momentum as we press on. Next up: let's talk about profit and people.

References

Clear, J (2018) *Atomic Habits: An easy and proven way to build good habits and break bad ones*, Avery, New York City

Delmonico, D (2016) Need to tame your active directory beast? Automate! *IT Briefcase*, 29 August, www.itbriefcase.net/need-to-tame-your-active-directory-beast-automate (archived at https://perma.cc/4YX7-ZYDS)

Duke, A (2018) *Thinking in Bets: Making smarter decisions when you don't have all the facts*, Portfolio, New York

Forer, B R (1949) The fallacy of personal validation: A classroom demonstration of gullibility, *The Journal of Abnormal and Social Psychology*, http://apsychoserver.psych.arizona.edu/JJBAReprints/PSYC621/Forer_The%20fallacy%20of%20personal%20validation_1949.pdf (archived at https://perma.cc/A9PS-MN42)

Jeon, S W and Kim, Y-K (2018) Application of assessment tools to examine mental health in workplaces: Job stress and depression, *Psychiatry Investigation*, www.ncbi.nlm.nih.gov/pmc/articles/PMC6018143 (archived at https://perma.cc/JN9Z-ACRH)

Kahneman, D, Slovic, P and Tversky, A (1982) *Judgment Under Uncertainty: Heuristics and biases*, Cambridge University Press, Cambridge

Kim, W C and Mauborgne, R (2015) *Blue Ocean Strategy*, Harvard Business Review Press, Boston

Lexico.com (nd) Key performance indicator, www.lexico.com/definition/key_performance_indicator (archived at https://perma.cc/YM4Q-RENZ)

London Business Forum (2016) Sir Dave Brailsford – The 1% factor (online video) www.youtube.com/watch?v=NQxYlu12ji8 (archived at https://perma.cc/T7XV-Y52H)

Meehl, P E (1956) Wanted – a good cook, *American Psychologist*, http://meehl.umn.edu/sites/meehl.dl.umn.edu/files/039cookbook.pdf (archived at https://perma.cc/C7DD-FEBE)

Mental Health America (2017) Mind the workplace, https://www.mhanational.org/sites/default/files/Mind%20the%20Workplace%20-%20MHA%20Workplace%20Health%20Survey%202017%20FINAL.pdf (archived at https://perma.cc/H585-NLLH)

Movieclips (2012) *Finding Forrester* movie clip – the Pulitzer Prize (online video) www.youtube.com/watch?v=A_lu5jmaUbU (archived at https://perma.cc/9UWL-QY9V)

Poe, E A (1844) *The System of Doctor Tarr and Professor Fether* (2017 reprint), CreateSpace Independent Publishing Platform, Scotts Valley, California

17

Profit and people

The information here is really targeted at CEOs and founders more than, say, chief human resources officers. However, the examples of strategic thinking should be instructive for any reader. In fact, at the risk of sounding like a broken record, the examples show the importance of *thinking deliberately and strategically* about everything you do.

IN THIS CHAPTER

- Let's talk money
- Kim's exit strategy
- Let's talk people

Let's talk money

The motivations for making money differ from person to person and, as a company leader, your motivation will depend on and shape the kind of company you are creating. We're going to provide some insight into planning for, managing and using money, so be sure you understand the type of business you have. These are the main types of businesses:

- A **lifestyle company** or lifestyle business has a central, defining strategy: to provide the owner with enough income to maintain their chosen lifestyle. Typically, lifestyle companies are smaller and more often involved in services or distribution rather than manufacturing. Examples include online drop-ship businesses and consulting agencies.

- A **growth company** allows the owner to reinvest in the business and to attract certain investors. To be a growth company, the business has to have a strong positive cash flow that increases faster than the overall economy or competitors. Many technology companies, such as Google, are growth companies.

- An **exit strategy company** is one in which the end goal of the owner or owners is selling the company for a profit. Typically the owner aims for a specific target, such as a certain level of revenue or market share percentage, and sells the company once they hit the target. Decision Toolbox is a great example of an exit strategy company, and we'll get into more detail on that company shortly.

Now that you understand the type of business you have, here are some considerations regarding handling money.

Pay yourself first

After all, you are investing time, energy and money, along with blood, sweat and tears, in either starting a virtual company or taking your existing company remote. This is, by definition, critical in a lifestyle company. Once the business is up and running, you need cash for operational costs and payroll. How to pay yourself in this model depends on a lot of factors – more factors than we have time to discuss here. The average annual salary for a small business owner in the United States is about $70,000, and some entrepreneurs take no salary in the first year (Payscale, 2020). However, Bryan Borzykowski (2020), an author focused on small business and investing, recommends that you set up at least a modest monthly salary.

In a growth business, assuming it is successful, the owner should be able to have a salary and a share of the profits. We referred to the tech industry above as examples of growth businesses, and quintessential examples of entrepreneurs living the growth company dream are Amazon's Jeff Bezos and Microsoft's Bill Gates. Of course, they represent the exception rather than the rule, so in your early startup days you should include a reasonable salary for yourself.

KIM'S EXIT STRATEGY

When Kim became partners with Jay Barnett in Decision Toolbox, they set a goal of growing the business to $10 million in revenue, and then selling it. Kim originally hoped it would take six years, but with the ups and downs of the economy, it actually took 18 years. She had to flex and adapt through those years, but one thing she could always depend on was the end goal.

Kim's experience is an example of why being strategic and deliberate is important in defining that end goal. Your goal gives you something to look forward to and keep yourself motivated. When things got tough, Kim would tell herself that, as soon as they reached that goal, she would have the time and resources to do whatever she wanted every day – even go to Disneyland.

With the exit strategy as a starting point, Kim and Jay could then set additional goals, which included:

- nurturing a unique company with an upbeat and fun culture – the kind of culture they wanted to work in;

- developing and refining an efficient, process-oriented approach to recruiting that distinguished them from high-priced competitors;

- creating and leveraging technology to make the recruiters' jobs easier and to keep costs down.

A thought may have already crossed your mind: what happens to the employees when the owners exit? Having an exit strategy created an emotional tug-of-war for Kim, between moving towards the end goal while also creating a tight-knit culture with highly engaged and strongly loyal employees. Ultimately, however, her advice is: don't be ashamed to set your exit strategy early.

Take the time to dream and define your goal, and then work hard to achieve it. Remember the sacrifices you are making to run a successful business, such as mortgaging your home for capital. As for the employees, keeping your exit strategy to yourself is probably best. We advocate transparency, but some things don't need to be shared with employees. In a sense, your exit strategy is part of that space where personal and business meet. We feel it lands in the personal category and is therefore private. In addition, being transparent about your exit strategy might undermine the sense of psychological safety that is so important for your employees. When Kim and Jay sold Decision Toolbox to Engage2Excel in 2016, all employees had the option to keep their jobs, and almost all stayed with the new organization.

The goal of creating technology, mentioned above, had a significant impact on the sale price of Decision Toolbox. The company originally developed an internal platform that combined elements of enterprise resource planning (ERP), applicant tracking (ATS) and human resources information systems (HRIS). Eventually they packaged it as Recruiting Machine and offered it to customers in a software-as-a-service (SaaS) model.

While Decision Toolbox was essentially a recruitment services company, Recruiting Machine made them also a technology company. When businesses are bought and sold, an earnings multiple is often used to arrive at a price. That is, you would multiply the earnings base of the company by the earnings multiple. Earnings multiples vary by industry, and for service companies like recruiting firms, investors usually use an earnings multiple of 3X. In contrast, for technology companies, the earnings multiple can be 10X. Because of Decision Toolbox's hybrid nature, Kim and Jay secured an earnings multiplier of 8.5X.

Avoid shiny objects

Stay true to your goal and avoid 'shiny objects' or offers and opportunities that look great but are likely to derail you in reaching the goal. For example, in 2016, Google reportedly offered to acquire Snapchat for $30 billion (Thubron, 2017). No typo there – that's 'billion' with a 'B'. A few years before that, Facebook supposedly had offered $3 billion, and Google had tried to outbid them by offering $4 billion (Souppouris, 2013).

So why didn't Snapchat CEO Evan Spiegel accept any of these offers? Certainly $30 billion is a *very* shiny object. According to Aaron Souppouris (2013), Spiegel was, in fact, considering a strategic alliance with Google, but declined the offers because Snapchat revenues were growing stronger. Perhaps he was interested in attracting strategic investors but not interested in being acquired outright. The point is, Spiegel stuck to his goals.

Pricing strategies

In Chapter 16 we talked about how to define your strategic advantage, and price plays a role in that definition. Here we want to point out that your pricing strategy should support your end goals. Recall that, at Decision Toolbox, pricing was a key part of the company's strategic advantage and helped support the exit strategy.

Kim knew she was leading a small company in competition with some very large recruiting agencies, like Robert Half, Korn Ferry and Adecco – all multi-billion-dollar companies with high-profile reputations and significant market share. If she was going to get little Decision Toolbox to $10 million, she was going to have to get over, around or through the industry Goliaths.

Along with partner Jay Barnett, Kim decided to embrace being small but with the smarts and spirit of David. They identified a hole in the Swiss cheese of the recruiting industry: few agencies were offering a low price. Kim and Jay then created a boutique recruiting firm with a low fee + high volume approach. The big companies would charge 20 to 30 per cent of an open position's salary, so Decision Toolbox offered to fill the same positions for 8 per cent of salary.

The low fees brought in the volume and helped them march steadily towards the $10 million target. But there was more to making this model work. To deliver $30,000 results for $8,000, Decision Toolbox had to be very, very efficient. We already talked about how their technology, Recruiting Machine, helped them with efficiency. But Kim also knew that clients would have to adapt to the model.

'If you want to save $22,000,' Kim told prospective clients, 'You have to be an active participant in the recruiting process, not a spectator.' Hiring managers, for example, had to provide timely feedback on candidates without the Decision Toolbox team hounding them. They also had to use Recruiting Machine throughout the process, to review résumés, provide feedback and more.

A company paying $30,000 can expect the vendor to adapt to them. But at a significantly lower price, Kim was able to compel them to become a partner more than a client. To give you an analogy, if you pay $125 for a massage at a high-end spa, you can expect little extras like Egyptian cotton towels, complimentary refreshments and more. However, you can get the same massage for $15 around the corner, just without the extras. Decision Toolbox provided exactly the same core service as their bigger competitors – qualified candidates to fill open positions – but without the spa extras.

By making clients into partners, Kim promoted a lot of repeat business, helping keep the volume and the revenue high. In contrast, as we've noted previously, Chris's approach at PeopleG2 is to appeal to companies that want background checks completed PLUS high-end customer service.

The takeaway here is, whatever your pricing strategy – basic, mid-level or luxury – define it and stick to it. But make sure it supports your overall goal. As entrepreneur Elon Musk, leader of Tesla and SpaceX, puts it, 'If you're entering anything where there's an existing marketplace, against large, entrenched competitors, then your product or service needs to be much better than theirs. It can't just be slightly better. It's got to be a lot better' (Bariso, 2017).

Fund initiatives

Now that you have set your goals and set your own salary, you should put careful thought into dividing up your profit pool. As a remote company, you will be saving in a number of areas in which your sticks-and-bricks competitors must spend, such as office space, furniture, payroll for positions like receptionist, and more.

One part of the profit pool can be set aside for initiatives and new ideas, essentially reinvesting in the company. Chris does this in a couple of ways at PeopleG2. He has a small fund in the marketing budget to allow the company to try things that may be viable, but also may be blue sky. For example, they recently created a marketing strategy to target a certain demographic that isn't really their main target audience. However, the demographic includes people who *influence* the target decision makers.

Another built-in fund originates from the tech side of the business and supports his sales team in experimenting and enhancing their efforts. Part of the PeopleG2 model includes integrating their system into the ATS and HRIS platforms of clients. Although paying programmers to create the integration bridge is a cost, Chris doesn't treat integration simply as a cost centre. Instead, he treats it as a business-within-the-business, and looks at how the integration generates profit as well.

Then 5 per cent of that profit is set aside for the sales team as a fund to pay for tactics and strategies that will bring in more business. In addition, Chris empowers the sales team to use the fund at their own discretion, without having to get permission. The fund is not only a great use of money, but the fund's existence and intent sends a message that Chris trusts his team to do the right thing.

Sharing the wealth

Many factors are involved in motivating and engaging employees, like recognition, culture and professional development opportunities. But pay is the most important. Dr Jack Wiley is an author, consultant, researcher and instructor who has focused his career on two big research questions: what do employees most want and what organizational factors best promote employee engagement, performance confidence and business success? Dr Wiley used 30 years of employee survey data to develop his RESPECT model (Wiley and Kowske, 2011), indicating that the most important things to employees are recognition, exciting work, security, pay, education and career opportunities, conditions and truth. 'Pay' may come fourth in RESPECT, but it is actually the most important item on the list – 25 per cent of the respondents ranked pay as highest, followed by recognition (20 per cent) and security (19 per cent).

You know already that there are different compensation schemes for different types of employees, such as commission plans for salespeople, bonuses, stock options for executives, and so on. As you construct your compensation plan, keep in mind two points:

- The best way to spend money is to share it with your best people, in the form of bonuses, raises or other rewards. This approach rewards the right people for the right behaviour – setting an example for others – and elevates the recipient's motivation and engagement.
- Replacing any employee is expensive and replacing your top people is especially expensive. A bonus or raise is an investment in retention.

You can also use bonuses to create exponential energy. Recall the way Kim did this with her VP of Recruitment and VP of Finance, as we described in the previous chapter.

Kim created another way of investing in business development: a channel partner programme. Decision Toolbox was too lean to have a formal sales team, so that job fell mostly to Kim. To get help, she reached out to her network, which included many people in or near human resources and recruitment. The offer: if you tell people about Decision Toolbox and they become a client, you will get a percentage of the revenue.

They didn't have to take a hard-sell approach; instead, they could just say, 'Decision Toolbox is good, fast and cheap. Here's Kim's number.' Others at Decision Toolbox pushed back on the idea, but it was successful. The company only had to pay out when it worked, and the programme brought in about $1 million in revenue each year.

Right size, right time

Another money consideration concerns the size and makeup of your team. For example, if you are a startup, consider bringing on generalist employees rather than specialists. In the early running, you and perhaps one partner have specialist expertise. However, if you hire several more specialists, you create a high risk that the basic, nuts-and-bolts tasks of running the company won't get done. If you need additional specialized support, consider outsourcing. This advice applies to companies at any stage of life. For example, Chris outsources both IT and marketing rather than bringing them into the company full-time.

At some point, whether you are running a startup or an established growing company, you'll be faced with expanding the infrastructure. Infrastructure may include tools, technologies or people. This decision is a tight-rope walk: if you expand too soon, you may decimate your cash flow, and if you wait too long, your operations may slow.

Ultimately, however, you have to decide for yourself. For example, conventional wisdom says that a small business should wait until the $5 million mark to expand. Kim, always suspicious of conventional wisdom, brought in a VP of Finance at $1.5 million. The members of her CEO roundtable warned her against it, but her reasoning was sound. At that time, Kim was balancing her CEO role with responsibilities on the finance side. The financial responsibilities began to interfere with business development efforts. She hired Loren Miner, a CPA, to oversee finances as well as operations, which freed Kim to focus on what she does best: business development.

While we can't tell you exactly when to expand, we have two pieces of advice. One is to think in terms of what you do best, as in the example above. Another is to plan ahead for your next organization chart expansion and run the numbers against your goals. If you feel you are on the cusp, but you're not quite sure, you can use outsourced vendors. If you were right and you continue to grow, you can replace the vendor with employees. If you were wrong, you can let the vendors go much more easily than terminating an employee contract.

This brings up an important point, especially if you are a startup or small business: if you are going to add another person at the leadership level, make sure they complement your own strengths. Kim is not a numbers person, so bringing on a finance professional made good sense. In fact, if you dig into it, you'll find that most successful CEOs have a background in either sales or finance. Call it covering your behind or knowing your blind spot, but if you are sales oriented, your number two leader should be cut from the numbers cloth, and vice versa. Importantly, whatever role your number two plays, make sure they own it completely. That way, you are free to do your job.

Another aspect of growth that can be challenging is determining whether your existing staff are the right team for the next level. Perhaps you have a team member who has been with you since the beginning, and who was instrumental in helping the company get to this point. However, your company's needs change as you grow – for example, you now need more

management, feedforward coaching *doesn't* involve assessing the past year's performance. Instead, it focuses on employee growth and development, an important factor in employee engagement. This type of discussion is an ongoing process that focuses on goals rather than standards. Goals should be set through a collaboration between manager and employee, and should be agile to change as situations change.

In addition, you should help your managers incorporate these suggestions:

- empowering with intention;
- focusing on teamwork and collaboration;
- focusing on behaviours you want by rewarding what is working and in line with company values;
- helping others;
- putting the client first;
- exceeding goals and KPIs;
- remembering the long-term career conversations;
- making the conversation a two-way street.

What employees want but won't tell you

These suggestions are more on the subjective side but are important. Chris's interest in this area is driven in part by his work as a consultant. In several cases involving diverse companies, he was asked to help reduce unusually high turnover rates. To uncover the causes, Chris conducted exit interviews with former employees as well as interviews with high-value and/or high-risk employees. He consistently found two things: there are things employees simply won't tell their supervisors and supervisors often assume that employees will and do share all their concerns.

However, if your employees don't get the things listed below from you, they are likely to find another job where they can get them. For a long time, Millennials had a reputation as job-hoppers, and hiring managers and human resources professionals blamed them for being entitled and spoiled. However, this is simply part of the Me, Inc. mentality: if this employer isn't giving me what I want, I'll find it elsewhere (Alton, 2018).

Here are some reasons Millennials and members of other generations leave within six months:

- the recruitment process was complicated and impersonal;
- the onboarding process was terrible;
- they feel pressure to agree and fit in… immediately;
- they lack a designated person to help them;
- they don't like their new boss.

With employees of all generations, it pays for managers/coaches to ask, 'What do you expect and need?' Here are some things we believe will be on employees' lists of what they desire from their managers:

- be brave;
- be inspiring;
- be upfront;
- be compassionate;
- be open;
- be okay with dissent;
- be the boss, not the friend;
- be clear;
- be rigid about the big stuff;
- be flexible about the small stuff;
- support work–life fusion.

In both consulting and in leading PeopleG2, Chris emphasizes that leaders need to let employees know that they value challenging feedback. For employees to perceive value requires that the employer emphasize creating trust and a safe psychological environment. Employees need to know that they can share frankly without fear of repercussions. For example, an employee might say, 'It seems like you are disorganized, and it is making my work difficult.' When an employee has a bad boss, they really only have two choices: leave or speak up. Make sure your people know you want to hear what they have to say.

What to look for

This is a good place to revisit some suggestions from Chapter 11, about what qualities are likely to help remote employees be successful:

- Hire proactive and not reactive people. If a person will just sit at their desk until someone gives them a task, they are the wrong person.
- Look for people who can prioritize effectively, and coach the rest of your team in this valuable skill.
- Find people who aren't afraid to ask questions – unless they ask too many.
- Hire people who have remote experience already, such as running a side business (freelancing or an online storefront) or working in the field. They'll have a head start.
- Look for experience with Scrum, Agile, Kaizen or other continuous improvement methodologies.
- Enforce a strict 'no jerks' policy. Hire people you want to work with.

A few other points, and then we will discuss an exercise for you to do. First, for many roles, you can interview candidates by phone or, even better, via video conference. However, for executives and other key roles, you probably want to do an in-person interview. Second, great candidates don't mind being tested – in fact, in our experience, most prefer it. Third, don't forget that being remote opens your candidate pool so you can include people in both rural and metro areas, military spouses, physically disabled people and other 'non-traditional' candidates.

TIGER TEAM EXERCISE

Leaders have a large portion of people's lives in their hands. Employees and managers spend at least a third of their weekday hours working and, for most people, work incorporates life goals as well as professional goals. For many, their work becomes part of their identity, both for their friends and family and for themselves, which is a big responsibility for you as a leader. This exercise will help you share a little of the responsibility with your employees, by gathering input.

As you recall from earlier in the book, a tiger team or Scrum session can be a great way to gather ideas and information. Here's what you do: depending on the size of your organization, divide the team up into multiple small groups of four or five. Ideally, create the groups so that they are cross-functional. Give each group a question about the relationship between employees and the company and let them brainstorm for an hour. The questions should ask for multiple suggestions. For example, you might ask:

- Imagine your perfect Me, Inc. world. What are the five most important elements shared by everyone in the group?
- What three things can the company provide that will make your work easier and more effective?
- Imagine you have $1 million to invest in improving the company. What are five ways the group would spend it?

When the hour is up, have each group share their answer. You should gain some valuable insights into your company culture and processes, and you probably will get some great ideas. Be sure to implement at least some of them, to ensure the team knows you listen and care.

Hopefully this chapter has made it clear that profit and people are connected in many ways. Regarding money and profit, you should pay yourself fairly, create an exit strategy, set aside funding for situations that arise, be strategic about growth and share the wealth with those who help generate it. And since it is the people who help you generate the profits and the success, you should be proactive not only about knowing what they want but also about giving it to them.

In the next chapter, we'll list some of the questions you should be asking yourself as you move forward. One question right now: have you signed up at https://chrisdyer.com/remotework? We're looking forward to hearing from you.

References

Alton, L (2018) Millennials aren't job hopping, young people are: 5 things to keep in mind, *Forbes*, 22 January, www.forbes.com/sites/larryalton/2018/01/22/millennials-arent-job-hopping-young-people-are-5-things-to-keep-in-mind/#640096ea10d8 (archived at https://perma.cc/H8BN-9YAU)

Bariso, J (2017) It took Elon Musk just 3 minutes to give the best business advice you'll hear today, *Inc.com*, 9 November, https://www.inc.com/justin-bariso/it-took-elon-musk-just-3-minutes-to-give-best-business-advice-youll-hear-today.html (archived at https://perma.cc/TY3V-DZ8B)

Borzykowski, B (2020) This is how much to pay yourself if you run your own business, *CNBC*, 29 February, www.cnbc.com/2020/02/28/this-is-how-much-to-pay-yourself-as-a-business-owner.html (archived at https://perma.cc/9PSS-83W3)

Buono, J (2018) Why your managers should be like coaches (not bosses), *Gallup*, www.gallup.com/access/243359/why-managers-coaches-not-bosses.aspx (archived at https://perma.cc/74TF-4PAZ)

Gallup (2020) Working remotely: Careers, management and strategy, www.gallup.com/workplace/316313/understanding-and-managing-remote-workers.aspx#ite-316508 (archived at https://perma.cc/H4JS-CPAF)

Kruse, K (2012) Stop giving feedback, instead give feedforward, *Forbes*, 19 July, www.forbes.com/sites/kevinkruse/2012/07/19/feedforward-coaching-for-performance/#7c5f46db235d (archived at https://perma.cc/NN4T-YYDG)

Payscale (2020) Average small business owner salary, www.payscale.com/research/US/Job=Small_Business_Owner/Salary (archived at https://perma.cc/U7AY-R92V)

Purdue University Global (2020) Generational differences in the workplace (infographic), www.purdueglobal.edu/education-partnerships/generational-workforce-differences-infographic (archived at https://perma.cc/6ZUF-DJPN)

Souppouris, A (2013) Google reportedly tried to outbid Facebook for Snapchat with $4 billion offer, *The Verge*, 15 November, www.theverge.com/2013/11/15/5106950/google-snapchat-4-billion-buyout-rumor (archived at https://perma.cc/U5LZ-EZL4)

Sutton, R and Wigert, B (2019) More harm than good: The truth about performance reviews, *Gallup*, 6 May, www.gallup.com/workplace/249332/harm-good-truth-performance-reviews.aspx (archived at https://perma.cc/XQE7-SFED)

Thubron, R (2017) Google reportedly tried to buy Snapchat for $30 billion, *TechSpot*, 4 August, www.techspot.com/news/70437-google-reportedly-tried-buy-snapchat-30-billion-last.html (archived at https://perma.cc/34K7-67HX)

Wiley, J and Kowske, B (2011) *RESPECT: Delivering results by giving employees what they really want*, Pfeiffer, Hoboken, New Jersey

18

Questions you should be asking yourself

A good leader pauses regularly to ask, 'What am I missing? What don't I know that I should?' The following are answers to questions that we asked ourselves, or were asked by others. The list is not exhaustive, so don't stop stepping back, taking in the big view, and asking yourself those questions.

IN THIS CHAPTER

We will cover:

- FAQs about going remote
- FAQs about operations
- FAQs about culture
- FAQs about leadership

Questions about going remote

How do I know if remote is for me?

We recommend you review Chapter 3, where we tried to be blunt about the challenges of taking your company remote. We both went remote out of necessity in response to a crisis, but we both now believe it made our companies stronger. But we recognize that it is not for everyone.

If you are not facing a crisis, then you have to weigh the advantages and disadvantages. You and your company will have to invest time and effort in a significant transition that may last a year. If you don't anticipate a positive return on that investment, or if you are not excited and enthusiastic about the growth potential inherent in change, you might want to stay in the office.

What is the most impactful thing I can do when I start a remote team/ company?

Create a recognition programme and/or habits to let your employees know that you value them. Recognition isn't about material rewards but about celebrating wins and saying thank you – all the time. Recognition is very important to employees and should start *before* the actual hire, during recruitment and onboarding. Engage2Excel and Dr Jack Wiley (we mentioned him in Chapter 17 – he is the one with 30 years of research into what employees want) conducted a survey of 1,500 job seekers and found that they believe praise and recognition are important during the pre-offer (67 per cent), post-offer (54 per cent), onboarding (56 per cent) and post-onboarding (77 per cent) phases (Engage2Excel, 2017). Further, the authors found that the number one reason employees leave a company is lack of respect, followed by compensation and job fit.

Recognition doesn't have to be extravagant. You can post kudos in the water cooler room of your chat platform or mention successes at team meetings. You might create a name for wins and successes, as Kim did with 'green flags'. In the next chapter, we'll tell you the innovative way she came up with the name (for now we'll just say it involved monkeys), but at Decision Toolbox, a green-flag email went out whenever they got a new project or whenever they filled an open position for a client.

You don't have to track kudos or keep score, and you don't need to give a gift card or physical gift. Sometimes a gift is appropriate, but kudos is just a way of saying 'great job' and sharing it with the company.

Another important thing to do from day one is to clearly define your culture. You can refer back to Chapter 13 for more insight, but you and your team need to be crystal clear and aligned on what your culture is and how it can be expressed.

What if I have a fixed team that is moving to remote, where do we start?

An important early step is to talk with your team about how things will be different at your company going forward. Chapter 2 dives deep into the new ways of thinking required in remote work. Remote work is a significant change, and you'll need to manage that change carefully and deliberately.

When Chris took PeopleG2 from office to remote, he and his team planned extensively, and then enacted the change all at once – almost like ripping off a Band-Aid®. However, if you have a large company, you may want to roll out the change incrementally. You might go remote one department at a time, so that teams are all on the same page. Consider starting with the departments that you feel will handle the transition best. Ask them to document what worked well and what didn't, so that the departments transitioning later can learn from the previous ones.

How do things get communicated across long-distance or anachronistic teams?

With team members in different time zones, you can't expect everyone to work the same hours. You need a way to document and record important information, and share it with those who are, for example, sleeping when other teammates are having a meeting. Chat platforms are a great solution here – designate a space for sharing information.

You also can schedule short standup meetings at 'shift change', like nursing staff do in hospitals, to download/upload information. However, consider whether or not an actual meeting is needed. If the information can be shared in an email or chat, that's one less meeting on your people's calendars.

You might recall from the Buffer case study in Chapter 10 that they used video messages to communicate across time zones. Many find this type of handoff easier than writing things down, and the video format enhances communication by displaying personalities, intonations and body language. Kim's VP of Creative, Joanna Sherriff, moved to New Zealand, putting her a full day ahead of the rest of her team in the US. Joanna worked unique hours to get some overlap with her team, and Kim would talk with her daily to ensure she was always up to speed.

One word of caution: if Team A, in North America, always expects Team B, in Asia, to join calls at off hours, tell them to switch it up and take turns. You'll find that Team A will become more empathetic, and the two teams are likely to come up with an even better solution that works for everyone.

Do people have to be on video? Or what if people won't turn on their video?

We recommend you establish a policy to clarify expectations. Call a tiger team session so that the team can decide together, whatever the decision is. Some things to consider in the tiger team:

- A videoconference usually means that people need to pay attention to their appearance, such as shaving or putting on mascara. Even if the policy says don't worry about that, some team members may still feel pressure to do so.

- Not all meetings need video. If you choose to use video to promote connections, consider alternating between video and phone meetings.

- Video offers the chance to share a smile. According to Ronald E Riggio, Professor of Leadership and Organizational Psychology at Claremont McKenna College, seeing a smile or (especially) smiling yourself activates neurotransmitters like oxytocin and endorphins in your brain (Riggio, 2012), a chemical cocktail that relaxes you and lowers heart rate and blood pressure.

- If the meeting involves strategy, deep thinking or brainstorming, consider making the video mandatory, so that the leader can 'read the room', albeit virtually.

- You might include, in your policy, the option to let individuals say, 'I can't do video today', with no questions asked. If you find people are doing this too often, you can set a limit, such as twice a month (depending on the frequency of the meetings).

Questions about business strategy

When will I know that my efforts are successful?

The simple answer is: when you hit your targets. Like most things, however, the answer isn't that simple. First of all, hitting a target almost always involves achieving a series of subsidiary targets. Remember Dave Brailsford's work with the British Cycling team in Chapter 16 (Clear, 2018)? He determined that champions weren't made from a single burst at the finish but from hundreds of incremental changes.

You should constantly reflect on what is going well and what is not and make adjustments to your subsidiary targets accordingly. Flexibility is an absolute necessity in the constantly changing business landscape.

Should I set my targets in stone or keep them fluid?

This question is an extension of the previous question and answer. For the most part we feel your end goal – your exit strategy – should remain constant to serve as a steady beacon. What can and often should change are the sub-targets and the action steps. However, even your end target can change. For example, let's say your exit strategy is to sell when you hit $20 million in revenue. You are currently at $19 million and starting to dream about the Turks and Caicos Islands. Your top salesperson comes to you and says, 'I'm working on a prospective deal that can take us to $30 million in two years.' Now is not the time to be stubborn.

At the same time, keep in mind that the deal is prospective, and this too can change. Be prepared to fall back to the original end target.

When is it time to consider an exit strategy?

Unless you are running a lifestyle company, you should define your exit strategy from the beginning. The exit strategy is your beacon and tells you where you are going. Without knowing that, you are simply wandering. You may turn a profit, but without a long-term goal it's not a business, but a hobby.

How long is my financial runway?

The best answer for this comes from our colleague Dave Berkus. We've mentioned him before. We both know him from our Adaptive Business Leaders (ABL) CEO roundtable, and he is a well-respected business consultant and angel investor. Dave addresses this question in his book *Extending the Runway* (2014) and compares running a company to flying a plane.

One of the first rules that new pilots learn is 'never run out of fuel'. Pilots not only check the tank but also calculate the rate of fuel used per hour, the length of the flight and the potential impact of wind and weather. In addition, they always add an extra 45 minutes' worth of fuel.

The point is, careful planning, including anticipating complications and problems, will help ensure you never crash – or run out of cash. But it's not a one-time planning session. Once you have plotted your fuel/cash usage over time, monitor it carefully to ensure you are on track and make adjustments before the engine starts to sputter.

To do this, use your experience and training and ask a lot of 'what if' and 'then what' questions to project your cash flow over both the short and long term. If you don't have strong financial savvy, get input from someone who does.

Money can disappear in unexpected ways, such as the loss of a major customer, market shifts, lawsuits or other involuntary expenses. As you plan, be aware that there are multiple sources of cash should you find yourself in a bind. More accessible cash sources include credit cards, slowing down payment to vendors, second and third home mortgages and taking on consulting gigs. Keep in mind, however, that these sources also carry significant risk. Other cash sources may be less accessible and may require the help of intermediaries. These resources include deal-packager finders, well-connected attorneys, venture capitalists and investment bankers.

Start building relationships *before* you need cash. Many funding sources will be available while the plane still has some fuel, but once the fuel has run out, funders will be more reluctant.

How do I determine what should be outsourced?

Chris uses outsourcing for different reasons. One reason is to get the help of an expert he can't afford to hire permanently but he can afford as a consultant. Plotting your cash flow might be a good time to seek out expert help. You could use this expert for a month or two to help you set up a system for predicting and tracking. Then, your own team can handle the execution moving forward. You get a fraction of an expert's time for a fraction of the cost.

Another reason to outsource is when your team doesn't have the bandwidth or expertise to handle complex issues. As a background check company, PeopleG2 handles a good deal of sensitive personal data. As you know, the stakes are high in this area, so Chris outsources cybersecurity. He might be able to bring cybersecurity inhouse for a little less money but he feels that outsourcing is worth it to protect people's data, his customers and his own company.

You also can use outsourcing as a bridge. In the previous chapter, we talked about how to decide when the time is right to expand your infrastructure. Instead of building a new call centre before you know that your new product will succeed, consider outsourcing customer service until your product does take off. Once the sales revenue justifies it, you can bring the function inhouse.

Kim used the bridge strategy when she was getting ready to expand, although what she did, technically, was insourcing. You may recall she brought Loren Miner onboard to provide both financial and operational support. However, for the first six months, Kim engaged Loren as a consultant rather than as an employee. This strategy provided Kim with two key advantages. First, while Kim paid Loren at a premium during those six months, Kim didn't have the same commitment to Loren that she would have had with a regular employee. Second, the outsourcing relationship created a 'try it before you buy it' situation for both sides. This tactic also can help you clarify what you need when hiring a regular employee.

Questions about operations

Why are things moving so slowly?

Chris worked as a consultant with Johnson & Johnson, IKEA, the United States Patent Office and others, and the issue of speed came up many times as those organizations deployed remote workforces. After going remote, leaders found that their teams weren't getting as much done as before – that's the opposite of what you should see in a remote setup. First, a couple of 'quick fixes':

- Stop having frequent one-on-one meetings. In the brick-and-mortar world, managers would pop by an employee's cubicle for a five-minute chat. But after going remote they were scheduling 30-minute meetings. Use platforms like Slack or Teams to replace the cubicle chat to get the right balance of communication and productivity.

- Stop having long video meetings. Some managers were holding three-hour meetings, sometimes without breaks. That's too long for people to remain focused. More importantly, long meetings keep people from doing their real jobs. Refer back to Chapter 15, where we discussed different kinds of meetings, and use the different types to ensure your meetings are effective and efficient.

Second, a longer-term fix is being deliberate about time management habits in the new remote setting. Kim got herself into the habit of using the think-launch-review method for different tasks, whether the task took 10 minutes or an hour. Here's the sequence:

- **Think** about your goals for the task, including understanding what the payout is. Consider the task in terms of return on investment (ROI) of time.

- **Launch** the execution of the plan and stick to it.

- **Review** when finished with the plan to make sure you have maximized your ROI. If not, what will you do differently next time?

You might even consider adding 'Reward' to this process. When you finish a larger task or several smaller tasks, pat yourself on the back. Reward yourself by getting a cup of coffee or taking the dog for a walk. Then get back to work refreshed.

What do I do when I'm having connectivity difficulties?

To be clear, here we're not talking about helpdesk problems like password resets but about a situation where you can't connect with the company systems. Maybe your power is out, your internet is down or your computer has crashed.

You need to prepare in advance for these scenarios and the first thing to do is make sure you have reliable service and equipment. This tip applies to both you and your employees. If you recall our case study about Adam Miller and Cornerstone OnDemand from Chapter 9, you might remember that his company provided equipment for employees making the transition to remote work. Ensure you and your people have reliable broadband service. You also can offer a monthly internet allowance.

For companies with employees in the United States, if the employee is in California, connectivity details get even more defined, and it is possible that other states will follow suit, so make sure you check your state's employment laws. For example, a new law in California states that, if an employer requires that an employee work from home, the employer is required to reimburse all costs associated with remote work (Bell, 2020). This may include furniture, computer equipment, internet service and even utilities.

However, even with the most reliable service you can experience problems. You and each employee should do some tsunami planning *before* an issue comes up. Anticipate different scenarios and come up with a plan. For instance, if the power goes out, you will do X, Y and Z. If the internet goes down, you'll do A, B and C. Having a plan prevents panic.

You also should consider a mobile back-up strategy. Rebekah Adams, Vice President of Customer Service at PeopleG2, had a close call that demonstrates the importance of having a plan. Just before a big meeting, she lost both power and internet connectivity in her home. However, because she had all of her necessary apps and programs also on her mobile phone, she made the switch to her mobile device without losing a beat. She and Chris are strong advocates of mobile redundancy, as it is known in the United States. Mobile redundancy is not complicated – remember that your phone or tablet is a computer. Determine which of the applications on your desktop or laptop are essential and make sure they are also on your mobile device. Keep that device charged, keep the apps up to date and also keep a power bank charged. With this contingency in place, if a connectivity disaster strikes, you should have access to your key platforms, email and even chat.

In an office you can always talk to someone to get a quick answer. How do I replace the office pop-in?

The best way to replace the pop-in is to adopt a chat/collaboration platform like Slack, Microsoft Teams, Google Chat (formerly Hangouts), Trello, Ryver or Flock. In addition to providing a chat space, these platforms allow you to create separate rooms, either temporary or permanent, for specific purposes. For example, Chris uses Slack and encourages his team to use Slack's water cooler channel to share kudos. You may recall from Chapter 13 that Chris also created an 'Oops – my bad' room where people can learn from others' mistakes.

With remote tools like these, the entire organization can 'pop in' and ask questions at any time. Communication and collaboration won't just happen in a remote model – you have to take a deliberate approach to selecting the best platform and establishing processes and habits for your team to make the most of it.

What if we get stuck? How do we get unstuck?

We like the approach for 'unsticking' developed by Dr Carol Dweck, a highly regarded researcher in psychology who worked at Columbia University and is now at Stanford. Through her research with students, she found that their attitude towards learning and growth has a significant impact on achievement. In her book, *Mindset: The new psychology of success* (2007), she states that students tend to take one of two approaches: a fixed mindset or a growth mindset. Students with a fixed mindset had more difficulty solving problems and achieved less, while the opposite was true for students with a growth mindset.

At the risk of oversimplifying, employees with fixed mindsets believe that there are limits to what can be learned. They may say things like, 'I'm just no good with technology' or 'Either I'm good at something or I'm not.' Because of those beliefs, these employees are disinclined to put in the effort necessary to learn. Conversely, employees with a growth mindset believe that they can learn new things and are willing to put in the effort. These employees say things like, 'I can learn anything I want' and 'Challenges help me grow'.

The good news is, mindsets can be changed. You can promote a growth mindset among your employees by letting them know that your organization values learning and perseverance rather than innate talent. Make sure the feedback you provide doesn't depend on absolute values like 'correct and incorrect' or 'success and failure' – focus instead on the process more than on the results. Embrace mistakes as learning opportunities.

Circling back to where you got stuck, you should first recognize that you and your team CAN solve the challenge. Then use a cockroach meeting to brainstorm – no idea is bad. You might try positive deviance, as described in Chapter 13; instead of focusing on what's not working, look at what does work. Engaging in problem-solving actually promotes a growth mindset.

What skills should I be looking for in a good remote employee?

Refer back to Chapter 11 for help with this question. To sum it up, you should look for many of the things that make a good employee in the office. However, in a remote model, these characteristics should be even stronger. You can vet candidates according to the hard skills, but you should hire for the soft skills. Look at your top performers and list what makes them stand out. We think that the skills that make them assets will include critical thinking, organizing, prioritizing, communicating and collaborating; however, the softer skills of goal orientation and a solid work ethic are also important.

Can firing an employee be made easier?

Firing is harder when you've waited too long to make the decision; maybe you tried to make the situation better. A good approach to making firing easier is to have a practice of hiring slowly and firing fast. Chris spent years coaching students in water polo and other sports and found that if he put time and energy into helping a particular student, the student could get better. However, it often took a long time. Knowing this made tryouts very important – identifying which students had the right stuff, which ones had potential and which ones clearly were not ready to compete was easy. Unlike in sports, we don't hold 'tryouts' for employment. However, testing candidates is acceptable using established assessments as well as hypothetical challenges.

Regarding culture fit, you have to assess that personally. As hard as you try, sometimes a promising candidate turns out to be all flash and no substance. Or, worse, they turn out to be a jerk.

Once employees are on board, a good leader encourages people to rise. Provide the support, training and tools they need, but set a timeframe for them to show that they can fit in and contribute. The longer you wait, the harder it will be.

Questions about culture

How do I know if they are working?

We hate this question because it suggests that the person who's asking isn't in the right frame of mind for remote success. Remember, working remotely requires new ways of thinking. The answer to the question is that you will know they are working because you monitor your employees' achievement according to established performance metrics.

But the first step to knowing whether they are working is to establish trust. Old-school managers used to say, 'Employees have to earn my trust.' In fact, in a remote model, trust has to be a two-way dynamic, and leaders have to take the first step to set the dynamic in motion. You trust first, which creates more trust. Remember the story about Southwest Airlines from Chapter 15? You need to trust your employees and empower them to achieve their goals independently.

When establishing performance metrics, measure what matters. How many hours employees work doesn't matter, nor does how many times they log onto your system or how visible they are on your chat platform. What matters is achieving their specified goals. Set and clarify the goals and metrics and set the employees free to achieve them. This approach allows you to trust but also to validate. And, if an employee can get their work done in less than 40 hours a week, congratulate them!

Isn't trust a two-way street?

In the answer above, we focused on leaders trusting their employees. But when you think about trust, be sure to ask yourself if your employees trust you. You want to avoid a work culture dependent on subservient or superior behaviours. Instead, promote a relationship in which you and the employees are partners in achieving goals. Be transparent, fair and supportive, and you should have a team that trusts you.

Is it lonely working from home?

Working from home can be lonely for both you and your employees. As a leader, you can provide fun and social interaction to minimize loneliness, but each employee also has to be deliberate and proactive about staving off loneliness. In the office, some people get almost all of their social needs met through work interactions. Those employees will need to find other sources of social interaction, like clubs, volunteer organizations or religious/spiritual communities. Chris found that, at PeopleG2, some employees don't want or need much social interaction from work, while other teams interact constantly in the remote setting, maybe even more than they would have in an office.

As promised, here are some of the things you can do to help prevent loneliness. You may recall that Kim formed pods at Decision Toolbox – groups of three or four recruiters who met once or twice a month. Pods evolved into cockroach meetings and best practices, but the pods' original purpose was to help employees fight loneliness. Another of Kim's tactics was identifying at least one customer located near each recruiter. Recruiters were based across the country, so pairing them with a local customer wasn't too difficult. She then asked the recruiter to call on that client once a month, which compelled the recruiter to suit up, shave, put on makeup and get out of the house. The frequent touch-base with the clients also helped keep relationships with those customers healthy.

Other ideas leaders can employ to ward off loneliness in the remote teams are contests, such as costumes at Halloween or ugly sweaters for the winter holidays, or monthly movie nights. Costume parties can be held on your chat platform or include sharing or posting pictures, and movies can be enjoyed in remote 'watch parties' where employees comment on the movie via the chat platform.

How important are 'soft' skills?

Very important in terms of both culture and performance. For decades employers dismissed employee soft skills. Anything too squishy to measure just dropped off the agenda of CEOs. Now, soft skills are 'in fashion' and we've talked about them throughout this book. As we mentioned above, regarding screening for remote effectiveness, soft skills are even more important in a virtual workspace than in the sticks-and-bricks office.

In terms of performance, a positive attitude may be the most important soft skill to have. An employee with a positive attitude is likely to have a growth attitude and therefore be good at solving problems. Communication, flexibility, self-discipline, critical thinking and teamwork are soft skills that set top performers apart. Think of soft skills as arrows in your quiver.

How do you on-board someone into a highly evolved culture?

You've invested time and energy in building a great culture, so it's important to give the same deliberate attention to the onboarding process. In Chapter 15, we gave some suggestions for creating and delivering onboarding (remember *mise-en-place* and giant fortune cookies?). What follows are some additional insights and recommendations.

Chris assigns new hires a peer mentor whose job is to ensure that the existing team fully embraces the new employee. Part of the peer mentor's task is showing the new person the ropes, but there's more to it than that. The new person needs to understand not just what the team does but *why* they do it. The peer mentor needs to express to the new employee the team's values, goals and interactive dynamics.

When bringing on a new executive or a new team leader, pay attention to credibility. Ensure that everyone knows why there is a new leader or manager joining, what that person is expected to accomplish (their targets), and what leadership expects from the rest of the organization to help integrate the new employee.

Even if you bring on a leader to drive change, that person needs to take time to understand the team and the culture before making large changes. The changes may be positive and beneficial, but the leader first needs to establish credibility and demonstrate an understanding of the culture and the relevant points of the team's history. If the leader pushes too fast and too soon, the change initiative is likely to fail.

A great leader will come in and adapt to the team and promote cohesion rather than cause divisiveness. Kim calls this 'waffle batter' – the leader changes and contorts to fill in gaps, like batter poured into a waffle iron, to give the team and culture strength and substance.

How do I stay connected to my people?

First of all, connectedness and communication are your responsibility. If you want the team to connect, you have to show up and engage. If you want strong communication, you have to practise good communication habits.

You have to figure out a way to be visible to all your employees, even if you are in Oregon and they are in Florida, for example.

We've mentioned chat platforms several times already, so if you haven't found one yet, start shopping. Once you are up and running with your chat platform, make a point of being virtually visible. For example, you might ping each employee once a month, just to check in. If you have 'social' chat rooms, like a water cooler room, be present in that space whenever possible. If you're new to chat programs, 'being there' just means that, at minimum, people can see your name in the list of room participants. More importantly, join in the fun periodically.

Recall that in Chapter 15, we recommended ditching annual reviews and instead setting up monthly or even weekly check-ins. Also in that chapter, we shared some of Chris's tactics for staying connected, such as sending out a 'question of the week' email.

What about employee health and burnout?

Employees may be tempted to sit at the kitchen table or even on the sofa when working at home, but ergonomics are just as important at home as in the office. The Mayo Clinic (2019) offers a how-to guide with details. Here are the highlights:

- use an ergonomic chair while sitting and stand when possible;
- use a footrest if your chair is too high;
- keep important and often-used objects (such as your phone, stapler, etc) close to minimize reaching;
- follow ergonomic guidelines for placing and using monitor, keyboard and mouse;
- if you use the phone often, consider getting a headset or putting it on speaker;
- make sure there is plenty of room under your desk for your knees, thighs and feet.

Sophie Downes, Assistant Editor of Inc., writes that, in the midst of the Covid-19 pandemic, large numbers of employees felt the impact of poor ergonomics, stress related to the pandemic, and stress stemming from the changes involved in working from home (2020). She gathered input from a number of business and ergonomics experts, including Chris, and came up with five key suggestions that should be considered routine actions at any time, pandemic or not:

- model best ergonomics practices and encourage your team frequently to follow those practices;
- ensure ergonomics are embedded in your work-from-home policies;
- offer to offset the cost of home office furniture and equipment (remember that in some US states you are obligated to do so);
- keep an eye out for mental strain;
- encourage people to let you know what they need.

In Sophie's article, Chris shared that even employees who were already working remotely were subject to higher stress during the pandemic. He observed changes in behaviour among some employees; for example, one employee who was almost never late to meetings started missing them or showing up late frequently. Chris learned that the individual had started drinking more to deal with the stress of the pandemic and helped the employee find professional help.

Chris also observed that different teams had different work ethics, and those who valued putting in more hours became angry with those who worked less. The teams were both accomplishing goals, but as resentment grew, Chris intervened with some exercises that broke down the 'silos' and promoted mutual respect.

Other ways to encourage health and wellness include:

- offering wellness programmes as part of your employee benefits, which focus not only on preventing illness but also on optimizing health through lifestyle choices;
- offering discount fitness club memberships (where applicable);
- encouraging employees with shared interests to form groups that do things together; at Decision Toolbox, for example, some employees formed a Weight Watchers group to help encourage one another;
- encouraging people to use the egg timer approach from Chapter 8, which incorporates small self-rewards for accomplishing goals. Better time management reduces stress, and the rewards could include healthy habits, such as taking a walk;
- encouraging people to build out their social networks, such as joining clubs, volunteering in the community or becoming more active in their religious community.

How do I ensure the culture really sticks?

Culture is a living, growing entity that needs regular attention, so you need to monitor it just as you monitor other important parts of your operations. You'll use more qualitative assessments, but you need to take the pulse regularly. Culture can also be nebulous. Seth Godin sums up culture in the phrase 'people like us do things like this' (2018), which is both accurate and intuitive. For more about measuring culture, refer back to Chapter 13 or to Chris's book, *The Power of Company Culture.*

You can reiterate and reinforce culture using meetings, pods and activities. We talked about using meetings to promote culture in Chapter 15. Whatever is discussed in a meeting should be framed by your culture and company goals. Therefore you need to be intentional about planning, or curating, your meetings. Create an agenda – if you don't have an agenda, you don't need a meeting. In addition, recall the three key rules about meetings: start on time, end early and keep it small.

Pods, or small teams, can help reinforce culture and, as we've said, help prevent loneliness. Pods can be made up of people who do the same work, so they can share ideas and best practices, or they can be cross-functional, to help your people know what's going on in other departments. We recommend you keep pods to five or fewer people.

Other activities to promote culture include monthly contests, such as posing a question and awarding a Starbucks gift card to the person who gives the best answer. Also consider birthday and anniversary celebrations, movie nights, book of the month clubs – you and your team can come up with even better ideas together.

A final word on culture: business circumstances can require that the culture change temporarily. For example, let's say your culture emphasizes autonomy and life balance, but then you land a large project that will require all hands on deck. You might let your team know that you expect the culture to change for the next, say, 90 days.

Questions about leadership skills

How do I distinguish a habit from a goal?

You can think of it this way: first, set a goal – something you want to achieve. Then, establish habits that will help you achieve the goal. For example, Chris wanted to exercise more during the day, with a goal of being more fit. He set up a habit in which, whenever he closed his laptop, he did 10 pushups.

For business-related goals and habits, you can use Kim's think-launch-review method, described earlier in this chapter. Be sure your habits support your goals and vice-versa. If your goal is to be a $25 million company, you have to develop $25 million habits.

As the leader, how do I look after my own well-being?

It is easy to find yourself alone on an island. You have to be your best self to your employees and even to your senior leaders. You can talk with them and commiserate to an extent, but absolute transparency could undermine your leadership and credibility. Sharing work concerns with your spouse or close friends can even be difficult, because it can strain those relationships.

To get off and stay off that island, build a network of peers and/or mentors who are external to your organization. An executive roundtable can fill some of this need, but you'll probably also need to make more personal connections with other C-level executives. These are 'professional friends' that you can call any time, who won't mind you blowing off some steam or having a good cry.

A mentor is someone you look up to and who has wisdom to share. They can help you solve your trickier problems, and reassure you that what you're experiencing is completely normal.

As we mentioned at the beginning of the chapter, this list isn't exhaustive, but we hope this chapter has given you some ideas and points to consider as you move forward. In the next chapter, we'll let you know some things to beware of, things that we have lived through. Hopefully the advice will help you avoid these situations or, if you can't avoid them, it will help you get through them.

References

Bell, J (2020) Do your work-from-home policies comply with California law? *SHRM*, 4 September, www.shrm.org/resourcesandtools/legal-and-compliance/ state-and-local-updates/pages/do-your-work-from-home-policies-comply-with-california-law.aspx (archived at https://perma.cc/6W7D-HEMY)

Berkus, D (2014) *Extending the Runway*, 2nd edition, Berkus Press, Los Angeles

Clear, J (2018) *Atomic Habits: An easy and proven way to build good habits and break bad ones*, Avery, New York City

Downes, S (2020) How to keep your employees healthy while they're working from home, *Inc.com*, 6 October, www.inc.com/sophie-downes/remote-work-home-ergonomics-stress-back-pain-health.html (archived at https://perma.cc/6UWM-Z64F)

Dweck, C S (2007) *Mindset: The new psychology of success*, Ballantine Books, New York City

Dyer, C (2018) *The Power of Company Culture: How any business can build a culture that improves productivity, performance and profits*, Kogan Page, London

Engage2Excel (2017) Trendicators Report: The role of recognition in recruiting, onboarding and retaining employees, http://info.engage2excel.com/2017-trendicators-report-the-role-of-recognition (archived at https://perma.cc/LF3V-Y3GY)

Godin, S (2018) Why people like us do this (online video) https://www.youtube.com/watch?v=he1Vji1n8z0&feature=emb_ (archived at https://perma.cc/KT8T-ZK3S)

Mayo Clinic (2019) Office ergonomics: Your how-to guide, *Mayo Clinic*, 27 April, www.mayoclinic.org/healthy-lifestyle/adult-health/in-depth/office-ergonomics/art-20046169 (archived at https://perma.cc/XN8G-FEBJ)

Riggio, R E (2012) There's magic in your smile: How smiling affects your brain, *Psychology Today*, 25 June, www.psychologytoday.com/us/blog/cutting-edge-leadership/201206/there-s-magic-in-your-smile (archived at https://perma.cc/HZ7V-SZ8A)

19

Story time

We thought of calling this chapter 'Beware – we've already lived this!' Not all of these stories are about avoiding pitfalls, but they all have a moral or a takeaway that you can use in leading your business to success. These are random musings, but all are true and all are proof that there's nothing common about common sense. We hope you will be able to take the learnings and apply them in your remote organization.

IN THIS CHAPTER

- Focus on what's important
- Big problem, big solution
- Big problem, simple solution
- Persistence beats panic
- Mistakes vs errors
- Don't overcomplicate things
- Remain open to opportunity
- Lingo strengthens culture
- The importance of integrity
- Sharing stories to unite the team
- Making an impact without spending a lot
- Networking tips
- Focus on the here and now
- How to scale yourself

Fish and focus

Chris and wife Jody adopted three children from Russia, which involved many flights back and forth between that country and the United States. Most often they took Aeroflot, the largest airline of the Russian Federation, and the route was familiar to them. On their final flight from Los Angeles International Airport (known as LAX to many), they took off as usual. But the plane hadn't gone far before things started to look very different.

The plane started moving erratically, lunging, and passengers were starting to grow concerned. Suddenly Chris saw liquid spewing from the wing. Most people on the flight spoke only a little English, but Chris finally found a fellow passenger who was an engineer, and together they figured that the pilots must be dumping fuel. However, there was no word from the cockpit or the flight crew.

After circling Southern California for about an hour, the pilot finally came on over the speaker and spoke for a few minutes in Russian. Looking at the faces around him, Chris didn't think the pilot's message was very reassuring. In a moment the pilot switched to English and said simply, 'We go back to LAX.'

At this point all the passengers were alarmed and upset, and as they spoke together a sub-conversation grew. 'We're dumping fuel in ocean, no? Bad for fish!' Chris realized that they didn't know where else to put their energy. However, indignation started to grow.

Chris started to stand up to speak. His wife grabbed his arm and told him to sit down and keep quiet. However, that's not really in his nature – you may recall that his DiSC profile shows him to be strong in the dominance area, meaning he is very comfortable taking charge and leading. He stood up and turned to his fellow passengers.

'The pilot has to dump the fuel,' he said.

'But it's bad for the fish,' came the reply from several people who were clearly very upset.

'It's for safety,' Chris explained. 'If we try to land with full tanks of fuel, we could die.'

It went silent for a minute. Then an older woman stood up. She fit the stereotype of a *Babushka*, a Russian grandmother from the old country. Chris nodded at her, inviting her to speak.

'To hell with fish,' she said simply, and sat down.

She had hit the nail on the head, and it ended the conversation about fish. The moral here is that you have to know where to focus, where to put your attention and energy. Chris certainly wasn't happy about the fuel pollution, but in the balance, dumping it was the right choice.

In many scenarios, 'where to focus' will be the same, whether you are in a remote model or in an office. However, working remotely can make it harder to see the obvious. Check in with your team regularly and monitor your KPIs. Once you have identified an issue, just remember to understand and focus on the most critical elements of it.

The pyjama solution

Prior to joining Decision Toolbox, Kim led a healthcare recruiting team with a couple of managers and several highly skilled recruiters. They worked in a hybrid on-site/remote model. She often bragged about having the best team ever, and she still feels that they were among the best. Full of confidence in this team, she took a well-deserved 10-day vacation in Honduras. She felt on top of the world. Until she came back

It seemed that all hell had broken loose. She could feel the tension in the office and there was an undercurrent of bickering. By the time she had sat down at her desk, there was a line of 10 people at her door. She listened to the first four or five, and she kept hearing the same story: 'My problem is bigger than everyone else's' and 'So-and-so isn't doing the right thing.' It seemed that everyone hated one another.

Kim had heard enough. It was clear that all the values Kim had tried to instil in the team had been tossed out the window. Where there used to be collaboration, cliques had formed to compete with each other. Proactive and constructive problem-solving had given way to reactive and disabling finger-pointing.

She came out of her office and sent everyone home, giving them the day off. 'But tomorrow,' she said, 'Show up in your pyjamas and bring a pillow.' This got some puzzled looks, but then some said quietly, 'Uh-oh. Mom's mad.'

Fortunately, everyone lived near enough to come into the office and, the next day, the team arrived to find the cubicles pushed to the walls, and mats on the floor. Kim gave each person a sippy cup of juice and some graham crackers. 'I'm treating you as the children you have become.'

She went on: 'We're fixing this today, or I will shut this team down. I'll fire all of you and start over. I don't care which – it's up to you.' She pulled names at random from a fishbowl to create small teams, and directed each team to problem-solve in different practice areas, such as intensive care (ICU), hospice, rehab, etc.

Off they went into their workgroups, sitting on mats in the jammies, with sippy cups and graham crackers. It was pretty hard, under the circumstances, for people to cling to their ire and their grudges. By the end of the day, many operational problems had been solved. More important, however, the collaboration and cohesive team spirit was back, stronger than ever. Kim watched as her team left, proudly strutting out to the parking lot with their pillows.

It's not impossible to hold a pyjama party remotely – you can do it via video conference. But the pyjamas aren't really the point – the message here is that if you have a big, hairy problem, you need to come at it with a big, hairy solution. And it definitely helps if the solution has a playful or light-hearted element to help cut through the negativity.

Big drama, simple solution

Chris dealt with a similar all-hell-breaking-loose problem when a single contact at a large client – let's call her Maria – took offence at a $10 charge on an invoice from PeopleG2. Maria worked for a large staffing firm that was, at the time, Chris's largest client. Maria called a customer service representative (CSR) and asked, 'What the heck is this $10 charge? We are leaving. Close our account!'

The CSR didn't have the authority to close the account, but escalated the situation. Meanwhile, Maria sent emails and even letters expressing extreme anger. Chris tried to contact Maria's boss and her boss's boss, but they were away at a conference. Maria started shutting down user accounts in her company, ensuring that her colleagues couldn't use PeopleG2. She had started a war, and Chris's team were beside themselves with anger and resentment.

Normally Chris lets his people work through problems, but this situation was becoming toxic quickly. He reached out to his team and told them all to take an hour to get some coffee and clear their heads. 'Then we'll come back and tiger-team this issue,' he said. 'But when we come back, be prepared to love Maria, not hate her.'

Those instructions got people to cool off, and Chris started the tiger team by saying, 'We need to solve this with a completely different perspective. Let's assume that Maria loves us, that she's a good person. Let's not focus on being offended, but on how we can help her.'

Based on the tiger team suggestion, Chris reached out to Maria and, without even mentioning the $10 charge, asked, 'In a perfect world, what would we do differently in order to be a better vendor?' Maria's momentary silence suggested to Chris that this was not what she had expected.

'Well,' she said, 'Right now we get multiple invoices. It makes it hard for me to reconcile all the charges, and I get in trouble. If we got just one comprehensive invoice from you, it would make my job easier.'

'We can do that,' Chris replied.

'You can?' Maria responded. 'That's great.'

And the war was over. In fact, Maria became a great ally and advocate of PeopleG2. She consistently provides great ratings, she helps promote the ongoing relationship between the two companies, and she refers PeopleG2 to others. Chris estimates that the 'war' over a $10 charge actually resulted in Maria sending him about $100,000 in business.

The moral? Instead of getting angry, focus on positives and remain solution-oriented. The anger can inflate an issue, whereas a fairly simple solution transformed it into a win-win.

Three yards and a cloud of dust

This story first appeared in Kim's collaboration with Dave Berkus, *Get Scrappy* (2015). All too often, leaders or teams will take on big goals that are overly ambitious. Kim compares this with a downfield pass in American football, also known as a 'Hail Mary' pass. If you're not familiar with a Hail Mary pass, this play is usually a last-ditch effort at the end of the game. The quarterback throws the ball as far down the field as possible, and the team prays that someone will catch it and score. Analysts differ on the exact probability of success for a Hail Mary, but most agree it is less than 10 per cent, and many put it at about 2.5 per cent (Burke, 2012).

A lot of business development teams are wired this way, to the extent that, all too often, they will resort to a Hail Mary pass. You may recall that Kim was the primary sales driver at Decision Toolbox, but there also were others who supported business development, mostly as an adjunct to their regular jobs. During a particularly slow month, this group became anxious and panicky, and started to talk about trying to land a single large deal that would save the day – a Hail Mary play.

Given the high-risk nature of this approach, Kim developed an alternative strategy for maintaining sales momentum at any time, but particularly during a down cycle. Sticking with the football analogy, she calls it 'three yards and a cloud of dust'. Fans of American football will recognize this as an emphasis on the running game. It means grinding out shorter runs over the four downs (plays) allotted to gain 10 yards, thus earning another four downs, and so on. It's very similar to Dave Brailsford's work with British Cycling (see Chapter 16) and the aggregation of marginal gains.

Kim and her team followed that approach for the next month. At the end of the experiment, everyone was closing new deals on a regular basis. They weren't game-changing huge deals, there was no flash, and no Hail Mary plays. But that month ended up yielding more sales revenue than the previous six months.

The message here is that slow and steady wins. It might take a while to reach the end zone and score, and it might not be pretty, but you reach it in the end and have smaller celebrations along the way.

Insights from a zip line

Responding constructively to mistakes is one of the seven pillars of culture in Chris's book, *The Power of Company Culture* (2018), and we discussed this in Chapter 13. You and your team can learn from mistakes, but you have to be able to distinguish between a mistake and an error. A mistake happens when an employee acts in good faith and believes they are doing the right thing – in spite of the fact that the results are not great. An error occurs when an employee is careless or ignores their better judgement. A good leader gives people autonomy and leeway, and that means mistakes can happen. Errors, however, can and should be avoided. We touched on the distinction in Chapter 13, but this story brings it to life.

Chris was in Porto, Portugal with his wife Jody and some friends. Outside the city is an attraction featuring the longest zip line in Europe, and the second longest in the world. A zip line is a cable stretched between a high point and a lower point, and riders use a pulley and gravity to slide down.

Chris's friends persuaded Chris and Jody to give it a shot and, of course, the friends insisted that Chris go first. It was the first zip of the day, so the staff sent a weight first to test the line and clear any moisture. Meanwhile, through broken English and limited Portuguese, the guide got Chris's weight, converted it from pounds to kilos and fitted him with the correct size harness.

Soon Chris was sailing down a cable almost a mile long. He couldn't yet see the end, but he could see beautiful woods, vineyards and even a waterfall below. Having seen videos of this zip line, Chris knew that he should be travelling close to 80 miles per hour (mph) – but towards the end he was going slower than that. Too slow to reach the end.

Staff members extended a broom into the air, signalling Chris to grab it. It was too far away, however, and he continued on, finally slowing to a stop – but only for a moment. He then started moving backwards along the cable for about five minutes, until he reached the lowest point of the cable's droop.

He was suspended over a highway, watching the traffic below. In his head, an epic battle raged between panic and logic. He worried about falling onto the highway. He feared that Jody, unaware of his dilemma, would come soaring down at 80 mph and collide with him. Chris hung there for 20 minutes until he saw a staff member, also suspended on the line, pulling himself manually towards Chris. The staffer attached a hook to Chris, said 'Okay' and pulled Chris to the landing.

At the landing, another staff member came to him and said, 'Don't worry – you can go again for free.' He declined. It turns out that Chris was never in any real danger. Staff told him that this happens only once in a while, but typically on the first ride of the day or with very light riders, like children. He also found out that the wind at the low end was a factor.

So was this an error? Should someone be fired? Chris thinks not. He believes that the staff took every precaution available to them (sending the test weight, accounting for Chris's weight, etc). Despite their best efforts, however, it happened. If there were anemometers – wind meters – along the route and the staff had failed to check them, then it would have been an error. But those weren't available.

In business, when someone does everything right and things still go wrong, it doesn't do any good to get angry or punish that person. Instead, you and your team should learn from the mistake. For example, the zip line staff might learn that it's a good idea to install anemometers. Don't forget to share the mistake as a learning opportunity, as Chris does in the 'Oops – my bad' room on Slack.

Simplify the sea lion way

The sales field is inundated with consultants, seminars, books, lectures, programmes and more, and that expertise can be useful. At the same time, a simple approach can be best. Kim worked with a husband-wife team based in Chicago who wanted to become channel partners for Decision Toolbox.

Both had a background in recruiting, but not a lot of experience in building sales strategy. They reached out to her frequently to ask questions and get advice, and it wasn't long before they were taking up too much of Kim's time.

Fortunately, Kim had an upcoming speaking engagement in Chicago, so she arranged to meet the couple for lunch. There they told her that their biggest challenge was knowing what prospects to target. Kim excused herself, went to the lobby and ordered a town car with champagne.

The couple was pleasantly surprised at this development. Kim instructed the driver to drive around the Loop, Chicago's central business district. She told the couple, 'Every sign you can see is a prospect. If we can see them, we want to own them.'

They passed signs for some major players, including Sears, Boeing, Walgreens, Abbott Labs, ConAgra, Kraft Heinz and others. And, at every sign, Kim said, 'Ours. Ours. Ours.' Say it out loud and you'll hear why Kim calls this the sea lion approach.

This is another example of how it's possible to over-complicate things. In many ways, a remote model simplifies things, such as eliminating infrastructure worries. However, any time you are creating something new, it can be tempting to develop unnecessarily elaborate solutions. Henry David Thoreau wrote it in 1854, and it's still true today: 'Simplify, simplify.'

The year of saying yes

When starting a new business, people often become highly focused, which can lead to tunnel vision. As your business grows you need to be focused, but in the early days you should take a broader view so that you can see all the opportunities available. Sometimes a new opportunity shows up where you least expect it.

Chris tried an experiment to avoid tunnel vision, and it started a chain reaction of unexpected opportunities. He decided that, for a year, if he could possibly say 'Yes', he would. It might be 'Yes, but...' or 'Yes, and...' but the idea was to be wide open. The first unique opportunity arose when he was asked to do a podcast. His first response was to resist, telling himself, 'I don't know anything about doing podcasts.' But he said yes anyway.

As a result of the podcasts, Chris was approached by publisher Kogan Page about writing a book. Again, Chris said to himself, 'I don't know anything about writing books.' But he said yes anyway.

The book, *The Power of Company Culture* (2018), got people's attention and they reached out to Chris, asking him to be a keynote speaker at different events. By now he knew better than to question fate. He said 'Yes' and ended up speaking all over the world, including Tokyo, Amsterdam, London, Paris, Belgium, Toronto, Johannesburg and Guatemala, near an erupting volcano.

Flying home from Guatemala, Chris met a physician who had been volunteering in that country's poorer communities. As the physician was returning to his seat, he passed out, landing in Chris's lap. Chris might have said, 'I don't know anything about medical emergencies,' but instead he stepped up. He got the physician into a comfortable position and then went searching for help. Two nurses stepped in to take over.

If Chris had said 'No' to any of these things, especially the podcast, he would have missed many great opportunities. During that year he said 'Yes' to many things that didn't really pan out, but the point is this: if you are willing to put yourself out there, you may be able to do things that you never imagined. You can always say 'Yes' at first and then say 'No' later, but if you are closed-minded, the opportunities will pass you by. You have already shown the courage to consider taking your company remote, and maybe you've already done it. Channel that courage into saying 'Yes'.

By the way, Chris's podcast is called Talent Talk, and he talks with talented people, mostly about talent management. It is available on Spotify, iTunes and just about anywhere else you get your podcasts.

Talking in tongues

Insider lingo and unique 'tribal speak' can help strengthen the fabric of your company culture. It reinforces the feeling of being part of the group. Often tribal speak starts as a clever comment someone makes. Others pick up on it and it becomes part of the woof and warp of your culture.

Kim recalls sending an email that was entirely written in Decision Toolbox tribal speak: 'Break out the green flag, just landed a chunky monkey. Flag the cockroach committed – dog has fleas.' You probably could guess at the meaning here, but just in case, it meant, 'Send a "we got a win" email, I just landed a large new client. Call a short brainstorm session because there are issues that will need to be resolved.'

The point is not that tribal speak is unintelligible to outsiders, but rather that team members know what it means and it is part of a lingo that they 'own'. Chris discusses tribal speak in The Power of Company Culture, and compares it to the experience of being in a foreign country where you don't speak the language. When you unexpectedly hear someone speaking your native language, you brighten up and pay attention. You might even go over and introduce yourself. Back home, if you passed that person in a Starbucks, you might not even notice them.

Chris provides examples from Walmart employees, who use a lot of acronyms. For instance, HEATKTE (Pronounced HET-Ka-Tee) means *High Expectations Are The Key To Everything*, and EDLP stands for *Every Day Low Price*.

Tribal speak is an important part of your company culture, and helps to build a sense of teamwork and belonging. It can be very useful in a remote model and is one of the ways you can be deliberate about defining and promoting culture when everyone works from home.

Walking the walk

A lot of companies, including PeopleG2, have a stated commitment to inclusion and diversity. It's the right thing to do, and it's smart business. A McKinsey & Company report, *Diversity Wins: How inclusion matters* (Dixon-Fyle et al, 2020) found that companies with greater diversity outperform less diverse ones. For example, highly diverse companies are 36 per cent more likely to deliver better financial performance than companies with little diversity.

Still, it's one thing to state a commitment to diversity, and another to follow through. Chris wanted to do more than talk the talk, so he took a deliberate approach to diversifying his leadership team. He started the company with two brothers, so it was three white males at first. He found a lot of groupthink going on, where people agreed based just on a shared background – there was limited innovation happening.

At the same time, he wanted to find the right talent. The talent market was then, as now, highly competitive. Chris found that it worked best to hire talented and diverse people at a level below their target level, and then coach them up. As we mentioned in Chapter 5, Chris used StrengthsFinder assessments to help ensure he was getting diverse strength profiles as well as diversity in gender and ethnicity. It took about three and a half years, but PeopleG2 is now far more diverse.

You may also recall from Chapter 1 that Chris and Kim both shopped around to find an executive roundtable that offered diverse opinions. They both ended up at one sponsored by Adaptive Business Leaders (ABL) in Santa Monica, which is west of downtown Los Angeles. As they both live in Orange County, that meant driving 50 to 60 miles just to attend the meetings.

They got diverse opinions, sure enough. One participant once told Chris that maybe he wasn't the right person to run a company. At first Chris was deflated, but he took the criticism as a kick in the pants, and worked on sharpening his skills.

There are a couple of messages here. One is that, to demonstrate integrity, you have to walk the walk. More importantly, you need to get your team out of the groupthink bubble. There should be disagreements and different points of view in your meetings. It's harder, but the payoff is worth it.

Stories unite the team

We've referred to the term 'green flag', which became tribal speak at Decision Toolbox for a win – landing a new project or filling an open position for a client. The phrase itself became part of the company's culture, but the story behind it made it even stronger.

In the late 1990s Kim was at the San Diego Zoo, at the primate enclosure. Along with about 30 other people she was watching the chimpanzees, mesmerized, as they slowly, rhythmically swung from branch to branch. Some of the older chimps sat on the ground, but everything about them was calm and restful.

Suddenly, out popped a small chimp from a hole in the wall, and he burst onto this peaceful scene screeching and jumping around like his tail was on fire. The crowd was immediately intrigued – what was up with this little guy? Was he hurt? No – he was excited. He ran around the enclosure screaming and waving something green.

As the crowd watched this monkey celebrate, Kim shouted: 'I've got the green thing! I've got the green thing!' Everyone laughed, and the whole crowd was buoyed by the joy the little guy was expressing.

That gave Kim the idea to call any win announcement a green flag. It was meant to spark the excitement the little monkey had. The message here is that it's easy to miss opportunities. But when you find something unique and share it, it strengthens the fabric of your culture.

Make a splash for $10

You don't always have to spend a pile of money to get results. Chris and PeopleG2 are often asked to help sponsor professional conferences and networking events. While competitors were handing over $500–$5,000 or more for a sponsorship, Chris and team would buy a few $10 bottles of wine and donate them as prizes. They made sure to plaster a big sticker with the company name and phone number on the bottles. At the events, the master of ceremonies kept holding up the bottles, with the phone number, and calling out 'Donated by PeopleG2'. It created a lot of visibility for the company, at a fraction of the price paid by their competitors.

Kim had a similar strategy at conferences. She knew in advance who she wanted to meet, so she had fruit baskets sent to those people's rooms. The baskets cost only about $20 each, but they created a buzz. People were asking, 'Did you get one?' and 'Why didn't I get one?' That made Kim's target people feel special, and typically they were open to meeting with her.

The moral? Invest a little creativity to save a lot of money, and make a big splash.

Octopus networking

Kim was coaching a friend in starting a new company, and the friend asked how to be a better networker. 'You're so good at it,' the friend said. Kim had never thought much about it – it came naturally to her. Not surprisingly, her StrengthsFinder profile rates her high in 'woo', or a drive to meet new people and win them over.

After giving it some thought, she came up with an approach that helped her: look for the octopus. At a conference or networking event, you only have so much time to make connections. Instead of trying to connect one-on-one, scan the room to find the octopus.

This is the person who is surrounded by eight other people and is 'holding court' as the centre of attention. Now join that circle and introduce yourself to the octopus. By extension, you also should be meeting and collecting business cards from the other eight people. That's phase one.

Phase two is to start sharing stories – perhaps like the ones in this chapter. One or two should be somewhat relevant to the theme of the conference, but once you have people's attention, you can talk about just about anything. Soon you should become an octopus, surrounded by your own court.

The key here, however, is to be a good storyteller. People want to be around storytellers. They want to sit at their table and join them for lunch. There are two reasons for this. First, other people don't have to work so hard at making conversation. Second, they like to be part of the 'inner circle' of an octopus.

If you are a shy wallflower, this probably isn't the strategy for you. However, if you think you just need a little practice in telling stories, you can do it in front of a mirror. Even better, find a local group like Toastmasters, where members develop communication and leadership skills by practising before a group that provides feedback.

Finding the octopus in a virtual world is a little harder, but you can leverage social media to help identify them. They will have lots of connections or followers. You'll need credibility before the octopi will accept your invitations to connect, and you build that with blogs, articles and other content that establishes you as a thought leader. We're in danger of wandering off topic here, so for more information, there are plenty of websites, consultants and platforms out there to help you build your personal/professional brand. You might start with our friends at Buffer.com, subject of a case study earlier in the book.

What makes sense *now*

Flexibility is essential for any business to adapt to market and competitive changes. You also need to be flexible in organizing and managing your teams. As a game-changer, the Covid-19 pandemic makes most market fluctuations look like tiny ripples on a calm pond. Chris realized that he had to change the organizational structure of his team to adapt. However, that doesn't mean the changes will be permanent – it means they make sense in the here and now.

PeopleG2 had been remote for years before Covid-19, but the pandemic still impacted his employees. Chris realized that team members were falling into two camps, and there was anger, resentment and guilt growing in and between the camps.

Similar to what Adam Miller found at Cornerstone OnDemand (remember that case study?), PeopleG2 employees tended to be either:

- people with no children or other extended family at home other than a partner or spouse. This camp tended to work extra hours and have greater schedule flexibility. They were becoming frustrated with the changed work ethic of the other camp;
- people with children and/or extended family (their older parents, for example) at home. This camp found that they had to manage their schedules around those of other family members now at home. For

example, children had to be online for school at specific times. This group began to resent the other camp's frustration while also feeling guilty about it.

Prior to Covid-19, everyone belonged to a finite team – sales, customer service, operations, etc – and those finite teams served as a kind of virtual homeroom. That's where they had stand-up meetings and got information, and usually finite team members worked similar hours.

Once the pandemic hit, however, finite teams were split into the two camps. Chris realized it made sense, here and now, to reorganize the team according to the camps. He created teams that worked similar schedules, regardless of function. That reduced the friction because people now were part of a team that understood one another's situations. Team members help each other, even across functional lines.

Another plus is that the cross-functional nature of the teams is helping people better understand PeopleG2's big picture, and some new ideas have emerged from the cross-pollination. Chris expects that, post-Covid, they will return to the previous organizational structure.

But maybe not. Maybe it will stay the same or change in new ways. After all, the moral of this story is that you should do what makes sense now, but remain flexible in order to adapt as things change.

Scale yourself with a mini-me

When you start your business, you'll be a Jack or Jill of all trades, getting involved in just about all areas of the business and handling more than your fair share of responsibilities. However, while it is fairly easy to scale your company, individual leaders can only scale so much. When you hit the limit of your scalability, it's time to clone yourself.

Here's how Kim did it without having to resort to recombinant DNA. She hired Sharene Cleveland as an executive assistant, which seems simple enough. However, the two of them created some unique processes to turn Sharene into Kim's mini-me.

First, Kim selected Sharene in part because she lived in the Eastern time zone, while Kim lives in California. Sharene had access to Kim's email, effectively expanding Kim's day by three hours – that's 15 extra hours a week.

Second, Kim prioritized her contacts according to the urgency of responding, and empowered Sharene to respond to the high-priority ones to set up a meeting.

Third, as Kim frequently attended speaking engagements, organizational meetings and other events, they set up a virtual closet. Kim took pictures of her different outfits, and Sharene kept track of when Kim wore what. That prevented Kim from wearing the same thing twice in a row to any group's meeting. It also allowed Sharene to suggest outfits. For example, if Sharene knew that Kim would be sitting near the CEO of St. John Knits, she would suggest that Kim wear something by that clothing company.

This created a few unique situations, but none of them was bad. For example, Kim chooses to fly first class to get the chance to meet other businesspeople. On one flight, the gentleman seated next to her ordered orange juice and, to break the ice, Kim said, 'I'll have my orange juice with champagne.'

The gentleman did the same and they started chatting over their mimosas. He had his laptop out and open, while Kim's was put away and under the seat. He told Kim, 'I just sent you a "connect" invitation on LinkedIn.'

A few seconds later, he gave Kim a surprised look and said, 'And you just accepted it.' It was, of course, Sharene who accepted the invitation, knowing that Kim was out of pocket.

The point here is that, by taking a very intentional approach, you can scale yourself in several different areas. It's easier to find the right person, since your available talent can be located anywhere. Added bonus: you might help develop your assistant to grow beyond that role. As a business development 'apprentice' to Kim, Sharene went on to build her own client base and become an account executive.

Up next

Usually, after story time, we drift off to sleep. We're definitely near the end, but before you nod off, there's one last chapter, about the Movement.

References

Berkus, D and Shepherd, K (2015) *Get Scrappy: Business insights to make your company more agile*, Berkus Press, Los Angeles

Burke, B (2102) Hail Mary probabilities, *Advanced Football Analytics*, 25 September, http://archive.advancedfootballanalytics.com/2012/09/hail-mary-probabilities.html (archived at https://perma.cc/QJ96-C3BZ)

Dixon-Fyle, S et al (2020) Diversity wins: How inclusion matters, *McKinsey*, 19 May, www.mckinsey.com/featured-insights/diversity-and-inclusion/diversity-wins-how-inclusion-matters# (archived at https://perma.cc/TW87-CM8H)

Dyer, C (2018) *The Power of Company Culture: How any business can build a culture that improves productivity, performance and profits*, Kogan Page, London

Thoreau, H D (1854) *Walden and Civil Disobedience* (2012 reprint), Signet Books, New York City

20

Paying it forward

The movement

Paying it forward refers to 'sharing' an act of kindness or generosity in a unique way. We're pretty sure you're familiar with the idea, but just in case, suppose Isabel does something nice for Jason. In turn, Jason could simply accept the kindness, repay Isabel, or he could pay the kindness forward and do something nice for a third person, such as Trinh. If Trinh then does something nice for Malika, we've got some momentum building.

That is our real motivation in writing this book. We both have dealt with setbacks and failures, but overall we have run successful businesses and built fulfilling lives. In a sense, the universe has been kind to us, and we want to pay that forward by helping you navigate the minefields on your way to your own success.

IN THIS CHAPTER

We'll share stories of tipping points and courage, including:

- The broken windows theory
- Tipping point for remote
- Nelson Mandela: hope in a rock pile
- Teddy Roosevelt on courage
- Inspiration from Viktor Frankl
- Rosie the tipping point
- Kim shocks the boys
- Chris creates a niche
- Next steps: the Remote Work Movement

And there's more. If you take some ideas from the book, chances are good that you'll tweak them to fit your business's needs. You may make the ideas much, much better. You might even come up with entirely new ideas of your own – chunky nuggets that deserve to be shared. We also hope that you'll pay it forward by sharing those ideas.

To make that easy we've created a Slack community, Remote Work Movement, at https://chrisdyer.com/remotework. We invite you to join the community, share your own ideas, see what others are doing, and help build the movement towards excellence in working remotely.

You are getting ready to launch or transfer your business into the ether, and this project will be very challenging. A concept that may be useful in taking on challenges is the tipping point.

Tipping points

Malcolm Gladwell's 2002 book, *The Tipping Point: How little things can make a big difference,* has been so influential that the phrase has become common. According to Gladwell, 'The tipping point is that magic moment when an idea, trend or social behaviour crosses a threshold, tips and spreads like wildfire.'

From the outside it may look like it doesn't require a lot of thought or planning, but in reality it requires *more* thought and *better* planning than working in an office. For many, successfully working remotely is a new challenge. As you work through the process, whether you are trying to solve a problem or reach a goal, keep an eye out for the potential tipping point. Once you've identified it, you can break down the big problems and come up with simple but effective solutions.

The broken windows theory

A great example of finding the tipping point comes from the New York City Police. Social scientists James Q Wilson and George L Kelling described their 'broken windows' theory in 1982. It states that an environment that persistently displays the impact of crime and antisocial behaviour – broken windows, graffiti, public drunkenness, etc – encourages more crime. It sends a message that no one cares about the neighbourhood, and sends an open invitation to criminals that this is a place where they are unlikely to be caught.

In the early 1990s, New York City Mayor Rudy Giuliani and Police Commissioner William Bratton implemented a broken windows approach, calling it 'quality of life policing' (Harcourt and Ludwig, 2006). Previously the police had tried increasing foot patrols and other extra security measures in problem neighbourhoods, but nothing worked. In order to implement the broken window approach, the police rounded up thugs from the subway station and other locations, repaired broken windows and kept them repaired, redecorated subway interiors, diligently painted over graffiti, and more.

All of these actions were designed to send a very visible message: we do care about this neighbourhood, and we will hold people accountable for crimes. The police followed the programme persistently, and the overall crime rate dropped measurably. More important, residents of the neighbourhood felt safer.

The tipping point was the change in the environment, the elimination of the broken windows. The police flipped the pyramid, investing time in developing a solution. They focused on the holes in the Swiss cheese to see what wasn't there now. They designed what they wanted.

Simple but visible acts can start a chain reaction. At PeopleG2, Chris and his team post their kudos and green flag messages in the Slack water cooler channel. It allows everyone to share at least a small part of the positive, and sets an example. Others are encouraged to share their kudos for others and their own personal successes. This kudos platform has gained momentum and started a movement among the PeopleG2 team to give one another virtual high-fives. Like fixing a broken window, this is a public gesture on a platform that is easy to see and easy to use. It shows that Chris and his leaders care, and the team has rallied about the kudos site to make it their own.

Rosie the tipping point

Another major tipping point is exemplified by Rosie the Riveter. You've probably seen the image of Rosie, wearing coveralls, hair bound up in a kerchief, rolling up her sleeve to show off her flexed bicep. Many versions of this image have the motto 'We can do it' (Pruitt, 2020). Rosie's determined look conveys the courage women would need to be part of a significant change in the United States brought on by the Second World War.

Rosie's character appeared in a poster created by Westinghouse Electric Corporation, and was used to recruit women to the labour force during the war. With so many men in the military, and increased demands for productivity, companies actively sought out women for jobs traditionally filled by men. This need drove changes in the attitudes of both men and women regarding women in the labour force (Schweitzer, 1980).

According to Schweitzer, some 6.5 million women entered the workforce between 1940 and 1945. Although many left the workforce after the war, things had changed, and previous barriers to employment for women were lessened or eliminated. Rosie remains a symbol of an important tipping point for women and has become an inspirational icon of the women's movement.

You will face challenges that test your courage and your will. Do you have what it takes to brass it out, suit up and get in the game? The following story shows how Kim's courage was tested, but her persistence created a tipping point.

Oh no, she didn't!

You may recall from Chapter 1 that Kim (Chris, too) had to shop around in order to find a CEO roundtable that would challenge her. Finally she had the chance to join the Adaptive Business Leaders group in Santa Monica. However, she would be the first woman to join, and the men in the group were leery. In fact, Kim had to audition.

At her first meeting the group discussed various topics, and then started going around the table, answering the question, 'What is keeping you up at night?' As the newcomer Kim would go last, so she listened as the others talked about ROIs, margins, year-to-date growth and other 'all business topics'.

There was something keeping Kim up, but it was very personal. She thought about sharing it, but then decided to go with a business topic. However, when her turn came, she felt she had to share the personal story.

'I'm being sued for palimony by a former life partner, and I'm getting ready to go to court.'

It was as if all the oxygen went out of the room. No one responded to her, and the meeting went on, but everyone was stone-faced. There was an elephant right in the middle of the roundtable. Kim felt horrible and, as she drove home after the meeting, she was sure she had blown her chance.

Just the same, two weeks later she was officially accepted into the group. At the next meeting she was determined to show that she could learn from her mistakes. When it came time to share what was keeping them up, Kim went first, and talked about debt-to-equity ratios or some all-business topic.

However, the next person talked about some issues he was having with his wife. After that a member shared that he worried about his daughter, who was off at college. A third talked about trying to help his son choose a profession.

Kim had taken a big risk in being honest and direct, but it changed the construct of the group: they were now 'allowed' to mesh the personal and professional. She might have been rejected, but instead members told her later that her honesty and courage turned a good group into a great group.

Tipping point for remote

For years leaders have resisted remote work, citing any number of reasons. We discussed many in Chapter 6. Employees have wanted it, while employers have resisted it. The Covid-19 pandemic was the tipping point that proved remote can work.

There are still broken windows in the remote landscape, however, and still a need for visible messages of hope and progress. We expect you will help us turn the Remote Work Movement into a source of those messages, the fuel for momentum and innovation.

Courage and inspiration

Whether you are taking an existing company remote, looking for better ways to remain remote in the future or launching an entirely new remote company, you're facing a significant challenge. We've already said it will require hard work, but it will also require inspiration to keep you motivated and positive. When we compared notes on the role models who inspire us, we discovered that they all were influenced by stoicism, which helped them overcome challenges.

Originating in ancient Greece, stoicism is based on the belief that what happens in life is neither good nor bad – it just is (Van Natta, 2019). For stoics, there is no cosmic mechanism by which good people are automatically rewarded and bad people automatically punished. You have to play the hand you're dealt. While the cards can evoke emotions from joy to despair, your response, your actions, should NOT be based on emotions. Instead, stoics believe that the best approach to life is to use reason to determine how to respond to whatever life throws your way. One important and inspiring role model for both of us is Nelson Mandela.

Hope in a rock pile

Mandela became President of South Africa, led the dismantling of apartheid and won the Nobel Peace Prize. Before that, however, he spent 27 years in prison for treason and attempting to overthrow the oppressive government of the white minority. We both visited Johannesburg to learn more about Mandela and his remarkable vision and leadership abilities.

We learned that Mandela read a number of books during that time, including *The Meditations*, by Roman philosopher Marcus Aurelius (2020; originally written circa 171–175 AD). The book is considered a classic text on stoicism.

Life threw a lot at Mandela. His mother and his son both passed away while he was in prison, and his pleas for a temporary release in order to attend their funerals were denied (Mandela, 1995). The horrifying Soweto uprising occurred in 1976, while he was in prison. The uprising started against a background of rising discontent, when school children took to the street to protest an edict requiring that school be taught in Afrikaans, the Dutch-based language of the minority government (Cummings and Holmes, 2016).

During the uprising police responded with particular brutality, including firing on and killing children. Many consider the Soweto uprising a tipping point to ending apartheid, galvanizing people in response to the bloodshed. Mandela, however, was powerless to do anything at the time. He would remain in prison for another 13 years.

Once released, Mandela could have focused on revenge. Instead, stoicism influenced him to take another course that would revolutionize South Africa and become a message of hope and reconciliation to people around the world. Even while in prison, Mandela engaged the guards, persuading them to improve conditions for his fellow inmates. Later, with a focus on the future and not on the past, he collaborated with F W de Klerk – President of South Africa and leader of the white government – to negotiate the end of apartheid. Mandela and de Klerk would later share the Nobel Peace Prize (BBC, 2008).

In 1995 Mandela attended a reunion with more than 1,000 former political prisoners at Robben Island, the maximum-security prison where they had all been held (Zlatos, 2015). In a gesture representing conciliation, Mandela and the others went to the quarry where they had previously done hard labour. They each removed a rock from the quarry, some using picks and hammers. They then followed Mandela to a point near the quarry entrance. Mandela placed his rock on the ground and, one by one, the others did the same. The rock pile is still there, a cairn marking their history as prisoners and, for many, their subsequent efforts supporting Mandela's crusade against apartheid. Today the former prison is a museum and UNESCO World Heritage Site.

Mandela's accomplishments make going remote look like a small task. Nonetheless, it will be a challenge, and there will be times when you need inspiration. What we have both learned from Mandela is that, when life throws obstacles in your path, stand firm. Focus on healing and building rather than on injury and division. Covid-19 is a great example, and challenges like it will continue to arise. Instead of letting the challenges get you down, be inventive. Ideate solutions. Get scrappy. Be courageous.

Courage from Teddy

In 1910, shortly after his second term as President of the United States, Theodore Roosevelt addressed students at the Sorbonne in Paris (Duxbury, 2011). One part of that speech has become well known for inspiring courage:

'It is not the critic who counts; not the man who points out how the strong man stumbles, or where the doer of deeds could have done them better. The credit belongs to the man who is actually in the arena, whose face is marred by dust and sweat and blood; who strives valiantly; who errs, who comes short again and again, because there is no effort without error and shortcoming; but who does actually strive to do the deeds; who knows great enthusiasms, the great devotions; who spends himself in a worthy cause; who at the best knows in the end the triumph of high achievement, and who at the worst, if he fails, at least fails while daring greatly, so that his place shall never be with those cold and timid souls who neither know victory nor defeat' (Duxbury, 2011).

President Roosevelt was also influenced by stoicism, and even carried copies of works by stoic philosophers Marcus Aurelius and Epictetus with him on the perilous 'River of Doubt' excursion in the Amazon Basin (Holiday, 2014).

Even before she became CEO of Decision Toolbox, Kim embraced this message wholeheartedly, and always carried Roosevelt's quote with her. The paper became dog-eared from all the times she pulled it out over the years to help her through challenging moments. In particular, when Kim took Decision Toolbox remote, there were no models for her to follow – at least, none she knew of. She got a lot of pushback about going remote from naysayers and critics, but in the end, she was the one in the arena and her efforts were successful.

Inspiration from a survivor

Another icon of courage and persistence is Viktor Frankl, an Austrian neurologist and psychiatrist who was also a Holocaust survivor. His book, *Man's Search for Meaning* (1946), is a memoir of his experience in Nazi concentration camps. Prior to his internment, Frankl had developed Logotherapy, a branch of psychoanalysis based on the existential concept of the will to meaning – that is, humans can find solace, purpose and motivation in meaning. Each of us must define the meaning of life – a specific meaning that adapts and evolves throughout life. Two quotes from Frankl's book stand out for Chris and Kim.

> 'Those who have a "why" to live, can bear with almost any "how".'
>
> 'Everything can be taken from a man but one thing: the last of the human freedoms – to choose one's attitude in any given set of circumstances, to choose one's own way.'

The second quote clearly resonates with stoicism, and Frankl's philosophy helped him survive Nazi concentration camps. Frankl originally published the book anonymously, feeling that the anonymity would give him more freedom as he wrote it. Nonetheless, it has become the most influential and popular of his 39 books. The US Library of Congress, in 1991, named it 'one of the ten most influential books in the US' (Fein, 1991).

Choosing an attitude

Chris faced a challenge that pales in comparison to concentration camp internment, but Frankl's story gave him the inspiration to overcome it. When he started attending the ABL roundtable, he felt like the mail clerk in the boardroom – he felt he didn't belong among this group of successful, intelligent people. No one in the group was evil or mean, but they were intimidating. For several meetings he sat quietly, waiting for someone to tap him on the shoulder and say, 'You're in the wrong room, buddy. Head down the hall to the room with the other bozos.'

Finally Chris realized that he had three choices: he could leave in shame, he could sit quietly until they found him out, or he could find a 'why' for his involvement with ABL. He decided to establish his place among the others. He looked at the holes in the Swiss cheese of the group: where does the group struggle?

One area was managing human capital, an area with which Chris is familiar and comfortable. He began to contribute insights around culture, talent management and working remotely. One of his earliest contributions came when another CEO said he thought he would have to fire an underperforming salesperson.

Chris asked if the CEO had considered taking the salesperson to lunch, expressing his concerns and asking what was up. Maybe it was a personal issue, or something going on at home. At first the others looked at him as if he were speaking a different language, but it wasn't long before Chris established himself as a subject matter expert. The group began to direct their culture, talent and remote work questions to him. In fact, other ABL groups asked him to come and present many times.

Instead of allowing the ABL group to push an attitude on him, Chris chose his own attitude in the tradition of Frankl: instead of crying about feeling like a fraud, he was proactive about designing a solution – he chose his own way. Chris credits the ABL group with helping him find other holes in his own cheese.

Looking back

As we stated in Chapter 1, crises drive innovation. At the same time, you don't need a crisis to push you to go remote. It's a great model and, we believe, an important part of the evolving future of work. The model won't work for every job, and it may not be a good fit for every individual. However, in our opinion, it's a great model for leaders, companies and employees.

We've introduced some concepts that will help you in your transition, including:

- Swiss cheese, or looking beyond the cheese to see unrealized potential in the holes.
- Design what you want, or deal with what you get – the power of taking a deliberate approach to just about everything.
- The importance of seeing and thinking in new remote ways.
- Scrum as a model for positive structure, process and team interaction.
- Performance-based management to monitor what you can't see.
- Autonomy, mastery and purpose to empower employees and build loyalty.
- The impact of an affirming, supporting culture.
- People, process, tools and technology as the building blocks of a sound company.
- The value of well-curated meetings.
- The Me, Inc. world and how a Tour of Duty approach supports it.

Those are just the highlights, but we hope you will take these ideas and put them to work. And that's just the beginning...

Looking (and paying it) forward

Chris and Kim became friends at ABL. With Chris's StrengthsFinder profile of ideator and Kim's profile of creator, they soon found a very comfortable space in which they brainstormed freely. When it happened at ABL meetings, the others would watch as the two leapfrogged each other, taking an idea, turning it into a concept and making a plan to implement it. Sometimes the other CEOs' eyes would glaze over, but they had learned that these sessions created good things, so they would ride it out.

We thank you for riding it out, too, but we want the book's end to be the beginning of a great game of brainstorm leapfrog. We've served up some fully baked offerings from our inner creators, ideators and implementers. Now we urge you not only to take these ideas, change them and evolve them, but also to share your stories. We're confident that your ideas and creations will improve upon ours and help others. Please sign up on the Slack community (https://chrisdyer.com/remotework) to become part of the movement. Working together, we can make remote the model of choice.

References

Aurelius, M (2020) *Meditations: The philosophy classic*, Capstone, Mankato, Minnesota

BBC (2008) 1990: Freedom for Nelson Mandela, http://news.bbc.co.uk/onthisday/hi/dates/stories/february/11/newsid_2539000/2539947.stm (archived at https://perma.cc/ZX7E-ZZXL)

Cummings, B and Holmes, M (2016) 'My activism started then': The Soweto uprising remembered, *Guardian*, 16 June, www.theguardian.com/world/2016/jun/16/my-activism-started-then-the-soweto-uprising-remembered (archived at https://perma.cc/5TLH-XY9S)

Duxbury, C (2011) It is not the critic who counts, *Theodore Roosevelt Conservation Partnership*, 18 January, www.trcp.org/2011/01/18/it-is-not-the-critic-who-counts (archived at https://perma.cc/57MU-JPDH)

Fein, E (1991) Book notes, *New York Times*, 20 November, www.nytimes.com/1991/11/20/books/book-notes-059091.html (archived at https://perma.cc/4ZXJ-ZYQD)

Frankl, V E (1946) *Man's Search for Meaning* (2006 reprint), Beacon Press, Boston

Gladwell, M (2002) *The Tipping Point: How little things can make a big difference*, Back Bay Books, New York City

Harcourt, B E and Ludwig, J (2006) Broken windows: New evidence from New York City and a five-city social experiment, *University of Chicago Law Review*, 73 (1), pp 271–320

Holiday, R (2014) Stoicism: Practical philosophy you can actually use, *Medium*, 13 November, https://medium.com/@RyanHoliday/stoicism-practical-philosophy-you-can-actually-use-f952d4002481 (archived at https://perma.cc/9E8V-2NL5)

Mandela, N (1995) *Long Walk to Freedom: The autobiography of Nelson Mandela*, Back Bay Books, New York City

Pruitt, S (2020) Uncovering the secret identity of Rosie the Riveter, *History.com*, 26 March, www.history.com/news/rosie-the-riveter-inspiration (archived at https://perma.cc/8CUR-69EC)

Schweitzer, M (1980) World War II and female labor force participation rates, *The Journal of Economic History*, www.jstor.org/stable/2120427 (archived at https://perma.cc/HBV2-2SKA)

Van Natta, M (2019) *The Beginner's Guide to Stoicism: Tools for emotional resilience and positivity*, Althea Press, San Antonio, Texas

Wilson, J Q and Kelling, G L (1982) Broken windows, *Atlantic Monthly*, March issue, www.theatlantic.com/magazine/archive/1982/03/broken-windows/304465 (archived at https://perma.cc/NLJ3-9S4G)

Zlatos, B (2015) A visit to Robben Island, Nelson Mandela's prison, *Pittsburgh Post-Gazette*, 5 December, www.post-gazette.com/life/travel/2015/12/06/A-visit-to-Robben-Island-Nelson-Mandela-s-prison-in-South-Africa/stories/201511290002 (archived at https://perma.cc/4XYB-YPHG)